C000212267

Walking the Victorian Streets

Sheila Rowbotham

WALKING THE VICTORIAN STREETS

Women, Representation, and the City

Deborah Epstein Nord

Cornell University Press
Ithaca and London

Copyright © 1995 by Cornell University

All rights reserved. Except for brief quotations in a review, this book, or parts thereof, must not be reproduced in any form without permission in writing from the publisher. For information, address Cornell University Press, Sage House, 512 East State Street, Ithaca, New York 14850.

First published 1995 by Cornell University Press.

Printed in the United States of America

Library of Congress Cataloging-in-Publication Data

Nord, Deborah Epstein, 1949–
    Walking the Victorian streets : women, representation, and the city / Deborah
Epstein Nord.
        p.   cm.
Includes bibliographical references and index.
ISBN 0-8014-2392-9 (alk. paper)
    1. English fiction—19th century—History and criticism.   2. Women and litera-
ture—England—History—19th century.   3. Feminism and literature—England—
History—19th century.   4. Marginality, Social, in literature.   5. City and town life in
literature.   6. Moral conditions in literature.   7. Social problems in literature.   8. Prostitutes in literature.   9. Sex role in literature.   10. Mimesis in literature.   I. Title
PR878.W6N67   1995
823'.809352042—dc20   95-10932

⊗ The paper in this book meets the minimum requirements
of the American National Standard for Information Sciences—
Permanence of Paper for Printed Library Materials, ANSI Z39.48-1984.

For Philip

Contents

List of Illustrations

ix

Acknowledgments

xi

Introduction: Rambling in the Nineteenth Century

I

PART ONE   STROLLER INTO NOVELIST

CHAPTER ONE   The City as Theater: London in the 1820s

19

CHAPTER TWO   *Sketches by Boz:*
The Middle-Class City and the Quarantine of Urban Suffering

49

CHAPTER THREE   "Vitiated Air":
The Polluted City and Female Sexuality in
Dombey and Son and *Bleak House*

81

Contents

PART TWO   FALLEN WOMEN

CHAPTER FOUR   The Female Pariah:
Flora Tristan's London *Promenades*
115

CHAPTER FIVE   Elbowed in the Streets:
Exposure and Authority in Elizabeth Gaskell's Urban Fictions
137

PART THREE   NEW WOMEN

CHAPTER SIX   "Neither Pairs Nor Odd":
Women, Urban Community, and Writing in the 1880s
181

CHAPTER SEVEN   The Female Social Investigator:
Maternalism, Feminism, and Women's Work
207

Conclusion: Esther Summerson's Veil
237

Bibliography
249

Index
259

Illustrations

Figure 1 Thomas Shepherd, "The Quadrant and Part of Regent Street." Thomas Shepherd and James Elmes, *Metropolitan Improvements; or, London in the Nineteenth Century* (1827).

26

Figure 2 Thomas Shepherd, "Burlington Arcade, Piccadilly." Thomas Shepherd and James Elmes, *Metropolitan Improvements; or, London in the Nineteenth Century* (1827).

28

Figure 3 I. R. and G. Cruikshank, "*Lowest 'Life in London.'* Tom, Jerry & Logic, among the unsophisticated sons & daughters of nature at 'All-Max' in the East." Pierce Egan, *Life in London* (1821).

32

Figure 4 I. R. and G. Cruikshank, "*Midnight.* Tom & Jerry at a coffee shop near the Olympic." Pierce Egan, *Life in London* (1821).

34

Figure 5 I. R. and G. Cruikshank, "*Bow Street.* Tom & Jerry's sensibility awakened at the pathetic tale of the elegant cyprian, the feeling coachman, & the generous magistrate." Pierce Egan, *Life in London* (1821).

47

Figure 6 George Cruikshank, "The Streets, Morning." Charles Dickens, *Sketches by Boz* (1839).

59

Figure 7 George Cruikshank, "Seven Dials." Charles Dickens, *Sketches by Boz* (1839).

67

Figure 8 George Cruikshank, "The Pawnbroker's Shop." Charles Dickens, *Sketches by Boz* (1839).

69

Figure 9 William M'Connell, "Two o'Clock A.M.: The Turnstile of Waterloo Bridge." George Augustus Sala, *Twice Round the Clock; or the Hours of the Day and Night in London* (1859).

78

Figure 10 Hablot K. Browne, "A Chance Meeting." Charles Dickens, *Dombey and Son* (1848).

89

Figure 11 Hablot K. Browne, "Florence and Edith on the Stairs." Charles Dickens, *Dombey and Son* (1848).

91

Figure 12 Hablot K. Browne, "Consecrated Ground." Charles Dickens, *Bleak House* (1853).

103

Figure 13 Hablot K. Browne, "The Morning." Charles Dickens, *Bleak House* (1853).

108

Figure 14 Eyre Crowe, "The Dinner Hour, Wigan" (1874).

140

Figure 15 J. Bernard Partridge, "Odds and Ends." Amy Levy, *A London Plane-Tree and Other Verse* (1890).

198

Figure 16 Gustave Doré, "London Charities." Gustave Doré and Blanchard Jerrold, *London, A Pilgrimage* (1872).

210

Figure 17 Hablot K. Browne, "The Visit at the Brickmaker's." Charles Dickens, *Bleak House* (1853).

211

Figure 18 "Jersey Dwellings, Ancoats, 1897."

213

Acknowledgments

It is a great pleasure to be able to thank those who have supported and inspired me through the years of writing this book. From one perspective the book had its origins in my years at the Society of Fellows at Columbia University and in the courses I taught there as Heyman Fellow in urban studies. From another, longer perspective it grew out of my training as a student of Victorian studies, as a Dickensian, and as a critic of nineteenth-century women's writing. The interdisciplinarity that is intrinsic to both Victorian studies and feminist scholarship has influenced my work in profound and lasting ways; and the centrality of urban experience and representation to our understanding of the Victorian period shaped my interests and my thinking. The mark of two of my teachers—Steven Marcus and the late Ellen Moers—can be detected on many of the pages that follow.

The writing of this book coincided with my coming to Princeton University and finding an academic home in the English department and the Program in Women's Studies there. Without the welcome and the support I have enjoyed in both, I doubt that this book would exist in its current form—or, perhaps, that it would exist at all. I particularly thank Elaine Showalter, who invited me to Princeton as a visitor, and Christine Stansell and members of the Women's Studies faculty, whose graciousness and confidence in me helped make it possible for me to stay. The friends and colleagues who have read or heard parts of the manuscript and given invaluable advice include Joseph Boone, Dana Brand, Patrick Brantlinger, Jerome Buckley, Dina Copelman, Deirdre d'Albertis, Laura Engelstein, Donald Gray, Olwen Hufton, Uli Knoepflmacher, Peter Mandler, Arno Mayer, Andrew Miller, Suzanne Nash, Jeff Nunokawa, Susan Pennybacker, Ellen Pollak, Ellen Ross, Bonnie Smith, Judith Walkowitz, and anonymous readers at *Signs* and Cornell University Press. Philip Collins put me on the trail of George Sala; Peter Keating's *Into Unknown England* introduced me to Mary Higgs; and years ago David Crew talked to me about Florence Bell. I also thank the students in my two graduate courses on the Victorian city for tolerating my hobbyhorses and adding their own insights and intelligence to our discussions. For listening to other kinds of obsessions I thank Maria DiBattista, Ellen Pollak, and Chris Stansell.

A grant from the American Council of Learned Societies helped in the very early stages of this project, and support from the Princeton University Committee on Research in the Humanities and Social Sciences buoyed me through its final stages. I have had wonderful research assistance over the years from Tova Perlmutter, Maria Davidis, Anne-Lise François, Julie Barmazel, and, above all, Lisa Sternlieb, who helped with crucial aspects of research and with the selection of illustrations. Beth Harrison and Barbara Gershen provided assistance in moments of crisis and calm. John Blazejewski photographed the nineteenth-century materials I have used for illustrations. I also thank Laura Moss Gottlieb for her superb work on the index and Carol Betsch for overseeing the production of the manuscript with intelligence and care.

Bernhard Kendler of Cornell University Press has been an encouraging and stalwart editor; I am grateful for his support, his patience, and the occasional sardonic nudge. Each generation of my family has contributed to the writing of this book in ways both direct and indirect. The knowledge of my mother's unflagging support of my work and of the personal decisions I have made has been a rare and precious gift. Both my mother and my brother, Jeremy, stand as inspiriting models of determination and character. My children, Joseph and David, have provided the distractions of joy which, I hope, find their way back into my work. Finally, I dedicate this book to my husband, Philip, who has listened endlessly, edited with alacrity, made me laugh, kept faith, and been my partner in all things.

An earlier version of Chapter 6 appeared under the title " 'Neither Pairs Nor Odd': Female Community in Late Nineteenth-Century London" (Summer 1990) in *Signs* and is reprinted here by permission of the University of Chicago Press (© 1990 by the University of Chicago. All rights reserved). Chapter 4 appeared in slightly different form in

Acknowledgments

Home and Its Dislocations in Nineteenth-Century France, edited by Suzanne Nash (Albany: State University of New York Press, 1993). Parts of "The Urban Peripatetic: Spectator, Streetwalker, Woman Writer," an article that appeared in *Nineteenth-Century Literature* 46 (1991), are dispersed throughout this book and are reprinted by permission of the Regents of the University of California, © 1991. I also thank the Manchester City Art Galleries, the Manchester Central Library: Local Studies Unit, and the Department of Rare Books and Special Collections, Princeton University Libraries, for permission to reproduce works in their collections.

D. E. N.

Yet perception of the new qualities of the modern city had been associated, from the beginning, with a man walking, as if alone, in its streets.

—Raymond Williams, *The Country and the City*

Who are those fair creatures, neither chaperons nor chaperoned: those "somebodies whom nobody knows," who elbow our wives and daughters in the parks and promenades and rendez-vous of fashion?

—William Acton, *Prostitution*

Sometimes, when I have been walking in Gray's Inn Road and seen one of those terrible old women that are so common there, the sense of agonised *oneness* with her that I have felt, that she was myself only under different circumstances, has stricken me almost mad.

—Olive Schreiner, letter to Karl Pearson, 1885

Introduction:
Rambling in the
Nineteenth Century

In the literature of the nineteenth-century city, the figure of the observer—the rambler, the stroller, the spectator, the flaneur—is a man. As Raymond Williams rightly remarks, the entire project of representing and understanding the exhilarating and distressing new phenomenon of urban life began, in some important sense, with this figure of the lone man who walked with impunity, aplomb, and a penetrating gaze. He begins as a visible character in the urban sketch, a signature—like "Boz" or "Spec"—who is both authorial persona and fictional actor on the city streets, and ends as the invisible but all-seeing novelist, effacing all of himself but his voice in the evocation of an urban panorama.[1] He delineates the spaces of modernity, the public realm of commerce and exchange, the alienation of the man in the crowd, and the display and selling of all things. The novelist-spectator passes invisibly through the crowd and then behind the facades of buildings, extending what Williams, thinking primarily of Dickens, calls a "potent and benignant hand, which takes off the housetops and shows the shapes and phantoms" within.[2] He discerns the patterns of

---

[1] Susan Buck-Morss writes, "The flaneur in capitalist society is a fictional type; in fact, he is a type who writes fiction." See Buck-Morss, "The Flaneur, the Sandwichman, and the Whore: The Politics of Loitering," *New German Critique* 39 (Fall 1986): 111. "Boz" is, of course, the name used by Dickens as urban spectator and sketch writer, and "Spec" was Thackeray's pseudonym for a series of London travels and sketches published in *Punch* in the 1840s (see Chapter 2).

[2] Raymond Williams, *The Country and the City* (London: Chatto and Windus, 1973), p. 156.

social relations that remain hidden to the uninitiated or the indifferent; he is investigator and theorist of poverty, disease, and class difference.

One of the major paradigms of urban spectatorship and observation in the nineteenth century emerges as a dialectic between alienation and contagion, between the sometimes liberating and sometimes disturbing sense that the crowd is distant, unknown, and unreadable and the anxiety that proximity to the crowd puts the spectator in dangerous contact with contamination and taint. The literature of rambling, the urban sketch, and the culture of bohemia fed on the exhilaration of disconnection and anonymity, of being, as Walter Benjamin writes, "at the margin, of the great city as of the bourgeois class."[3] The detachment of the marginal man, the artist, gave him the status of stranger and fostered his identification—although not necessarily his sympathy—with the outcast, the pariah. For the bourgeois novelist—for Dickens, and for Victor Hugo as contrasted with Baudelaire—the city could be read as a place of coincidence, unseen connection, and imminent contagion.[4] The novel itself, unlike the sketch, made manifest in its very structure patterns of relationship and alliance; it incorporated into the world of the familiar what might in other forms have remained exotic or ephemeral. The novelist-spectator took on the task of representing the poor and the outcast as features of middle-class experience and of illustrating the invasion of disease and disgrace into the homes of the respectable.

At the very center of this dialectic stood the figure of the fallen woman, the woman of the streets. Her role in the evocation of the nineteenth-century city, from Charles Lamb's "London-with-the-many-sins . . . City abounding in whores" to the high-capitalist London of *Mrs. Warren's Profession*, established the particular sexual politics of urban spectatorship and helped to shape narratives of urban experience throughout the period.[5] An inquiry into the masculinity of the spectator and into the role of woman as either spectacle or player on the rambler's stage suggests that the fallen woman's meaning was by no means monolithic. She could stand variously as an emblem of social suffering or debasement, as a projection of or analogue to the male stroller's

[3] Walter Benjamin, *Charles Baudelaire: A Lyric Poet in the Era of High Capitalism*, trans. Harry Zohn (London: New Left Books, 1973), p. 170.

[4] Benjamin distinguishes between Baudelaire, the flaneur, and Hugo, the *citoyen*, who celebrated the crowd as hero and placed himself comfortably within it (ibid., p. 66).

[5] Lamb's phrase comes from a letter to Thomas Manning written in November 1802. See *The Letters of Charles Lamb*, ed. E. V. Lucas (London: J. M. Dent, 1935), 1:223. George Bernard Shaw's *Mrs. Warren's Profession* was written in 1894.

alienated self, as an instrument of pleasure and a partner in urban sprees, as a rhetorical and symbolic means of isolating and quarantining urban ills in the midst of an otherwise buoyant metropolis, or as an agent of connection and contamination.

If the rambler was a man, and if one of the primary tropes of his urban description was the woman of the streets, could there have been a *female* spectator or a vision of the urban panorama crafted by a female imagination? And if such a vision were possible, under what conditions and with what distinctive features might it have been created? These are questions of history, about who was on the street in which urban neighborhoods and at what times of day and night, and questions of representation, about the cultural meanings ascribed to men and women in the context of urban literature and analysis. Social historians have begun to tell us about the public lives of women during the last decades of the nineteenth century, when they began to move about the city with some freedom, but it remains difficult to track the street lives of women in the 1840s, 1850s, and 1860s except through memoirs and fiction.[6] We have the overwhelming sense, however, that women alone on the street in the mid–nineteenth-century city were considered to be, as one American historian has put it, "either endangered or dangerous."[7] Martha Vicinus asserts that, even late in the century, a "lady was simply not supposed to be seen aimlessly wandering the streets in the evening or eating alone."[8] Virginia Woolf's middle-class Pargiter sisters,

---

[6] Recent historical works that recover the urban experiences of nineteenth-century women include: Ellen Ross, *Love and Toil: Motherhood in Outcast London, 1870–1918* (New York: Oxford University Press, 1993); Martha Vicinus, *Independent Women: Work and Community for Single Women, 1850–1920* (Chicago: University of Chicago Press, 1985); and Judith R. Walkowitz, *City of Dreadful Delight: Narratives of Sexual Danger in Late Victorian London* (Chicago: University of Chicago Press, 1992). Mary Ryan's *Women in Public Places: Between Banners and Ballots, 1825–1880* (Baltimore: Johns Hopkins University Press, 1990); and Christine Stansell's *City of Women: Sex and Class in New York, 1789–1860* (New York: Alfred A. Knopf, 1986), are invaluable works about the American scene which also shed light on Britain.

[7] Ryan, *Women in Public Places*, p. 86.

[8] Vicinus, *Independent Women*, p. 297. The question of the presence of working women on the streets has to be addressed in a slightly different manner. A rich source is the diary of Arthur Munby, who described London Bridge in 1861 as "the great thoroughfare for young working women and girls." He writes: "One meets them at every step: young women carrying large bundles of umbrella frames home to be covered; young women carrying cages full of hats, which yet want the silk and the binding, coster-girls often dirty and sordid, going to fill their empty baskets, and above all female sack-makers." Given Munby's sexual interest in working women, his description is not devoid of the eroticizing gaze of the male spectator, despite its evocation of a mundane and quotidian scene. See Derek Hudson, *Munby, Man of Two Worlds: The Life and Diaries of Arthur J. Munby, 1828–1910* (London: John Murray, 1972), p. 99. For working women in the metropolis, see

coming of age in the 1880s, "could not possibly go for a walk alone. ... Bond Street was as impassable, save with their mother, as any swamp alive with crocodiles. The Burlington Arcade was nothing but a fever-stricken den as far as they were concerned. To be seen alone in Piccadilly was equivalent to walking up Abercorn Terrace in a dressing gown carrying a bath sponge."[9] Even the West End, Woolf implies, where shopping offered new legitimacy to women's presence in public, conjured up the danger of exposure and contamination.[10]

Given their absence, their dubious legitimacy, their status as spectacle, and the eroticization of their presence on the streets, the relationship of women to spectatorship itself remained a vexed and nearly irresolvable one. If the rambler or flaneur required anonymity and the camouflage of the crowd to move with impunity and to exercise the privilege of the gaze, the too-noticeable female stroller could never enjoy that position. Baudelaire compares the spectator to the "prince who everywhere rejoices in his incognito," suggesting that by disguising his rank, the extraordinary man can "be at the centre of the world, and yet ... remain hidden from the world."[11] Sex, unlike rank, admitted no such easy camouflage; and though women such as George Sand and Vita Sackville-West did try from time to time to go about in public dressed as men, most women could not with any facility make themselves invisible and ignored.[12]

The bohemian or man at the margins in the early decades of the nineteenth century tended to celebrate the woman of the streets as his

---

Sally Alexander, *Women's Work in Nineteenth-Century London: A Study of the Years 1820–50* (London: Journeyman Press, 1983).

[9] Virginia Woolf, *The Pargiters* (New York: Harcourt Brace, 1977), p. 37.

[10] In the West End women were still part of the spectacle, and, as Judith Walkowitz and Martha Vicinus both suggest, it was while doing charity work in the East End that middle-class women felt most free to navigate the streets (Walkowitz, *City of Dreadful Delight*, pp. 52–53). Walkowitz includes an entire chapter on those urban residents she calls "new social actors"; she includes in this group "shopping ladies," charity workers, single women or "glorified spinsters," the matchworkers at Bryant and Mays, and Salvation Army lasses. For women shopping in the West End, see also Griselda Pollock, "Vicarious Excitements: *London: A Pilgrimage* by Gustave Doré and Blanchard Jerrold, 1872," *New Formations*, no. 4 (Spring 1988): 38–41.

[11] Charles Baudelaire, "The Painter of Modern Life," in *The Painter of Modern Life and Other Essays*, trans. Jonathan Mayne (New York: Garland, 1978), p. 9.|

[12] See Chapter 4 for George Sand's and Flora Tristan's efforts at masculine disguise. "I never felt so free," Vita Sackville-West wrote of dressing as a young man in her diary, "alone, and knowing that if I met my own mother face to face she would take no notice of me." Quoted in Nigel Nicolson, *Portrait of a Marriage* (London: Weidenfeld and Nicolson, 1973), p. 111.

double, as a symbol of his own rebellion against respectability, and as an element of his participation in what Benjamin, writing of Baudelaire, calls the "asocial."[13] For Baudelaire fallen womanhood is "woman in revolt against society"; for Thomas De Quincey she is the mirror image of his own status as "peripatetic," as "walker of the streets."[14] Like the ragpicker, the prostitute appears to the artist as a type of himself, a resourceful collector who makes a living off of the debris of the streets and sells her wares in the marketplace.[15]

The prostitute epitomizes the fleeting nature of urban relations, the lack of permanent connection. In her sexuality she marks "the ephemeral, the fugitive, the contingent," those very qualities that Baudelaire associates with modernity.[16] The young prostitute Ann in De Quincey's *Confessions of an English Opium Eater*, which Baudelaire translated and emended as *Un mangeur d'opium* in the 1850s, appears miraculously to save his life, becomes his close companion, and then disappears into the crowd never to be found again.[17] She becomes an emblem not only of what is of necessity lost in the city streets but also of the likely proximity even of those things that remain out of reach: "Doubtless we must have been sometimes in search of each other, at the very same moment, through the mighty labyrinth of London; perhaps even within a few streets of each other."[18] In this Ann resembles Baudelaire's "passante" in the sonnet Benjamin quotes to exemplify the erotic life of the crowd. A woman dressed in mourning—not a prostitute at all—passes by and becomes his "beauté fugitive," kindling a desire that thrives on her disappearance. "The delight of the city dweller," Benjamin writes, "is not so much love at first sight as love at last sight."[19] This form of erotic delight originates not only out of the woman's evanescence but also out of the male spectator's own potential transience. Both De Quincey and Baudelaire can move in and out of the position of urban margin-

---

[13] Benjamin, *Charles Baudelaire*, p. 171. Benjamin continues, "He achieved his only sexual relationship with a whore."

[14] Baudelaire, "The Painter of Modern Life," p. 37. Thomas De Quincey, *Confessions of an English Opium Eater* (Harmondsworth: Penguin, 1971), p. 50.

[15] Benjamin, *Charles Baudelaire*, p. 79.

[16] Ibid., p. 13.

[17] See Jessica R. Feldman, *Gender on the Divide: The Dandy in Modernist Literature* (Ithaca: Cornell University Press, 1993), pp. 97–101. Feldman writes that Baudelaire "saw in De Quincey a writer who told his, Baudelaire's, story. He wanted to lend his own voice to a tale that, though it chronicled the life of an English opium addict, seemed coincidentally to describe the life of a French artist and dandy" (p. 98).

[18] De Quincey, *Confessions*, p. 64.

[19] Benjamin, *Charles Baudelaire*, p. 45.

ality. In addition, De Quincey is a descendant of the eighteenth-century hero of *Bildung* who comes to the metropolis, tastes its pleasures and pains, and retreats again to the provinces.

Whether by the anonymous and transitory act of sex itself or by the suddenness of her appearance from and evaporation into the crowd, the sexually tainted woman (or the woman found and lost) serves to represent the experience of the masculine spectator. These women themselves gaze at the crowd, Baudelaire remarks, "as at a river which reflects their own image. In truth, they exist very much more for the pleasure of the observer than for their own."[20] The poet, exemplifying so much of the literature of urban spectatorship, cancels out the subjectivity of the woman of the streets. Paradoxically, by suggesting that she is a Narcissus who can see the streets only as a reflection of herself, he makes her into the spectator's mirror and the masculine observer's spectacle.

The fallen woman can also mark the observer's distance from the urban panorama he surveys by representing for him what is radically alien and relentlessly unsettling about the experience of the city. Wordsworth, in book 7 of *The Prelude*, uses the figure of fallen female sexuality in just such a manner. He recalls his introduction to London as a youth, "a transient visitant" unable to read the faces, the shows, the sights he sees.[21] The phantasmagoria of images and Babel of tongues thrill and frighten him; and he is "baffled" by the thought of "how men lived / Even next-door neighbors, as we say, yet still / Strangers, not knowing each the other's name" (ll. 116–18). He scans the crowd for what is decipherable and fastens on those people and edifices that carry their identities as texts upon themselves: the shops whose signs, "with letters huge inscribed," announce their names and trades "in allegoric shapes . . . / Or physiognomies of real men"; the beggar in sailor's dress who lies in the street forming letters with chalk on the paving stones beside him; and the blind beggar who wears his story written on a piece of paper hung around his neck. These text-bearing figures appear as types of the poet himself, transforming identity into language and offering it up to the spectator to be read. The poet's encounter with the blind beggar finally teaches him that the

---

[20] Baudelaire, "The Painter of Modern Life," p. 35.

[21] William Wordsworth, "The Prelude, or Growth of a Poet's Mind," bk. 7, l. 68, in *Selected Poems and Prefaces*, ed. Jack Stillinger (Boston: Houghton Mifflin/Riverside Press, 1965), p. 274; subsequently cited in the text. Stillinger uses the 1850 version of Wordsworth's poem.

man's label—perhaps like the autobiographical poem Wordsworth
writes—serves as the limit of what can be known of the self "and of
the universe."

If this admonition "from another world" seems an insufficient response to the disturbing mysteries of the city streets, it is, at least in
part, because embedded within this "London" book of *The Prelude* is a
series of female figures who tell a different story about human identity.
Between lines 315 and 400 of book 7 the poet introduces in an apparently aimless narrative a trio of women who represent different
forms of fallen female sexuality.[22] First, his memory sparked by a London play, he meditates on the woman whose legend inspired it, the
"Maid of Buttermere." A woman seduced and abandoned, the Maid
and her buried child rise up in his recollection as pure, chaste, and
untouchable. She lives "without contamination" beside the grave of
her dead baby, who is "fearless as a lamb" and safe in its shelter from
raging storms. Not so another mother and child he remembers from
his youth, a gaudy, painted actress and the beautiful son whose essential
purity is threatened by exposure to his mother's world:

> . . . Upon a board
> Decked with refreshments had this child been placed,
> *His* little stage in the vast theatre,
> And there he sate surrounded with a throng
> Of chance spectators, chiefly dissolute men
> And shameless women, treated and caressed. (ll. 355–61)

In this book of *The Prelude*, filled with references to London theatricals
and entertainments, Wordsworth registers the common association between actress and prostitute. Both, as Nina Auerbach has pointed out,
lived as "public" women who displayed themselves, performed for
men, and were paid for doing so.[23] Just as the actress falls from respectability by making herself a spectacle, so might this child be tainted by
even the gaze of those questionable creatures who look at him. The
strumpet-mother has faded from the poet's memory, he tells us, but
the boy remains, in the end an image of innocence untouched by the
dissolute crowd, "like one of those who walked with hair unsinged /

---

[22] For a closely related argument, see Lawrence Kramer, "Gender and Sexuality in *The
Prelude*: The Question of Book Seven," *ELH* 54 (Fall 1987): 619–37.

[23] Nina Auerbach, *Ellen Terry: Player in Her Time* (New York: W. W. Norton, 1987), pp.
38, 138.

Amid the fiery furnace." What might have become of the boy the poet knows not, but he conjectures that the child could have grown to be the kind of man who had reason to envy the Maid of Buttermere's dead infant, its life arrested in a pristine form.

Finally, the poet moves on to his third case, a nameless and indeed faceless prostitute, the first such woman he had ever seen, encountered while "traveling southward"—presumably toward London—"from our pastoral hills." For him this woman, "utter[ing] blasphemy" and exposed to "open shame" and "public vice," serves as confirmation of the complete and unbridgeable division between types of humanity ("splitting the race of man / In twain") and stands in for the extremity of experience the city encompasses. She embodies in a distilled and absolute form the separateness and alienation he feels from those who pass before him in London. There is no reading this woman, no admonition or consolation from "another world" that her unreadability partakes of a universal human condition. Although the poet can see the blind beggar as a type of himself, in these narratives of defiled female sexuality he is allied primarily with the chaste children of suspect mothers and, more precisely, with the actress's precariously innocent son. (It is interesting to note that later in book 7, in lines 602–19, he imagines the tender and protective parent of a living child as a *father*.) In these female figures he can represent not only the radical lack of connectedness he experiences in the city but also his anxiety about his own exposure to contamination and a consequent irreversible loss of innocence. By confining corruption to an association with femaleness—much as he cordons off the three female figures within that one section of the book—he proposes to keep the anxiety contained. Paradoxically, however, by sexualizing corruption he also makes it an uncontainable and unavoidable threat.

What Wordsworth tries to keep at bay in this London book of *The Prelude*—the danger of contamination embodied in the prostitute—emerges in the mid-nineteenth century as a dominant trope of urban description. In the Victorian dialectic of disconnection and contagion, the figure of fallen female sexuality shifts from marker of individuality and alienation to agent of connection and of disease both physical and social. As early as Blake's "London," in an image that introduces what Raymond Williams calls "a new way of seeing the human and social order as a whole," the "Harlot's curse" joins respectable with outcast London:

> But most thro' midnight streets I hear
> How the youthful Harlot's curse
> Blasts the new born Infant's tear
> And blights with plagues the Marriage hearse.[24]

Blake's insight—that the venereal disease associated with prostitution could serve as metaphor for a web of connection linking upper with lower classes, birth with death, bride with fallen woman, and innocence with experience—would become a theme of fiction, social investigation, sanitary reform literature, and journalism in the 1840s and 1850s.

The novelist or investigator of these decades registered the anxiety of the middle classes about the incursion of urban blight and disease into the preserves of their rank and fostered the notion that maintaining distance between classes in the city was neither wholly possible nor even desirable. The promotion of reform indeed depended on the threat of contagion, and the woman of the streets became the symbolic nexus of a variety of social and physical contaminants. She was allied metaphorically with the unsanitary conditions of urban life, with the refuse of the streets, with diseases such as cholera and typhus, with destitution and vagrancy, with the spread of vice and corruption of all kinds.[25] The prostitute Martha in *David Copperfield* (1850) wanders to a London riverside neighborhood where, legend had it, "one of the pits dug for the dead at the time of the Great Plague was hereabout, and a blighting influence seemed to have proceeded from it over the whole place."[26] Dickens's narrative joins Martha not just to the river's ooze and stench but also to a history of rampaging disease and death. This widely used imagery of contamination and pestilence culminated in a sense in the appropriately named Contagious Diseases Acts, passed by Parliament in the 1860s in an effort to contain the spread of venereal disease, especially in port towns, by forcing prostitutes to undergo med-

---

[24] Williams refers to Blake's "making of new connections" as "a precise prevision of the essential literary methods and purposes of Dickens" (*The Country and the City*, pp. 148–90).

[25] For the imagery associated with prostitution, see Alain Corbin, "Commercial Sexuality in Nineteenth-Century France: A System of Images and Regulations," in *The Making of the Modern Body: Sexuality and Society in the Nineteenth Century*, ed. Catherine Gallagher and Thomas Laqueur (Berkeley: University of California Press, 1987), pp. 209–19.

[26] Charles Dickens, *The Personal History, Adventures, Experience and Observation of David Copperfield, The Younger of Blunderstone Rookery* (New York: Signet, 1962), p. 677. In her *Myths of Sexuality: Representations of Women in Victorian Britain* (Oxford: Basil Blackwell, 1988), Lynda Nead comments on this same passage: "All the elements of the sanitary debate are there: the tainted air and impure water, the miasma from metropolitan burial-grounds, all festering and decomposing at this spot" (p. 127).

ical inspection. The acts themselves gave weight to the powerful notion that such women existed to ensnare men and to defile their bodies with disease.[27]

The narratives of prostitutes' lives that began to appear in certain midcentury treatises and investigations encouraged the idea that the woman of the streets was not wholly separable from the respectable bourgeois home. The influential French physician Alexandre Parent-Duchâtelet, expert on sewers and prostitution alike, stressed in his 1836 study that for many working-class women prostitution was a transitional occupation, not a lifetime identity.[28] Following suit, the English venereologist William Acton argued in the 1850s that prostitution might simply be a stage in a woman's life, and that she might gravitate eventually toward respectability and family life.[29] Any of these women, Acton writes, might become the "wife of an Englishman and the mother of his offspring."[30] Eliding the issue of class difference by making the prostitute's potential husband simply an "Englishman," Acton achieves his goal of bringing the problem of venereal disease close to home. Diseased women might become the mothers of Englishmen's offspring and thereby disrupt the process of inheritance. How much better, then, to police their activities and their bodies while they were still on the streets. Bracebridge Hemyng, in "Prostitution in London," his contribution to Henry Mayhew's *London Labour and the London Poor*, makes similar observations about the fluidity of the prostitute's status. The majority of such women, although not by any means all, he notes, "eventually become respectable, and merge into the ocean of propriety."[31] Hemyng includes the words of one relatively prosperous streetwalker, who ends by claiming, "We often do marry, and well too; why shouldn't we, we are pretty, we dress well, we can talk and insinuate ourselves into the hearts of men by appealing to their passions and

---

[27] See Ryan, *Women in Public Places*, for a superb discussion of a number of these issues in the American context. Ryan writes of this midcentury rhetoric that cast prostitutes as victimizers and "bloodsuckers" of men, as wanting to trap, rob, and infect their male captives (p. 72).

[28] On Parent-Duchâtelet's *De la prostitution dans la ville de Paris* (1836), see Judith R. Walkowitz, *Prostitution and Victorian Society* (Cambridge: Cambridge University Press, 1980), pp. 36–37; and Jill Harsin, *Policing Prostitution in Nineteenth-Century Paris* (Princeton: Princeton University Press, 1985), pt. 1, sec. 3.

[29] Walkowitz, *Prostitution and Victorian Society*, p. 46.

[30] William Acton, *Prostitution* (1857; rpt. London: MacGibbon and Kee, 1968), pp. 75–76.

[31] Bracebridge Hemyng, "Prostitution in London," in Henry Mayhew, *London Labour and the London Poor*, vol. 4 (1861–62; rpt. New York: Dover, 1968), p. 214.

their senses." He offers this woman's testimony as sufficient evidence to dispel the myth that "the harlot's progress is short and rapid."[32]

These investigators into the state of prostitution do much to close the gap between fallenness and respectability, in part to arouse the concern of complacent readers and in part to undercut the fictions about women of the streets which still prevailed in the popular imagination. At the same time, they provided material for new kinds of myths and anxieties: the specter of disease invisibly invading the middle-class home, the chance that the apparently chaste bride had a secret past, the unsettling possibility that "bad" women and "good" women were interchangeable. The streetwalker took on a newly powerful meaning as an agent of far-reaching contamination, and the rambler as investigator or novelist deployed the imagery of prostitution to evoke the inescapable web of connections that made up urban experience.

Recent critics, especially those interested in the connection between urban culture and the problem of modernity, have taken note of the virtual impossibility of the *flâneuse*. As a character, Janet Wolff remarks, she did not exist; or, writes Susan Buck-Morss, if one could identify the female version of *flânerie*, it would be prostitution. The flaneur, says Buck-Morss, "was simply the name of a man who loitered; but all women who loitered risked being seen as whores."[33] If we return to Raymond Williams's assertion that the apprehension of "the modern city" begins with "a man walking," we have a point of view compatible with these feminist notions of the masculinity of a modern urban vision. But if we follow Williams's statement back to the text of chapter 20 of *The Country and the City*, we observe that this assertion is followed by the illustrative examples of Blake, Wordsworth, Dickens's Florence Dombey, and Elizabeth Gaskell.[34] Unlike Wolff and Buck-Morss, Williams is not conscious of gender as an issue, and so he unself-consciously contradicts himself on the subject at the very start. But this lack of self-consciousness provides a challenge to the notion of the utter impossibility of female spectatorship and of the absence of a female urban vision. The inclusion of Florence Dombey leads us to contemplate how

[32] Ibid., p. 219.

[33] Buck-Morss, "The Flaneur, the Sandwichman, and the Whore," p. 119; Janet Wolff, "The Invisible *Flâneuse*: Women and the Literature of Modernity," in *The Problems of Modernity: Adorno and Benjamin*, ed. Andrew Benjamin (London: Routledge, 1989), pp. 141–56.

[34] Williams, *The Country and the City*, p. 233.

Dickens used the vulnerability and anxiety about exposure of female characters such as Florence, Esther Summerson, and Lady Dedlock to tell a particular kind of urban story. When a female character walks the streets, what happens to the portrait of the city the novelist represents? What occurs when a narrative tries to evoke the subjectivity of the always objectified female figure? What happens to the urban landscape when the hunted female herself becomes a decipherer of the crowd, a pursuer and a detective?

The inclusion of Gaskell in Williams's group of examples seems unremarkable: she was, after all, a great observer of the industrial city. In the context of the present discussion, however, her sex becomes a complicating issue, an ostensible obstacle to her spectatorship and to her presence on the street. How does the "impossibility" of the *flâneuse* or female spectator influence Gaskell's narratives of industrial life? How is the vulnerability of the female observer written into her narrative? And how does her own suspect status, as both street walker and woman writer, make its way into her subjects, her plots, and her characters?

My argument in this book is that the particular urban vision of the female observer, novelist, or investigator derives from her consciousness of transgression and trespassing, from the vexed sexuality her position implies, and from her struggle to escape the status of spectacle and become a spectator. The "respectable" middle-class woman creating her own city spectacle had to come to terms with woman's place in a well-established literary tradition of urban description as well as with her relationship to the poor women, the female beggars, the factory workers, and the prostitutes she observed on her own tentative rambles. Associated by gender with the very emblems of poverty, disease, and fallenness in urban panoramas created by novelists and social reformers, women writers had to contend with split identifications: they wrote with the cultural (and class) authority of the writer and with the taint of their sex's role in the urban drama. Rather than assume the absence of a female spectatorship, we might ask instead what circumstances and discourses shaped it and what typified its forms and contradictions.

In Part 1, "Stroller into Novelist," I explore the formal progression from sketch to novel and a parallel shift in the stance of the male spectator from one of detachment and transience to one of engagement and an awareness of possible contamination. From the 1820s, when the city was frequently represented as a stage, as a panorama to be viewed and savored from a distance, to the 1850s, when an overwhelming consciousness of the web of social connection dominated urban description, the metropolis became the central symbol of social crisis and the frequent object of investigation and acute concern. In 1800 only a minority of the English population resided in urban centers; by midcentury more people lived in cities than in rural areas.[35] Overcrowding, poor sanitation, unemployment, epidemic diseases, dangerous working conditions, inadequate housing, and unsettling changes in family patterns became features of daily life for many and issues of pressing national concern for more. The cities, especially London and the larger industrial towns, had become imaginatively and psychically inescapable. The figure of the fallen woman—the street prostitute and ultimately the bourgeois wife with a past—served as a means of representing first the novelty and buoyancy and then the danger and inevitability of urban experience.

In Part 2, "Fallen Women," I turn to the efforts of two women, Flora Tristan and Elizabeth Gaskell, to take on the role of urban spectator, Tristan as traveler and stroller in London, Gaskell as novelist of industrial Manchester. The texts composed by both women reflect their consciousness of the urban iconography of tainted female sexuality. Both bear marks of the authors' struggle to occupy the position of spectator when, at the same time, they themselves are part of the urban spectacle. In her *London Journal* Tristan takes advantage of her status as foreign observer to survey London and offer a critique of its social inequities and hypocrisies; but the economic and sexual marginality characteristic of the female travel writer's situation is accentuated and given a treacherous dimension within the urban context. Gaskell extended the role of social mediator typically available to the middle-class minister's wife into the sphere of novel writing, taking as her subject class conflict and its transcendence in the industrial town. *Mary Barton* and *North and South* are marked by the struggle to assume authority in a sphere of masculine concerns and by anxiety about the public exposure that attends such authority. Gaskell's narratives evince an interest in the connections between working women, prostitutes, female activists, and, by implication, female authors. They betray a nervousness about the inevitable eroticization of the woman—whether as author or as charac-

[35] See Asa Briggs, *Victorian Cities* (New York: Harper and Row, 1970), p. 12. See also Penelope J. Corfield, "Walking the City Streets: The Urban Odyssey in Eighteenth-Century England," *Journal of Urban History* 16 (February 1990): 147. Corfield writes: "Eventually, in the long term, worldwide urbanization has meant that the town has become less the exception, much more a routine social norm. That has blurred the sense of drama engendered by early growth. Undoubtedly, in eighteenth-century England, urban residents were still a minority of the total population, in 1800 as in 1700."

ter—who bears witness in a public manner about matters of injustice, class politics, or bigotry.

Finally, in Part 3, "New Women," I turn to the last decades of the century and to the fictions, poetry, and social investigations of women bolstered by the rise of new possibilities for urban female community and by a new set of social questions which women were, ostensibly, ideally suited to answer. In the 1880s and 1890s unmarried middle-class women began to find it possible to navigate the city on their own, leave families behind, and settle in flats or dwellings with others like themselves. New opportunities for education and for work fostered networks of independent women; and living outside of conventional domestic arrangements altered women's perspectives about marriage, sexuality, work, and social relations generally. Settlement house work, rent collecting, and a proliferation of philanthropic activities made urban centers, especially London, not only places in which to live and work but the very subjects of work—of writing, investigation, and social activism. The marginal and precarious social position of some of these women gave their evocations of urban life distinctive dimensions; they rewrote London out of a new relationship to its dangers, fascinations, and pleasures.

The late-century figures with whom I end this study mark the full-scale entry of women into the field of social investigation. Inspired by the work of Charles Booth and trained in the customary middle-class activity of "visiting," these women undertook lengthy and detailed examinations of urban working-class life. The elevation of domestic life to an issue of national concern in the last decade of the nineteenth century gave these female investigators an opportunity to marshall their acknowledged expertise on questions that were considered legitimately their own province. As urban spectators they entered private spaces rendered public by their writing and by the political and social agendas of the day. They assumed the authority of their class in relation to the poor and that of their sex in relation to men of their own class. In their investigations, however, their professional and personal dedication to the domestic realm invariably came into conflict with their own aspirations to escape the domestic sphere and claim the public one, the sphere of work, as their own. The one woman in this group of investigators who remained in the world of rambling—Mary Higgs, who produced a proto-Orwellian exploration of "going on the tramp"—discovered very quickly that, in her words, "the harlot *is* the *female tramp.*" She also learned that, disguised as a tramp for the purposes of investigation, she was subject to taunts and jeers, and that the "bold, free look of a man at a destitute woman must be felt to be realised."[36]

The subject of this book—the role of the woman on the street in the creation of a literature of rambling and urban investigation—touches on a number of larger issues of genre, literary persona, and the gendered province of authorship. As an emblem of alienation and social dislocation, the streetwalker figured in the construction of a certain type of urban artistic personality and in the depiction of the city as theater, carnival, and diversion. As a way of figuring webs of social connection, the image of the "public" woman helped to generate and give structure to the panoramic novel of urban life. Her powerful place in the evocation of the city, however, impinged on and indelibly marked the female spectator's ability to ramble, to see without being seen, and to represent her own urban experience. Although the female bohemian who strolled and looked with freedom could not exist in the nineteenth-century city, women were indeed on the streets; and, though their movements and their authority were hampered by urban realities and discourses alike, they ventured into public spaces and into their own project of representation. It is my intention in this book to acknowledge both their confinement within a tradition of masculine spectatorship and their efforts to reconfigure that tradition from within the contradictions and constraints of their experience and of their relationship to culture.

[36] Mary Higgs, *Glimpses into the Abyss* (London: P. S. King and Son, 1906), p. 94.

PART ONE

Stroller into Novelist

❧ ONE ❧

The City as Theater:
London in the 1820s

Early nineteenth-century London was a city in transition, no longer Augustan and not yet Victorian, no longer the buoyant, bawdy city of Boswell and not yet the menacing labyrinth of the later Dickens.[1] In the first three decades of the century, and particularly in the aftermath of Waterloo, the nation celebrated itself and its metropolis, keeping at bay an awareness of the new social realities that would ultimately dominate urban consciousness. The harsh facts of poverty and urban squalor, slums and homelessness that later troubled and animated the Victorian imagination made themselves felt in the most peripheral and subliminal of ways; they were detected but generally resisted as social problems worthy of attention and action. The urban observers and writers of these decades reflected this transitional state in their essays and sketches. They continued to employ the literary conventions of eighteenth-century urban description and tried in large measure to retain the equanimity about urban life that their predecessors had expressed. But their faithfulness to convention ultimately came under stress, and their writing betrayed ill-suppressed anxieties about the urban scene and the society that had spawned it.

The 1820s in particular saw the creation of a distinctive London character, shaped by such disparate cultural events as the reordering of city streets under George IV's "London improvements"; the ap-

[1] For a discussion of eighteenth-century London, see Max Byrd, *London Transformed: Images of the City in the Eighteenth Century* (New Haven: Yale University Press, 1978). Byrd writes, "When Boswell's soul bounded toward happy futurity, London had not yet become Cobbett's great wen nor had its furnaces and factories yet become satanic mills" (p. 1).

pearance of the famed literary monthly the *London Magazine*, with its
self-consciously urban identity; the proliferation of a popular urban
literature, most notably the works of Pierce Egan; and the creation of
new urban amusements that occupied the reconstructed capital and
made it their very subject. We see in the 1820s a society that regarded
the metropolis as a stage on which to perform and witness its own
civility, grandeur, and ebullience. The image of theater is crucial to
urban representation in the early nineteenth century, for it suggests
not only entertainment and performance but also a relationship of distance and tentativeness between spectator and the action on the stage.
The urban spectator of this period, whether writer or imagined subject,
experienced the sights and people of the street as passing shows or as
monuments to be glimpsed briefly or from afar. This distance helped
to obscure and control all that was seen, however arresting or unsettling, and it helped, too, to ensure that whatever did unsettle the spectator would not be understood as a symptom of some larger social
disturbance.

During these years of what one urban historian has referred to as "a
period of self-satisfied urban pride and grandiose speculative projects,"
a number of writers with a more skeptical relationship to the theatrical
city began to represent the metropolis from the marginal position of
the artist.[2] Although their portraits of urban experience were not as
celebratory as the theme of "metropolitan improvements," they signaled their aloofness from urban strife in terms of nostalgia, insouci-
ance, or bohemian detachment. Among many of these evocations
the prostitute figures as female partner to the rambler, at times a feature of the theatricality and high-spiritedness of city sprees, and at others the embodiment of transience, ephemerality, and estrangement. As
marker of the urban demimonde, she could represent both the liberating attractions and the victimized underclass of city life. The specta-
tor-reveler regarded her as an emblem of pleasure and diversion, while
the bohemian found in her not an object of pity but a reflection of
himself.

In August 1822 a fairly unexceptional sketch by Cyrus Redding, titled
"The Tea Garden," appeared in the *London Magazine*, which first published Lamb's "Elia," De Quincey's "Opium Eater," and Hazlitt's "Ta-

---

[2] Donald J. Olsen, *The City as a Work of Art: London, Paris, Vienna* (New Haven: Yale
University Press, 1986), p. 21.

ble Talk." In this brief piece the narrator takes a familiar evening ramble up Primrose Hill in the north of London for the often-sought "bird's-eye view" of the metropolis. Here, from a considerable height and distance, he achieves a vision of what for this particular writer is the essential London, not a "mighty heart lying still" but the active, powerful, and glorious center of the Western world: "Royalty, legislation, nobility, learning, science, trade, and commerce, were concentrated before me in a mightier whole than had ever before been in the history of the world; and its fame and glory had gone forth and been felt in the most remote corners of the earth."[3]

This London spectator, full of pride and pleasure in his city and his nation, moves on to Chalk Farm, a celebrated tea garden on Primrose Hill, where he is accosted by a clarinet-playing beggar. The beggar proceeds to tell the rambler all about his plan for ridding England of poverty and "achieving a more equitable distribution of the good things in life," until their chat is interrupted—much to the rambler's relief—by a procession of little girls from a charity school. The girls are about to have tea to celebrate their annual public day when, the author tells us, they are "marshalled to gratify their patrons." His response to this custom is quite different from that of Blake, who, as the poet of "Experience," cursed the "cold and usurous hand" that fed the miserable babes of his second "Holy Thursday" poem. The sight of the little girls moves our rambler to meditate on the virtue and generosity of the English people, on their "stock of pure unadulterated feeling—a redeeming charity of the most exalted kind." He goes on, echoing his pride in the greatness of the capital, "No nation under heaven has ever yet come near us in deeds of charity."[4]

I begin with this sketch because it embodies, in a characteristic and uncritical way, two dominant perceptual and literary modes of evoking the early nineteenth-century city: the panoramic view and the sudden, instructive encounter with a solitary figure. These are found in a variety of different forms of urban representation during this period, in literary and graphic portraits of the city, in urban entertainments, and even in the renewal and reconstruction of the city under George IV. The literary use of these devices can be seen in Wordsworth's two very different poetic evocations of London: the view from Westminster Bridge,

---

[3] "The Tea Garden," *London Magazine* 6 (August 1822): 137. Frank P. Riga and Claude A. Prance identify the author as Cyrus Redding in their *Index to the London Magazine* (New York: Garland, 1978), p. 61.

[4] "The Tea Garden," p. 140.

which partially subverts the image of the imperial capital by wedding it to the image of nature, and the epiphanic encounter with the blind beggar in book 7 of *The Prelude*. In this London section of *The Prelude* Wordsworth transposes the experience of what Geoffrey Hartman has called the "halted traveler" from the bucolic to the urban scene.[5] In fact, this mode of urban encounter—the revelatory meeting with a solitary figure—is inherited from romanticism and, before that, from eighteenth-century conventions of the sublime.

Panoramic descriptions replicate in literary form the topographic views of the city which proliferated in nineteenth-century illustrations of London and which had their origins in eighteenth-century graphic representations of European cities after the manner of Canaletto. And descriptions of chance encounters with street figures have their pictorial analogue in the sketches of London types that were collected in bound editions and exhibited singly in printshop windows to entice buyers and to provide free entertainment for those who could only afford to look.[6] Panoramic London also provided forms of amusement, both as it could actually be seen on Sunday outings from vantage points such as Primrose Hill and as it was depicted in panoramas and dioramas, those new popular entertainments of the period.[7]

These two modes, panoramic and episodic, though radically different in structure and content, convey an essentially coherent and consistent interpretation of urban experience. Cyrus Redding's rambler offers a fairly crude version of this interpretation. He loves to view London from afar, to see it as a stage set, a mural, or a panorama in order to take in without obstruction the grandeur, the splendor, and the monumentality of the city. As Donald Gray has observed, the descriptions of London that accompanied nineteenth-century collections of graphic views are filled with "such words as 'elegant,' 'grand,' 'beautiful and var-

[5] Geoffrey H. Hartman, *Wordsworth's Poetry, 1787–1814* (New Haven: Yale University Press, 1964), pt. 1.

[6] For more on visual representations of London, see two very fine essays, Donald J. Gray's "Views and Sketches of London in the Nineteenth Century" and Will Vaughn's "London Topographers and Urban Change," in *Victorian Artists and the City*, ed. Ira Bruce Nadel and F. S. Schwarzbach (New York: Pergamon Press, 1980), pp. 43–58, 59–77. In this same volume see Guilland Sutherland's "Cruikshank and London" (pp. 106–25) on the viewing of graphic satire as popular urban entertainment.

[7] For outings to Primrose Hill, see M. Dorothy George, *Hogarth to Cruikshank: Social Change in Graphic Satire* (London: Penguin, 1967), p. 77; for panoramas and dioramas, see Richard D. Altick, *The Shows of London* (Cambridge: Harvard University Press, 1978), esp. chaps. 10–12.

ied,"noble,' and 'princely.' "[8] Panoramic London is not only highly picturesque but also artificial. Topographers altered the scale of streets and buildings to accentuate the stateliness, symmetry, and sheer beauty of the city; and they imagined the streets themselves as largely devoid of people, and certainly of the chaos—not to say anarchy—of the London scene.[9] The ideological message of this perspective seems clear: here is an ordered and virtuous capital, emblematic of a majestic and great society, indicative of a nation fit to rule a great and growing empire.

If panoramic views of London speak unequivocally to a buoyant and untroubled confidence in the grandeur of English society, traditional encounters with the urban solitary seem at first glance less convincing as emblems of Regency smugness. Again, Redding's rambler provides us with an unsubtle version of the way in which the urban solitary can confirm the complacency that a panoramic view from Primrose Hill inspires in the observer. The rambler is accosted by the clarinet-playing beggar only to be diverted by the procession of charity girls, a timely reassurance that all is right with English social justice and with the English national character. But in some important sense the romantic moment of revelation has been aborted, or at least subverted, in this case. The rambler never receives the lesson—moral or philosophical— that the beggar might offer, and indeed derives quite a different one by turning his attention to the orphans. It is as if he introduces the beggar only to deny his significance, to defuse the obvious social question that his existence raises, both in life and in literature. So in this *London Magazine* sketch the urban solitary does little if anything to disturb the equanimity achieved by that splendid "bird's-eye view."

In a larger sense, literary representations of isolated urban encounters—as well as graphic sketches of street types—share with panoramic views of the city the element of theater or spectacle. The urban solitary becomes, as we shall see in the essays and literary sketches of the period, an act in the passing show of London, an object to consider, observe, and appreciate. He (or she) exists for the sake of the spectator's pleasure or education rather than as a character in his or her own right or as an introduction to the wider social scene of which the character is a part. Walter Benjamin, writing of an analogous genre of urban

[8] Gray, "Views and Sketches," p. 45.
[9] Vaughn, "London Topographers," pp. 59–60.

representation, observed that in the French feuilleton the urban worker appeared for the last time outside of and separated from his class, as a "stage extra in an idyll."[10] This is equally true of the English sketch, both graphic and literary, of the period. While the spectator remains invisible, his *experience* is paramount; the urban "type" is visible, fully exposed, yet his or her thoughts, feelings, and experience of life remain mysterious.

In eighteenth-century traditions of the lowlife sketch, typical street figures—ballad singers, chimney sweepers, dustmen, prostitutes, pickpockets—were, as Dorothy George has phrased it, "a subject for ridicule, not compassion."[11] In the early part of the nineteenth century, ridicule gave way to detached amusement, as well as to the "scientific" impulse of cataloguing and sorting. It has been remarked that in early nineteenth-century sketches the crossing sweep was depicted in a manner and tone not unlike that used to represent outings at Blackheath or Vauxhall Gardens: both were entertainments, and their juxtaposition or disjunction signaled no cause for alarm, no grounds for social criticism.[12] To include and embrace all of London—its low as well as its high life, its orphans, prostitutes, and beggars as well as its monuments and grand edifices—was to disclaim the anxiety about urban life and British society that existed just below the surface in an as yet unconscious and unarticulated form.

Another way to understand the link between these two seemingly distinct ways of seeing the city is to refer to Michel Foucault's evocation of the Panopticon, the Benthamite device for surveying prisoners from a central tower. The Panopticon—which, Foucault speculates, owed something to the concept of the early panorama—afforded the surveyor or spectator both a panoramic view of the whole prison scene and the ability to scrutinize individual prisoners isolated in their cells.[13] As in the case of the panorama, the privileged central vantage point of the Panopticon gives the surveyor control over what he sees, control that is heightened by his own invisibility. "He is the object of information," writes Foucault, "never a subject in communication."[14] Similarly, the urban spectator of this period remains anonymous and

[10] Walter Benjamin, *Charles Baudelaire: A Lyric Poet in the Era of High Capitalism*, trans. Harry Zohn (London: New Left Books, 1973), p. 161.

[11] George, *Hogarth to Cruikshank*, p. 73.

[12] Gray, "Views and Sketches," p. 47.

[13] Michel Foucault, *Discipline and Punish: The Birth of the Prison*, trans. Alan Sheridan (New York: Pantheon, 1977), p. 317, n. 4.

[14] Ibid., p. 200.

invisible, always an observing eye whose own presence is suppressed. As the sketch of the urban type separates the potentially dangerous or unsettling face from the crowd in order to tame it and to defuse its mystery, so the Panopticon abolishes, in Foucault's words, "a compact mass, a locus of multiple exchanges, individualities merging together, a collective effect," and replaces it with a "collection of separated individualities."[15] Whether viewed from afar, atop the dome of St. Paul's or Primrose Hill, or at close range as in isolated encounters or images, the city's disruptive nature, like the prisoner's, is muted and controlled.

The image of London as a great world city possessed of an expansive and charitable spirit was embodied in George IV's grand scheme for rebuilding the capital during the era of "metropolitan improvements." With the help of his architects John Nash, John Soane, and Robert Smirke, George—first as regent and then as king—oversaw the transformation of the West End. These men re-created Regent's Park in the north and St. James's Park in the south in their modern forms, linked the two by extending Regent Street, built Trafalgar Square and its grand monuments, reconstructed the west end of the Strand, transformed Buckingham House into Buckingham Palace, and erected the Hyde Park arch and screen.[16] Nash's original plan for the West End amounted, in John Summerson's words, to a "highly picturesque conception of a garden city for an aristocracy, supported by charming panoramas showing a composition of alluring groves and elegant architecture of a somewhat Parisian character."[17] Although only a fraction of the original plan was carried out, these London "improvements" gave the city a new sense of grand scale, classical stateliness, openness, and prosperity, and provided spectators, artists, and writers alike with panoramic views and unbroken vistas. This transformation expressed what one historian has referred to as the "euphoria" of the years between Waterloo and the Reform Bill, the belief of the many that London was "healthy, happy and beautiful."[18]

[15] Ibid., p. 201.

[16] For the best account of the changes London underwent during the Regency, see John Summerson, *Georgian London* (Harmondsworth: Penguin, 1978), chap. 13. He writes: "Once, and only once, has a great plan for London, affecting the development of the capital as a whole, been projected and brought to completion. This was the plan which constituted the 'metropolitan improvements' of the Regency" (p. 177).

[17] Ibid., p. 178.

[18] Donald J. Olsen, *The Growth of Victorian London* (London: B. T. Batsford, 1976), p. 38. Olsen writes: "Chadwick and Shaftsbury and Mayhew had yet to point out that Lon-

Figure 1 Thomas Shepherd, "The Quadrant and Part of Regent Street." Thomas Shepherd and James Elmes, *Metropolitan Improvements; or, London in the Nineteenth Century* (1827). Department of Rare Books and Special Collections, Princeton University Libraries.

If these Regency improvements accentuated the beauty and grandeur of London, they also enhanced, to some degree, its quality of theatricality and sheer spectacle. London took on a new aura of artifice and became not only a more easily navigable city but one more readily viewed as an enormous stage set. A number of decades later George Moore observed, as others must have done, that the "circular line" of Regent Street itself resembled an amphitheater (figure 1). Parks and museums were at the center of the new plan, for amusement, as well as taste and power, was essential to the character of the metropolis. Theaters, too, had their place in the refashioned city: Covent Garden and Drury Lane had both been rebuilt earlier in the century, the former by Robert Smirke himself. Smirke gave Covent Garden its Doric portico and grand staircase, and in the 1820s Benjamin Wyatt added porticos to Drury Lane. The Theatre Royal, Haymarket, was rebuilt in 1820–21, designed by Nash as part of the program of metropolitan improvements.[19] The grand neoclassicism of the theaters' facades complemented the monumentality and stateliness of Regent Street and the

don was unhealthy, overcrowded, and miserable. . . . Street and park seemed to point the way for the positive transformation of London into a city that would stir the pride and command the affection of the whole British people, and represent to the world the taste and humanity of the British nation" (p. 38).

[19] Summerson, *Georgian London*, pp. 254–56.

Hyde Park arch, and the porticos provided opportunities for promenading, loitering, and enjoying a space both interior and exterior (figure 2).[20] The entertainments outside the theater, both elegant and
lowlife, competed with those inside. The theaters and adjacent coffeehouses and cafés were the provinces of male sociability and slumming.[21]

As if to underscore this connection between the "new" London and
urban entertainment, buildings erected expressly to house the panoramas and dioramas of the 1820s were planned as part of the Regent's
Park area. The first London diorama opened in 1823 in a Georgian
building designed by Augustus Pugin, at that time employed by John
Nash, at the southeast corner of the park amidst the most fashionable
new mansions of the day.[22] The diorama, designed by its French inven-
tor Louis Daguerre, fed the public taste for "romantic topography, the
stuff of picturesque art and of sentimental antiquarianism," the same
taste that shaped, or at least responded to, the new look of the West
End.[23] Even more obviously emblematic of the tie between Regency
improvements and the London of artifice was the Colosseum, the
Greek Revival building that housed an extraordinary panorama of London as seen from a bird's-eye view atop St. Paul's.

Decimus Burton, designer of the triumphal arch and screen at Hyde
Park Corner, planned the Colosseum as a "magnificent palace-for-
profit, dedicated to the more seemly pleasures of Regency society . . . a
kind of public counterpart of Carlton House, the sumptuous mansion
in Pall Mall on which the Prince Regent . . . had squandered a fortune."[24] The creator of the panorama, Thomas Hornor, described a
number of years later as a "compound of Barnum and Nash," captured
a rounded panorama of the city from its highest point, a view of an
"absolutely ideal" London without smoke, clouds, or fog. The Colosseum, which took almost the entire decade of the 1820s to complete,

[20] See Walter Benjamin on the arcades of Paris as the perfect site for strolling, as "a
cross between a street and an *intérieur*" (*Charles Baudelaire*, pp. 36–37).

[21] In many larger towns in England a "red-light district" was located near places of
entertainment, especially theaters. See Penelope J. Corfield, "Walking the City Streets:
The Urban Odyssey in Eighteenth-Century England," *Journal of Urban History* 16 (February
1990): 148. Thomas Burke, in *English Night-Life: From Norman Curfew to Present Black-Out*
(London: B. T. Batsford, 1941), describes Covent Garden in the eighteenth century as a
place where wealthy rakes would sit in carriages and watch the "up-and-down procession"
of women of the streets in the piazzas nearby (p. 49).

[22] See Altick, *Shows of London*, pp. 163–64. Augustus Charles Pugin was the émigré
architect father of the author of *Contrasts*.

[23] Ibid., p. 166.

[24] Ibid., p. 142.

Figure 2 Thomas Shepherd, "Burlington Arcade, Piccadilly." Thomas Shepherd and James Elmes, *Metropolitan Improvements; or, London in the Nineteenth Century* (1827). Department of Rare Books and Special Collections, Princeton University Libraries.

became the most celebrated entertainment of its day. It was built, appropriately, on "one of the most desirable sites in London," next to the grand terraces surrounding Regent's Park.[25] What visitors came to see depicted in the panorama they could also see in actuality by mounting to a lookout point atop the Colosseum. "Winding still higher," wrote James Elmes in his lengthy description of the extraordinary building in *Metropolitan Improvements,* "the spectator suddenly emerges into an extensive gallery, built round the exterior of the building, where it is no longer a picture that is before him, but a living panorama of the whole circle around him."[26] This experience must have helped to blur the distinction between representation and reality for the viewer and to make the city and its entertainments seem as one.

The bird's-eye view from St. Paul's or the Colosseum and the refashioning of Regency London both worked to obscure the poverty that was built into the very structure of the modern city. H. J. Dyos writes that although the Regency improvements were not designed to affect slum areas in any direct way, their presumably incidental result was to

[25] Ibid., pp. 141, 149, 142.
[26] Thomas Shepherd and James Elmes, *Metropolitan Improvements, or London in the Nineteenth Century* (London: Jones and Co., 1827), p. 78.

reinforce and sharpen the already existing geographic separation
between classes and to contain the slums of the West End.[27] An article
in the July 1825 issue of *London Magazine* celebrated the projected improvements of St. James's Park and berated the "sentimental philanthropy" of the day that "indulges itself in weeping over the
inconveniences of those who must be removed."[28] According to the
author of this article, too much concern had been wasted on the plight
of the poor and criminal classes, and clearing them out of certain areas
and public spaces would not be a bad thing. Systematic slum clearance
would be a project of the post–Reform Bill future, but the desire to
make slums less visible, even invisible, to the upper classes was already
finding expression in Nash's plans. Nash spoke explicitly of making the
line from Charing Cross to Oxford Street a "boundary and complete
separation" between the dwellings of the nobility and those of the commercial classes. It was implicit in his scheme—and went without say-
ing—that the poor would remain completely out of sight.[29]

The comments in *London Magazine* and Dyos's analysis of the implicit
motives of those who were reshaping London in the 1820s suggest that,
as in the case of Redding's rambler, there was a persistent consciousness of urban poverty even as it was being denied, contained, and min-
imized. Among the writers, planners, and observers of this period there
seems to have been a need to raise the social question if only to ab-
negate it. One such case is the dedication to George IV that prefaces
Thomas Shepherd and James Elmes's impressive volume of prints and
descriptions of new London sites, *Metropolitan Improvements, or London
in the Nineteenth Century,* published in 1827. In Elmes's homage to the
king he compares the British monarch to the emperor Augustus and
the new London to ancient Rome. But, as Elmes is careful to remark,
in Rome "the few were prodigiously rich, and the mass of the people
as wretchedly poor; in Britain, the *converse* of this unhappy condition
prevails: and the majority of your MAJESTY's subjects are in the secure
enjoyment of liberty, prosperity and happiness."[30] The beggar is present, as he is in the rambler's outing to Primrose Hill, but he is acknowledged only to be dismissed. It was not *his* story, the story of the

[27] H. J. Dyos, "The Objects of Street Improvement in Regency and Early Victorian
London," in *Exploring the Urban Past: Essays in Urban History,* ed. David Cannadine and
David Reeder (Cambridge: Cambridge University Press, 1982), pp. 82–83.

[28] "On the Projected Improvements of St. James's Park," *London Magazine,* n.s., 2 (July
1825): 446.

[29] Quoted in Dyos, "The Objects of Street Improvement," p. 82.

[30] Shepherd and Elmes, *Metropolitan Improvements,* pp. iv–v.

"wretched poor," that was to be revealed in the period of "metropolitan improvements."

If journalists and George IV's planners and architects represent the dominant official vision of London in the early decades of the nineteenth century, writers such as Charles Lamb, Thomas De Quincey, and Pierce Egan mirror and yet transform that vision in their literary evocations of the metropolis. That these writers, bohemian and peripheral to the middle class as they were, should echo many of the sentiments and attitudes of Redding's chauvinistic rambler can be explained, at least in part, by their very marginality. They remained outside the class relations they saw enacted on the city streets, disengaged from the social struggle they watched as observers.[31] But as they reaffirmed the conventions of urban writing within which they worked, so too did they subvert and reshape them, betraying varying degrees of discomfort with the obliviousness to social suffering that these conventions reinforced.

All three writers, deeply influenced in a variety of ways by eighteenth-century traditions of urban description, mark a period of transition that looks backward in tone and form and yet forward to the subjects and concerns of Victorian urban spectators. Their marginality allows them to see a wider drama of urban life than many of their contemporaries did, but they stop short of framing the full critique of society that this drama would later elicit. The personae they create—Egan's Tom and Jerry, Lamb's Elia, De Quincey's Opium Eater—remain observers, perhaps (as in the case of Egan's swells) participating briefly in city sprees, but withdrawing again, looking in from the outside like an audience at a play, a window-shopper on the boulevard, a flaneur. Elia and the Opium Eater remain invisible, virtually anonymous, only tentatively engaged in the urban scene. Similarly, the implied reader of Egan's *Life in London* is invited to observe the urban scene vicariously and invisibly by reading Egan's book.

The forms these three writers employ reinforce, indeed mimic, this tentativeness. Lamb's essay or sketch, the strange, seemingly formless prose of De Quincey, the nonnovelistic fiction of Egan bring us in touch with the city without sustaining our involvement or resolving the questions these tantalizing glimpses often raise. These episodic forms, more akin to anecdote than story, are what Walter Benjamin would call

---

[31] The flaneur, writes Walter Benjamin, "still stood at the margin, of the great city as of the bourgeois class. Neither of them had yet overwhelmed him. In neither of them was he at home. He sought his asylum in the crowd" (*Charles Baudelaire*, p. 170).

"dioramic literature" (the French edition of Egan's *Life in London,* published in 1822, was titled "The English Diorama; or Picturesque Rambles in London"). Individual sketches of street characters in the popular press, he comments, can be compared to the "plastically arranged foreground of the dioramas," while their "documentary content" corresponds to the "painted backgrounds" of these entertainments.[32] The city—the social setting—of these dioramic forms is an unchanging backdrop; their representations of human life are static, not unfolding or changing but captured in a frozen state. The form of the literary sketch reproduces the brief encounter, the moment of viewing the urban scene. It tells no stories, nor does it sustain the encounter between author and reader any more than the content of the sketch itself sustains the relation between the urban observer and what he observes.

Pierce Egan's *Life in London, or The Day and Night Scenes of Jerry Hawthorne, Esq. and his Elegant Friend Corinthian Tom in their Rambles and Sprees through the Metropolis,* illustrated by Isaac Robert and George Cruikshank, owes much to Elizabethan forms of popular literature that featured the underworld of London with its rogues, criminals, and prostitutes, and at the same time anticipates both fictional and journalistic Victorian accounts of the London scene.[33] Egan employed the well-established device of sending a country gent—in this case Jerry Hawthorne—around London in the company of a swell—here his urbane cousin Corinthian Tom—to "SEE LIFE." The principle that organizes their sprees around town is that of contrast: high life and low life, industry and idleness, religious virtue and criminality, usefulness and dissipation, charity and wickedness. Glittering scenes of wealth alternate with scenes of poverty, crime, and drunkenness; the sights of London are valued for their variety and, above all, for their novelty. The metropolis, we are told, is a "complete CYCLOPEDIA," each street a volume of intelligence."[34]

As in contemporary collections of graphic sketches of London scenes and types, contrast works here only inadvertently as a tool of social

[32] Ibid., p. 161.
[33] See J. C. Reid, *Bucks and Bruisers: Pierce Egan and Regency London* (London: Routledge and Kegan Paul, 1971), pp. 50–52.
[34] Pierce Egan, *Life in London . . .* (London: John Camden Hotten, 1869), pp. 51–52; subsequently cited in the text. Carol L. Bernstein, in *The Celebration of Scandal: Toward the Sublime in Victorian Urban Fiction* (University Park: Pennsylvania State University Press, 1991), discusses *Life in London* in the context of the "fashionable novel" and dandyism (pp. 86–91).

Figure 3 I. R. and G. Cruikshank, "*Lowest 'Life in London.'* Tom, Jerry & Logic, among the unsophisticated sons & daughters of nature at 'All-Max' in the East." Pierce Egan, *Life in London* (1821).

criticism and functions primarily as a mode of entertainment and a source of delight. One of the book's most popular set pieces, for example, consists of a visit to "All-Max," a dive in the East End where gin and lowlife types dominate the scene (illustrated in figure 3), followed immediately by a trip to "Almacks," a grand assembly room in the West End where Tom, Jerry, and their man-about-town companion Bob Logic will have to mind their "P's and Q's." All-Max impresses even the jaded Bob Logic as "one of the greatest *novelties* that he had ever witnessed in low life" (p. 322; emphasis added). But it is the contrast between the two homonymous places of amusement that provides these swells with the most intense pleasure. "This will be a rich treat to you JERRY," Tom assures his friend, "and the contrast will be delightful; more especially, as the time is so short that we shall pass from ALL-MAX in the East to ALMACKS in the West almost like the rapid succession of scenes in a play" (p. 325). London is very much a "play" for Tom and Jerry, and its "scenes" are put together not to tell a story but to amuse, surprise, or shock simply by appearing side by side. As in a "CYCLOPEDIA," the juxtaposition of items promises no revelation of plot and no discernible connection between those chosen for inclusion.

Life in London puts its readers in the audience with Tom and Jerry and offers to protect them from the dangers of urban experience. It insulates its readers and, as we shall see, its heroes from the ultimately disturbing scenes of poverty and human degradation that it nevertheless represents. At the outset the narrator offers his audience what he calls a "*camera obscura*" view of the city, "not only [for] its safety, but because it is so snug, and also possessing the invaluable advantages of SEEING and not being seen" (p. 46). We can read about the most dangerous characters and parts of London and remain perfectly safe, keep our participation vicarious, even voyeuristic, sit by the fireside, see "LIFE," and emerge unscathed. Egan makes explicit what many urban observers of his age only implied: that they wished to maintain their own invisibility and invulnerability while enjoying, and even learning from, the "shows" of the city.

Tom and Jerry reproduce this avoidance of real danger—physical, social, and moral—in their own rambles and adventures. At a number of points Egan brings his genteel young men face to face with the hardcore underworld of the city. Tom and Jerry visit a sluicery (gin shop) to drink "blue ruin" and there observe two figures who give them— and the reader—pause: an aging, gin-sodden streetwalker, "Gateway Peg," and a barely clothed urchin begging for gin to take home to his ailing mother. The narrative response to Gateway Peg is cold-blooded; she offers an opportunity for moralizing rather than for pity or understanding. "This *lump* of *infamy, disease* and *wretchedness*," Egan writes, "was once a well-known toast among the *bon-vivants* for her elegance of person" (p. 218). The urchin is harder either to censure or to dismiss flippantly, so instead the narrator turns away almost without comment, assuring his readers that this unexceptional scene can be observed nightly "in *much more depraved* colours," as he declares with a parting flourish that this is, after all, "LIFE IN LONDON" (p. 219). This final phrase abruptly cuts off the possibility of commentary on the boy's circumstances and reabsorbs him into London's passing show.

After consuming too much gin, Tom and Jerry enter a coffee shop in the same neighborhood, and here they are greeted by "a complete picture of . . . drunkenness, beggary, lewdness, and carelessness" (a scene illustrated in figure 4). The narrator responds first by praising the gruesome scene as "quite *new* to thousands" and then by resorting to an all but incomprehensible vocabulary of London slang (p. 219). The slang allows the narrator to describe in a coded manner a group of "Cyprians," or prostitutes, but it also places psychological distance between him and the lowlife gang he brings into view. Indeed, the chapter takes on the quality of a split narrative, with a boisterous run-

Figure 4 I. R. and G. Cruikshank, "*Midnight.* Tom & Jerry at a coffee shop near the Olympic." Pierce Egan, *Life in London* (1821).

ning commentary on the "Cyprians," "Lady-birds," or "Fancy Pieces" and their pimps and procuresses in the main part of the text and a lament about the abuse and exploitation of prostitutes in the footnotes. "In the motley group," writes the narrator from the point of view of a swell delighted to have come across such a scene in his rambles, "are several *Coves of Cases* [proprietors of brothels] and procuresses, keeping a most vigilant eye that none of their 'decked-out girls' *brush off* with the property intrusted to them for the night; and other persons of the same occupation, may be *seen* closely WATCHING the females belonging to their establishments" (pp. 215–16). The lengthy footnote to this passage includes an account of how procurers keep women "as dirty as sweeps" until they go out on the town; berate, starve, and beat them if they bring home no earnings; search them after they have been with a client; and do not allow them to keep any money of their own. "The life of a PROSTITUTE," reads the footnote, "is of itself a most severe *punishment*, independent of *disease* and *imprisonment*. A volume would not unfold the *miseries* allied to such a character" (p. 216). Whether a volume would suffice or not, Egan's tour of London does not set out to tell the prostitute's story from her point of view. Instead, his volume presents the drama of pimp and streetwalker as a sight to be consumed. And yet the notes introduce a counternarrative of protest against a system of abuses that leaves its traces and prefigures a later Victorian theme.

Egan's central narrative, however, does work to keep sentiments of concern and guilt at bay. In the penultimate chapter Tom takes Jerry to the "back slums" of the "Holy Land" to see the cadgers. Here the beggars of London are unmasked, exposed as hypocrites and impostors. An apparently pregnant woman removes the pillow from under her stays; a crossing sweep manages to drink and feast grandly; a blind beggar turns out to see quite well; the poor woman with twins returns her "children" to the people from whom she has hired them (p. 375). This exposé, coming as it does at the end of numerous ostensibly amusing but potentially uncomfortable scenes of London low life, partly reassures the reader that what has seemed so disturbing should not be contemplated with too much concern after all. The real victims of urban life turn out to be those "charitable and humane persons" (p. 375) who have been taken in by the beggars' disguises.

It is during Tom and Jerry's visit to Newgate Prison on the morning of execution, however, that one senses most palpably Egan's anxiety about the cruelty of urban life and his desire to represent and yet repress its implications. Once again he is on the verge of evoking in both his heroes and his readers feelings of sympathy and horror, only to retreat into speechlessness. "Neither the PEN nor the PENCIL . . . can do it justice, or convey a description of the '*harrowed feelings*' of the few spectators that are admitted into the Condemned Yard upon such an occasion," he writes (p. 315). The swells decline the opportunity to get a bird's-eye view of the prison yard during their tour and hastily quit the "gloomy falls of Newgate" to join the "busy hum and life of society" (p. 317) at the Royal Exchange. The avoidance of grim social reality that this quick exit represents is underscored a number of episodes later when Tom and Jerry return to Newgate briefly on their way to the docks. When they now climb up to get their bird's-eye view, it is not the condemned prisoners but the order pervading the prison that impresses them. They "expressed themselves much pleased, on looking down into the different yards, and witnessing the excellent mode of discipline practised in that prison, of sorting the criminals into classes, according to their distinction of crimes" (p. 261). The brutal sight of men about to be hanged is exchanged for a vision of penal rationalism.

The view from the top of Newgate calls to mind the views from Primrose Hill and the dome of St. Paul's as well as Bentham's Panopticon. Here, in *Life in London*, we have a much more explicit expression of the need to achieve distance—and height—in order to see modern life at its best, its most palatable, and its most easily celebrated. The view of the prison yards serves almost as a parodic panorama: it brings order into relief while it obscures suffering, and it ensures the power to see without being seen.

Although the world of Egan's bucks and swells would seem remote from the bittersweet nostalgia of Lamb's Elia essays, the two can be found in close proximity in the August 1820 number of John Scott's *London Magazine.* In that month Elia made his first appearance as the author of "Recollections of the South Sea House," and J. H. Reynolds published an enthusiastic review of Egan's *Sporting Anecdotes.*[35] Despite what separates their two quite distinct styles of writing about and perceiving the world, the element that brings Egan and Elia together in this particular journal is their love for an older London, an older England. The antiquarian character of Lamb's essays is echoed throughout *London Magazine,* from its frontispiece reproductions of classical busts and antique friezes to its nostalgia for bygone urban festivals and its laments for the passing of the coaching days. Meanwhile, what particularly attracts Reynolds in Egan's work is his knack for keeping the tradition of older sports and amusements alive. We find Reynolds the following month praising Egan's account of dogfighting, which he regards as a tribute to the Elizabethan age, the "golden age of poetry and bear-baiting."[36]

The backward-looking nature of the Elia essays—their nostalgia, their distaste for utilitarian reform, their mockery of the future—has a complex origin in Lamb's experience of personal loss, in his sense that London itself had changed radically in his lifetime, and in the highly crafted literary voice he had chosen for these particular reflections.[37] As has often been noted, Lamb writes about many different Londons. The language and tone he uses to evoke the city in his early letters, for instance, differ dramatically from those of his later essays. The London of a November 1800 letter to his friend Thomas Manning resembles Egan's London, or even Boswell's, far more than it does Elia's:

Streets, streets, streets, markets, theatres, churches, Covent Gardens . . . noise of coaches, drowsy cry of mechanic watchmen at night, with bucks reeling

[35] [J. H. Reynolds], "The Jewels of the Book," *London Magazine* 2 (August 1820): 155–58. The author is identified in Riga and Prance, *Index to the London Magazine,* p. 18.

[36] "The Jewels of the Book," *London Magazine* 2 (September 1820): 272.

[37] The personal tragedy to which I refer is, of course, Mary Lamb's murder of her mother in 1796 and the periodic insanity that left Charles his sister's guardian for the rest of their lives. Something froze in him during the last years of the eighteenth century; his growth was irrevocably stunted in some profound way.

home drunk; if you happen to wake at midnight, cries of Fire and Stop Thief; inns of court . . . just like Cambridge colleges; old book-stalls, Jeremy Taylors, Burtons on Melancholy, and Religio Medicis on every stall. These are thy pleasures, O London with-the-many-sins. O City abounding in whores, for these may Keswick and her giant brood go hang![38]

The exuberance of this description and the explicit opposition Lamb sets up between urban and rural pleasures (with Keswick he alludes to his poet-friends' beloved Lakes) are present, too, in his well known "Londoner" essay of 1802, in which he declares that he takes far more delight in a "mob of happy faces" crowding before the pit door of Drury Lane than in "all the *silly sheep* . . . of Arcadia or Epsom Downs."[39]

This London of the early Lamb is a nighttime London, a fallen city ("London with-the-many-sins") inhabited by workmen and swells, arsonists and thieves, book browsers, theatergoers, and whores. It is the masculine city we have seen in Egan, in which pleasures and entertainments abound, all laid on for the consumption of the nocturnal male rambler. In the "London" essay Lamb presents himself as a man of the crowd ("I was born . . . bred, and have passed most of my time, in a *crowd*") and praises the effects on his humor of the inspiriting flow of humanity on the Strand—"like the shifting scenes of a skilful Pantomime."[40] London here is not merely a city of whores and passing shows. It is also the city as mother: "Where has spleen her food but in London—humour, interest, curiosity, suck at her measureless breasts without a possibility of being satiated. Nursed amid her noise, her crowds, her beloved smoke—what have I been doing all my life, if I have not lent out my heart with usury to such scenes?"[41] Whether whore or suckling mother, the city as female provides for masculine desires and breeds "the Londoner," who never gets his fill of urban pleasures.

In the guise of Elia some nineteen years later, however, Lamb transforms the London of his youth into a prelapsarian, nearly pastoral place. In "The Old Benchers of the Inner Temple" Elia remembers the gardens and courtyards of the Temple, where he passed the first

[38] Letter to Thomas Manning, November 28, 1800, in *The Letters of Charles Lamb*, ed. E. V. Lucas (London: J. M. Dent and Sons, 1935), 1:223.

[39] Charles Lamb, "The Londoner," in *The Works of Charles Lamb*, ed. William MacDonald (London: J. M. Dent and Co., 1903), 4:8. The essay first appeared in the *Morning Post*, February 1, 1802.

[40] Ibid., pp. 317–18.

[41] Ibid., pp. 318–19.

seven years of his life, as a small paradise, an Eden, with sundials, fountains, and "antique air." Marshaling the support of Adam and Marvell, he asks why the now bricked-over fountains of his childhood cannot be allowed to remain: "Why not, then, gratify children, by letting them stand? . . . Why must everything smack of man, and mannish? Is the world all grown up? Is childhood dead?" His focus shifts back to the Edenic city of his childhood while his persona grows older, now a "superannuated" and celibate man, a "bachelor" who complains about the "behaviour of married people" and dreams of the fantasy children he will never have.[42] He longs for the presexual innocence of childhood and reconfigures London as the sexless city he remembers and experiences once again in his superannuation. Girl children rather than whores populate the metropolis, and the masculine appetites of "the Londoner" have been replaced by the bittersweet celibacy and nostalgia of Elia.

In the Elia essays it is difficult to separate what Lamb himself referred to as Elia's resentment of the "impertinence of manhood" from his discomfort in a changed city; and the change was taking place as much within Lamb's own life as it was in the city of George IV. Writing to Bernard Barton in 1829, after he had retired to Enfield, Lamb spoke of London as a graveyard: all the old friends were gone, the houses and old haunts now "empty caskets," the bodies he had cared for "in graves, or dispersed."[43] It is, however, most often the pastoral city he praises in the Elia essays, not the boisterous, teeming London he described to Manning or the joyful city of the "Londoner" essay. The city now becomes a living museum, a collection of "magnificent relics" like the old South Sea House, or an archaeological site at which to mine the past and view the layers of personal and urban history.

Elia sees the city from a distance and, in Hazlitt's phrase, "through the film of the past." But distance is achieved as well by seeing London as a stage—a "pantomime and masquerade"—and by the use of persona and pseudonym. This latter convention, so common in the journalistic tradition of which Lamb was a part, seems to underscore the writer's tentative relationship to what he observes and records. "Elia" is not, in fact, so much a person as a signature, the mark of someone who briefly notes or remembers and then walks off—or signs off. The

---

[42] Charles Lamb, "The Old Benchers of the Inner Temple," in *The Essays of Elia and Eliana* (London: George Bell and Sons, 1883), p. 114. The essay was first published in *London Magazine*, September 1821.

[43] Charles Lamb to Bernard Barton, July 25, 1829, in *Letters*, 3:224.

anonymity, not to say invisibility, of the spectator is preserved, the scene not entered, the proscenium not crossed. The form of Lamb's essays or sketches recalls Benjamin's notion of episodic or dioramic literature and Egan's vision of the city as an encyclopedia. Scenes, people, events appear and recede. The essays, like the "physiologies" Benjamin describes, deny narrative and continuity. "Narrative teases me," writes Lamb in discussing his preference for the essay or the literary anatomy. "I have little concern in the *progress* of events. . . . The fluctuations of fortune in fiction—and almost in real life—have ceased to interest me."[44]

But distance is achieved above all, especially in those Elia essays that meditate on the strays and waifs of the city streets, through the use of irony, a tool both of distance and of a barely declared social criticism. This irony, which at certain moments flares into bitterness, is never totally separable from Lamb's nostalgia for a beloved, remembered London, and its real import, therefore, is not always easy to discern. The very titles of two of the Elia essays exemplify this doubleness: "The Praise of Chimney Sweepers" and "A Complaint of the Decay of Beggars in the Metropolis" are both laments for an older, socially simpler, paternalistic England and, at the same time, seemingly ruthless portraits of social inequity and inhumanity. In "The Praise of Chimney Sweepers" Elia teeters between a sentimental recollection of the myth of the sweep as orphaned nobleman and a bitter sense of the fragility of these wasted young lives. He alludes to two older representations of the child sweep: Blake's young chimney sweeper in *Songs of Innocence and of Experience* and Hogarth's boy, in his drawing of the March to Finchley, "grinning at the pieman . . . with a maximum of glee."[45] Lamb would appear to stand between and yet encompass both of these visions, the harsh Blakean knowledge of these "dim specks—poor blots—innocent blacknesses" about to fade to an early death and the Hogarthian celebration of innocence and urban festival. The tension between these two impulses remains unresolved (this is the art of Lamb's irony), and so the essayist's ultimate detachment from the social question is maintained.

[44] Charles Lamb, "Mackery End, in Hertfordshire," in *Essays of Elia*, p. 98; emphasis added.

[45] There is evidence that Lamb was familiar with Blake's poem "The Chimney Sweeper," which he referred to in a letter to Bernard Barton as the "Sweep Song" (see *Letters*, 2:425–26). Lamb's "*peep-peep* of a young sparrow" in the first paragraph of "The Praise of Chimney Sweepers" is a possible echo of Blake's " 'weep! 'weep! 'weep! 'weep!"

In "Complaint of the Decay of Beggars" Elia's explicit target is the reforming zeal that would remove beggars from the streets and drive them into the poorhouses. He prefers the anarchy of the streets and regrets this ostensible progressivism not only for its inhumanity to the beggar, deprived of liberty and companionship, but also for its effect on the spectators of London, for whom the beggars are the "standing morals, emblems, mementos, dial mottos, the spital sermons, the books for children, the salutary checks and pauses to the high and rushing tide of greasy citizenry."[46] Like Wordsworth's leech gatherer on the heath or, indeed, the blind beggar of *The Prelude*, Elia's beggars remind us of our humanity and act as moral instructors. In his "Londoner" essay Lamb describes this romantic philosophy of the streets: he can learn more of the "universal instinct of man" from observing a pick-pocket than from "an hundred volumes of abstract polity," just as the inhabitants of Shakespeare's Arden read much in the stones and brooks of the forest. Thus, he concludes, "an art of extracting morality from the commonest incidents of town life is attained by the same well-natured alchemy."[47]

Although this emphasis on the salutary influence of beggars does not absolutely reduce their humanity, it does help to accomplish Elia's transformation of the beggar into an object, an artifact. The beggar is a "grand fragment, as good as an Elgin marble"; he is one among London's "shows, her museums, and supplies for ever-gaping curiosity." And, he asks, "what else but an accumulation of sights—endless sights—is a great city; or for what else is it desirable?"[48] The literal and ironic meanings of these questions cannot be unraveled. Yes, we answer, a great city should be an accumulation of endlessly amusing, edifying, surprising sights, but no, a city must also be a place where each person's humanity is remembered and preserved. Elia struggles to remain the spectator, the audience at the shows of London, but Lamb the critic and ironist forces his hand.

One year after Elia's first appearance in the *London Magazine*, De Quincey's Opium Eater joined the ranks with his *Confessions*. With an introduction from Wordsworth in hand, De Quincey had come down to London in 1821 to make his living as a journalist. He had already

---

[46] Lamb, "A Complaint of the Decay of Beggars in the Metropolis," in *Essays of Elia*, pp. 150–51.

[47] Lamb, "The Londoner," p. 318.

[48] Lamb, "A Complaint," p. 154.

broken with *Blackwood's*, where he was to have published the *Confessions*, and now secured lodgings in a tiny set of rooms in Covent Garden in which to write his opium memoir for the *London Magazine*. Here he began by writing of the winter of 1802–3, when he was seventeen, poor, hungry, and alone in the metropolis.

The early parts of the *Confessions*, in which London figures prominently, seem at first glance to be peripheral to the central preoccupations, indeed obsessions, of De Quincey's idiosyncratic text. They also differ radically from the jaunty or benignly nostalgic renderings of the city in Egan and Lamb. It seems to me, however, that the London episode is crucial to the meaning of the *Confessions* and, more important, that it enacts in a hallucinatory way the essential nature of the London experience which I have been describing. The *Confessions* also articulate the centrality of female sexuality to the evocation of the city's meaning and the construction of bohemian identity. Here, female sexuality both chaste and fallen acts as a unifying narrative thread, externalizing male experience and drawing together the disparate episodes of the Opium Eater's life.

De Quincey noted that the introductory section of his *Confessions* made his entire work intelligible since, "without this narration, the dreams (which were the real object of the whole work) would have no meaning."[49] The dreams or images of the London experience were to act as a thread connecting his early with his later days, his waking moments with his trancelike ones, his conscious with his unconscious thoughts. That a London seen through unintoxicated eyes should be so linked with a later, postaddictive state is somewhat paradoxical. Not only did images of the city establish the texts of his future opium dreams, however, but there is also evidence that in his own life De Quincey needed opium to recover the otherwise irretrievable repressed memories of his London sojourn.[50] For him London and opium addic-

[49] Thomas De Quincey, *Literary Reminiscences* (Boston: Ticknor and Fields, 1851), 1: 114.

[50] Alethea Hayter notes that in a diary De Quincey kept in Everton, near Liverpool, in 1803–4, he never once mentions his then very recent sojourn in London. A year later, after taking opium for the first time, he had visions that blended his earliest childhood memories with recollections of his London experiences. Hayter writes, "The events of his London destitution were no longer shut off from his idea of himself; they were being integrated into his personality by the agency of dreams produced by opium." See Alethea Hayter, *Opium and the Romantic Imagination* (Berkeley: University of California Press, 1968), p. 119. See also De Quincey, *Literary Reminiscences*, 1:114, for a description of how he wrote the beginning section of the *Confessions* with the aid of an increased dose of opium.

tion were inextricably connected, first, because he believed the London experience to have been the cause of the gastric illness for which he later took the drug, and second, because in memory the metropolis was enveloped in the haze of addiction.

After a Fieldingesque start in which the young orphaned hero runs away from unsympathetic guardians to seek liberty and fortune, the narrative shifts radically to the description of a hallucinatory London, and we begin to understand why these months in the city were, as the author says, crucial for his opium experience. Young De Quincey leaves the world of bildungsroman for the rambling narrative of bohemia. We see, too, how De Quincey's London narrative serves as an unwitting commentary on the nature of urban life—especially the life of the streets—in the early nineteenth century. What is implicit in the relations between observer and Londoner in Egan and Lamb here absolutely determines the Opium Eater's every urban experience and makes each one surreal and inexplicable. This London is a place of sudden events, unidentified people, bizarre coincidences, and unexpected intimacies, all of them ultimately without explanation. The links between people or events that we have missed in Egan's *Life in London* and in Elia's essays are here relinquished as well, even though the *Confessions* takes the form of neither sketch nor essay but an apparent autobiographical narrative.

At the very start, for instance, an empty house inhabited by an always nameless ten-year-old child presents itself conveniently but mysteriously as shelter. More striking, perhaps, than this odd coincidence is the inability, or lack of desire, of the Opium Eater to discern or uncover the meanings of such unexplained circumstances: "Whether this child were an illegitimate daughter of Mr. ———," he writes, "or only a servant, I could not ascertain; she did not herself know."[51] Knowing neither her origins nor her name, he nevertheless sleeps on the floor of the unoccupied house with the girl wrapped in his arm and loves her as his "partner in wretchedness" (p. 49). His relationship with this nameless girl prefigures the more dramatic but equally mysterious and decontextualized relationship with Ann, the young prostitute. His expression of excessive gratitude to her for saving his life with a glass of sherry, his failure either to learn or to remember her surname, his vague appointment to rejoin her after a trip to Eton to get money, and

---

[51] Thomas De Quincey, *Confessions of an English Opium Eater* (Harmondsworth: Penguin, 1971), p. 47; subsequently cited in the text.

his ultimate and inevitable loss of her are all perplexing, inexplicable aspects of their acquaintance.

He is drawn to Ann, as he is drawn to the nameless orphan, because she mirrors his own isolation and his status on the streets: "Being myself at that time of necessity a peripatetic, or a walker of the streets, I naturally fell in more frequently with those female peripatetics who are technically called street-walkers" (p. 50). Ann enacts for him the relationship between bohemian and prostitute. She mimics his marginality and homelessness, and in his romanticization of her he dramatizes his own position. Later in the narrative, under the heading "The Pleasures of Opium," he talks of his tie to the proletarian figures of the city in a similar way. He delighted in wandering about London on Saturday nights, he tells us, frequenting the markets where the poor purchased their food for the week. Cloaked in the incognito of the classless stroller, he would eavesdrop on family negotiations and experience as a silent observer people's "wishes, . . . difficulties, . . . and opinions." Unlike most members of his own class, who "show their interest in the concerns of the poor, chiefly by sympathy . . . with their distress and sorrows," he was "disposed to express [his] interest by sympathising with their pleasures" (p. 80). What distinguishes the rambler's or the flaneur's stance from that of the social investigator or reform-minded novelist is this identification with and delight in the privileges of the poor. The flaneur sees the poor and the prostitute not as victims or objects of pity but as urban actors free from the constraints of bourgeois life.

De Quincey focuses on Ann because her condition is emblematic of urban alienation and therefore serves as a projection of the male observer's state of being and mind. Not only is her solitary condition symbolic of urban experience, however, but also the relationship between client and prostitute exemplifies the transitory and anonymous nature of the relationship between urban spectator and the people of the streets. Like Baudelaire's "passante," she represents the erotic tenor of the crowd and the quintessential urban phenomenon of discovery and loss.[52] The Opium Eater's tie to Ann is apparently not a sexual one but an intensely felt platonic bond that nevertheless mimics the fleeting, strangely impersonal encounter between prostitute and client: they meet, become intensely attached, learn nothing of each other, separate, and never meet again. He is at pains to tell his readers

[52] See Benjamin, *Charles Baudelaire*, pp. 44–46.

that, because of his weakened and impoverished state, his connection with Ann "could not have been an impure one." And yet, as if contradicting himself, he insists that "at no time in my life have I been a person to hold myself polluted by the touch or approach of any creature that wore a human shape" (pp. 49–50). The question of pollution and of the Opium Eater's susceptibility or immunity to its effects becomes a crucial leitmotif later in the *Confessions*. Ann is at the center of the Opium Eater's London and remains a powerful figure in his imaginative life because she epitomizes urban marginality, the disjointed, inexplicable images of opium reveries, and the paradox of the chaste sinner.

As in an opium dream images and people appear in De Quincey's London and fade away, seemingly unlinked to one another by lasting ties, unconnected textually by any interpretive or narrative thread. In this way the urban apparitions of the *Confessions* resemble and indeed prefigure one of the strangest characters in the later part of De Quincey's text: the Malay who suddenly appears at the Opium Eater's home in the Lake District and proves to be a source for his opium nightmares. The Malay also plays a role in the Opium Eater's obsessions with innocence and pollution which center on female sexuality: the "Oriental" comes to represent the sin that *can* pollute, and he is immediately contrasted with a chaste femininity that harks back to Ann. When De Quincey first sees the Malay in his cottage kitchen, it is as part of a tableau that the turbaned foreigner forms with the young English servant girl who works in the Opium Eater's home. The visual contrast between Malay and servant girl carries with it for De Quincey an implicit moral contrast: "A more striking picture there could not be imagined, than the beautiful English face of the girl, and its exquisite fairness, together with her erect and independent attitude, contrasted with the sallow and bilious skin of the Malay, enamelled or veneered with mahogany, by marine air, his small, fierce, restless eyes, thin lips, slavish gestures and adorations" (pp. 90–91). The racialist distinctions available to De Quincey—clear-eyed, pure, self-respecting Englishwoman versus tainted, unhealthy, groveling Asian—intersect here with a sexual imagery of chastity and defilement.

Indeed, when the Malay later "fasten[s] upon" De Quincey's dreams, bringing with him "other Malays worse than himself" who "[run] 'a-muck'" at the Opium Eater, he unleashes in the Englishman's imagination a nightmare that culminates in the infectious kisses of crocodiles (pp. 92, 109). In the section titled "The Pains of Opium"

De Quincey describes the hideous dreams he claims were shaped both by his London experience and by the sight of the Malay. Clotted with every sort of "Asiatic" image, from Chinese to African to Egyptian to Indian, the dream leaps from Vishnu and Siva to Isis and Osiris and ends: "I was kissed, with cancerous kisses, by crocodiles; and laid, confounded with all unutterable slimy things, amongst reeds and Nilotic mud" (p. 109). The crocodile, like the Malay, seems an externalization of the narrator's own sin—his addiction as well as his guilt toward those he feels he has betrayed—and the homoerotic, not to say autoerotic, gesture of the kiss suggests an inescapable circuit of contamination.[53] A subsequent dream does, however, offer resolution and escape, and it is through the figure of Ann the prostitute that he finds, or rather dreams, redemption.

In this dream an "Oriental" scene merges with the iconography of an Easter Sunday. The Opium Eater can see the domes of a celestial city much like Jerusalem in the distance. Here the "Oriental" has been domesticated and sanctified, the demonic and pagan replaced by a Judaeo-Christian setting and imagery. Seated next to him, "shaded by Judean palms," is a woman who turns out to be his lost Ann. He embraces her with words of relief and delight—"So then I have found you at last"—and sees that her face is unchanged, that she has never grown older and is indeed even more beautiful. He recalls the last time he kissed her lips: "lips, Ann, that to me were not polluted" (p. 112). Then a cloud comes between them, all vanishes, and within the dream he finds himself back in London, walking again with Ann, "just as we walked seventeen years before, when we were both children" (p. 112). Not only does this dream fulfill the Opium Eater's wish to find Ann again and to assuage the guilt he had felt at abandoning her, but it also redeems the city itself and breaks the circle of contamination represented by the crocodiles' cancerous kisses. London now shares something of the glory of Jerusalem and, perhaps more important, becomes a place of reunion and reconciliation rather than of separation

[53] A number of readers of the *Confessions* and other autobiographical writings have traced a connection between De Quincey's loss of his sister Elizabeth, who died of hydrocephalus in childhood, and his feelings about other young women, who seem to have taken her place or merged with her in his imagination. Ann is one such figure, as are the nameless orphan who inhabits the large London house and Wordsworth's young daughter Kate, who also died as a child. In a fascinating study, John Barrell focuses on De Quincey's guilt surrounding his sister's death and connects it to an extensive imagery of contamination and racism in his writing. See John Barrell, *The Infection of Thomas De Quincey: A Psychopathology of Imperialism* (New Haven: Yale University Press, 1991).

and loss. De Quincey himself regains the innocence of his youth and through Ann recovers the possibility of a kiss that is not polluted or polluting. The crocodile, a monstrous reification of his own sin, traps him in guilt and degradation; Ann, his erstwhile double, offers the possibility of reconciling sin and innocence. The prostitute, a reflection of his own street-walking, peripatetic self, emerges as a marker of voluntary bohemianism, to be distinguished from the inescapable nightmare of opium madness.

The Malay, like the figures of the unredeemed city, serves as an emblem, an image that appears without explanation, lends coherence to the text by virtue of its symbolic weight, and disappears from the narrative. The text of the *Confessions* can be read as a dream is deciphered: the narrative synapses are missing, but figures and events accrue meaning as symbols do, by repetition or association. De Quincey's text, like the London of his youth, can be explained or interpreted not according to the logic of linear narrative but only according to the logic of the Opium Eater's psyche.[54]

Despite the distinctive, idiosyncratic quality of De Quincey's vision, then, his representation of London in the early part of the *Confessions* seems a surreal expression of the early nineteenth-century observer's quintessential experience and view of the city. De Quincey declines to tell or invent the story of what he sees, to give to urban experience or to his own narrative what one critic has called its own "discursive interpretation."[55] He does not "read" the city as we try to read his narrative. And what he declines to read is not only the story of the individual life but the collective story of the social life of London. What kind of place, what sort of metropolis, generates the abuse and abandonment of children, abject poverty, child prostitution? These are simply not the questions De Quincey asks. As V. A. DeLuca has observed, De Quincey's work represents the "sufferings of urban experience" without acknowledging what systemic repression might have caused them or imagining what sorts of responses might change them.[56]

In one of the many odd passages in De Quincey's *Confessions*, the

---

[54] See J. Hillis Miller, *The Disappearance of God: Five Nineteenth-Century Writers* (Cambridge: Harvard University Press, 1963), p. 29, for the analogy between De Quincey's city and his prose.

[55] V. A. DeLuca, *Thomas De Quincey: The Prose of Vision* (Toronto: University of Toronto Press, 1980), p. 13.

[56] Ibid., p. 16.

Figure 5 I. R. and G. Cruikshank, "*Bow Street.* Tom & Jerry's sensibility awakened at the pathetic tale of the elegant cyprian, the feeling coachman, & the generous magistrate." Pierce Egan, *Life in London* (1821).

Opium Eater laments that the "stream of London charity," though "deep and mighty," is "yet noiseless and underground" (50–51). If only this charity could be "better adapted," he believes, the orphans and prostitutes of the city would not have to suffer. With the social solution of charity we come back to where we began with Redding's rambler on Primrose Hill. The rambler's unquestioning belief in the efficacy of English charity and De Quincey's more qualified faith in the power and usefulness of a perhaps temporarily inaccessible charity point to the common vision of urban reality that underlies all the representations of the city I have introduced here. For all of these shapers and observers of the London scene regarded the social reality of the city as part of a *natural order,* a system of social relations that was fundamentally organic and not to be challenged or radically transformed. At the very end of Egan's chapter on the bawdy coffeehouse frequented by an array of streetwalkers, he includes a sentimental narrative about one young woman, seduced and ruined, who had been dragged before a magistrate by a coachman to whom she owed a fare. After hearing that she had no money, no residence, and no friend in the world, the magistrate paid the coachman and gave the woman herself three shillings (see figure 5 for an illustration of this scene). The narrator marvels at the generosity and charity of the magistrate and at the touching effects of the story on everyone who heard it. Indeed, he concludes, "it was a fine scene altogether. It was one of NATURE'S richest moments" (p. 226).

The beauty and stateliness of the city could be enhanced, as in the "improvements" of the Regency, and its appearance brought closer to what already lay within the British nation and character. The grandeur and scope of the city could be captured or exaggerated in a panoramic view, or in the sudden encounter with an urban solitary recorded in its momentary form. But the questioning or probing of complex social relations was avoided by architect, essayist, and graphic artist alike.

What concerned these early urban observers was the experience of the individual as he is acted upon by the metropolis, not the power of the individual to act upon or change the city. As Egan's Tom and Jerry conclude their urban rambles, the narrator of *Life in London* tells us that they have seen the best and the worst, the most virtuous and most depraved, and so have learned the "advantages resulting from the connexions with one, and the evils arising from associating with the other" (p. 394). The individual spectator can be enlightened, corrupted, instructed, or even, as in the case of the Opium Eater, injured both physically and psychologically, but the spectator can always retreat or escape; his experience of the life of the streets is always temporary and fleeting. The people of the street are signs to be read only for the moral edification of the spectator, or left unread as part of the unraveled urban mystery, but they are not to be taken as manifestations of a wider social disturbance, a systemic fault in need of fixing or even of detecting. Neither are they to be understood as figures whose stories must be teased out and told. They are creatures of a scene or a moment, not characters or actors in an ongoing narrative. Whereas the experience or vision of the spectator remains paramount, the people of the streets remain objects, sights, landmarks, images in the spectator's dreams. Like the prostitute, who plays a role in all the urban evocations I have mentioned, the crowd comes and goes, bringing pleasure or illumination, and offering the observer only a reflection of himself or a spectacle to consume.

⚘ TWO ⚘

Sketches by Boz:
The Middle-Class City and
the Quarantine of Urban Suffering

With his scenes of London's "every-day life and every-day people," Boz the inimitable reinvented the urban sketch. Although he joined the popular literary tradition so successfully practiced by Pierce Egan and reproduced some of the pre-industrial nostalgia of Lamb's Elia, he also created a new audience, introduced a new cast of characters, and forged a new vision of the city.[1] In the decade of reform, Dickens created a metropolis that was populated by members of the middle class. He deliberately, almost militantly, took both the delights and the pitfalls of the city out of the aristocratic realm and replaced the Eganesque swell with the shabby genteel, the apprentices, and the newly rich of London. Dickens constructed this middle-class London out of his own past, and for an audience whose experiences mirrored his own. Boz's urban vision, though it encompassed and kept alive the profusion of theatrical metaphors and the emphasis on urban entertainments that characterized earlier representations of the city, also fostered a sense of familiarity and know-

---

[1] Dickens's sketches have been compared to those of Pierce Egan, Thomas Hood, and Theodore Hook in Virgil Grillo, *Charles Dickens' "Sketches by Boz": End in the Beginning* (Boulder: Colorado Associated Press, 1974), pp. 55–63, and to the London sketches of Leigh Hunt in Robert Browning's "Sketches by Boz," in *Dickens and the Twentieth Century,* ed. John J. Gross (Toronto: University of Toronto Press, 1962), pp. 22–23; and more recently in F. S. Schwarzbach, *Dickens and the City* (London: Athlone Press, 1979), pp. 35–37. See Carol Bernstein's chapter titled "Nineteenth-Century Urban Sketches," in which she argues that Dickens's sketches "break away from the taxonomy, articulation, and system that govern so many of the nonfictional sketches and instead regard the city as a more mysterious text." Carol Bernstein, *The Celebration of Scandal: Toward the Sublime in Victorian Urban Fiction* (University Park: Pennsylvania State University Press, 1991), p. 45.

ability rather than of remoteness and alien spectacle. As he collapsed the class distinctions between reader and subject, he emphasized not the distance but the correspondence between the observer and the urban scene.

In this chapter on *Sketches by Boz* and other early works by Dickens, as well as the sketches of some of his predecessors, contemporaries, and disciples, I focus on two crucial elements of the literary creation of a middle-class city: first, the continuing sense of distance from the "lower orders," now juxtaposed with a new awareness of possibilities for sympathizing, if not identifying, with the poor; and second, the development of a middle-class discourse about the presence on the city streets of the sexually tainted and victimized woman. Both elements distinguish the vision of Boz's sketches from the urban evocations of the 1820s and from the bohemian stance of alienation mingled with a sense of abandon. Although Dickens's most notable achievement in the *Sketches* amounted to a veritable cataloguing of urban middle-class types, his portraits, as a contemporary reviewer for the *Metropolitan Magazine* remarked, also "descend[ed] with a startling fidelity to the lowest of the low."[2] Yet in these portraits of street folk, criminals, slum dwellers, and other highly visible but socially marginal types, Dickens hesitated to assert absolutely the intimate connection between reader—or spectator—and subject. The relationship between the middle-class reader and the urban underclass is never fully resolved in *Sketches*, and at times Boz is at pains to isolate, to cordon off, the disturbing realities of city life.

These efforts to separate out social misery can be described as a form of quarantine, the imagery of separation and containment appropriate to an age in which the language of disease—of contagion and contamination—began to invade the language of urban description. The ambivalence of the middle class about its connection to the lower classes and its possible vulnerability to the social and physical taints of urban life emerged in this period in debates on cholera and in discussions of poverty and slum life, and they are reflected in Dickens's *Sketches*. *Sketches by Boz* is a text that fosters and yet limits notions of social connectedness, pressing on its audience the links between observer and observed, and insisting nonetheless that what Alexander Welsh has called the "city-as-problem" existed as a sharply delimited phenomenon.[3]

[2] *Metropolitan Magazine* (March 1836), quoted in Walter Dexter, "The Reception of Dickens's First Book," *The Dickensian* 32 (1936): 48–49.

[3] See Alexander Welsh, *The City of Dickens* (Cambridge: Harvard University Press, 1986),

One of Dickens's essential strategies for delimiting this problematic view of the city is the use of the female figure, especially the sexually fallen woman, to embody and contain the dangerous or disturbing aspects of the urban condition. If the tradition Dickens inherited and then modified was aristocratic and bohemian, it was also a masculine one. Not only were authors and fictional spectators male, but so was the readership of the journals and weeklies in which almost all such sketches appeared. When Dickens's sketches were first published in the *Morning Chronicle*, the *Evening Chronicle*, *Bell's Life in London*, and other such papers, his readers were exclusively male, not the mixed audience of husbands, wives, and children who would ultimately read his works by the family hearth. Indeed, as he collected the sketches for publication, first in two volumes and then in a single one, his awareness of an audience that was becoming increasingly female and more distinctly familial, prompted him to bowdlerize his material.[4]

It was with an implicitly male audience in mind, then, that Dickens deployed figures of female sexuality as a means to objectify, from an insulated point of view, urban pains that could be regarded as separate but present. The female figure allows him simultaneously to isolate and to expose social misery: he quarantines that misery by sex and yet suggests the threat of contamination that women—particularly fallen women—always represent. For if the tainted or suffering woman could be used to separate the problems of the streets from the rest of the urban scene, she also represented a potential danger: like the cholera that first invaded England in the early 1830s, she threatened to infect the upper and middle classes with the diseases associated with poverty and debasement. As the middle class claimed an exuberant metropolis as its own and celebrated the opportunities it offered, it also found an imagery for the misery which, in the 1830s, still touched it only remotely.

In the early 1830s the middle class was concerned in a variety of ways with its political and economic ascendancy. It felt itself coming into at least partial possession of the city and, as a consequence, into a position of responsibility for its fate. The city ceased to be a remote stage on which to view the alternately entertaining and disquieting extremes of high and low life. Neither comfortable nor convincing in the role of

---

chap. 2. Welsh argues that the "city-as-problem" replaced the "city of satire" at some point in the middle of the nineteenth century.

[4] See John Butt and Kathleen Tillotson, *Dickens at Work* (London: Methuen, 1968), p. 48.

observer, the middle class could no longer see the city as pure spectacle. The rise of the middle class, which began only slowly in the 1830s, altered the face of the city itself, as well as the language of urban description and the images of metropolitan life that dominated politics, journalism, and literature.

The passage of the first Reform Bill in 1832, which the young Charles Dickens would have witnessed and recorded as a neophyte parliamentary reporter, began to give some segments of the middle class a new political, economic, and social power. In London in particular large numbers of lower-middle-class and even working-class householders were enfranchised by the L10 clause of the bill.[5] The Reform Bill, as well as other efforts at reform, were ultimately to lead to a greater degree of middle-class control over the way in which money was spent by local governments. Predictably, middle-class Victorians (and proto-Victorians) had little sympathy with or enthusiasm for the aristocratic aspirations of recent "metropolitan improvements."[6] They preferred that money be spent for the practical—sewers, bridges, roads—rather than for the merely beautiful. In his history of Victorian London, Donald Olsen quotes the historian Archibald Alison, who declared in 1836 that "fine architecture was impossible in a democracy" and belonged rather to "aristocratic government."[7] Critics saw Regency changes as pompous, ostentatious, and wasteful; they wanted a metropolis that would provide comfort, cleanliness, and health for the many, not a city to advertise the triumphs and prosperity of the few. New utilitarian and democratic values undermined the "complacency [and] optimism . . . of the decade between Waterloo and 1825," and by 1837 moral scruples about display, poverty, and disease had contributed to a new vision of the ideal city.[8] A decade later, in a gesture more symbolic than practical, John Nash's colonnades were removed from the Regent Street Quadrant.[9]

The rising urban middle class also provided an audience for a new

[5] For Dickens as a parliamentary reporter, see Edgar Johnson, *Charles Dickens: His Tragedy and Triumph* (Harmondsworth: Penguin, 1977), pp. 51–53. Asa Briggs makes the point that because rents were so high in London, most genuine householders were enfranchised by the Reform Bill. In other cities with uniformly low rents, almost no working-class residents got the vote. Asa Briggs, *The Making of Modern England, 1783–1867: The Age of Improvement* (New York: Harper and Row, 1965), p. 262.

[6] Donald J. Olsen, *The Growth of Victorian London* (London: B. T. Batsford, 1976), p. 40.

[7] Ibid., p. 42.

[8] Donald J. Olsen, *The City as a Work of Art: London, Paris, Vienna* (New Haven: Yale University Press, 1986), p. 21.

[9] Olsen, *The Growth of Victorian London*, p. 45.

kind of popular press and supported journals with a distinctly urban character.[10] The 1830s saw the creation of a number of satirical magazines with a London flavor—Gilbert à Beckett's *Figaro in London* and Douglas Jerrold's *Punch in London* were but two—and a host of "scandalous journals" that contained gossip concerning men about town and prurient stories and jokes. Donald Gray has analyzed the readership of one such journal, *The Town*, with interesting results. The male audience of this bawdy paper consisted not of gentlemen but of "apprentices, shop assistants, clerks and other young men who were coming of age in the first Victorian decade of manifest political and social changes and chances to ride them to new social identities."[11] Artisans and clerks could afford the paper because it was "unstamped" and therefore cheap. They found in it sketches about brothels and courtesans as well as gossipy notes about recognizable characters of their own social class: marine store dealers, tailors, bakers, shopkeepers, piano teachers.[12] They also found tales and sketches of London life and London types which owed something to Dickens's *Sketches* as well as to other city scenes depicted in the more "respectable" press. The readers of *The Town* regarded themselves as young men on the way up, citizens of a world full of possibility, and they took delight in being portrayed as participants in all the city's pleasures and as beneficiaries of all of its opportunities. No longer just for the likes of Jerry Hawthorne, Esq., and Corinthian Tom were the sprees and revels of the city. Now the apprentice and the clerk could also begin to imagine themselves in the role of urban swell. Interestingly, the kind of journalism *The Town* exemplified did not last much beyond the mid-1840s. Gray sees it as a cultural phenomenon inseparable from the period of the 1830s and 1840s, a time of "audacious speculation and self-promotion."[13] This was an age of perceived social fluidity for certain members of London's

[10] Michael Wolff and Celina Fox observe: "The relationship between the press and the city is very close for, against a background of industrial and technical development, only city-dwellers can ensure a mass readership capable of escalating faster than their own numbers. The growth of the Victorian press, much more rapid than that of the Victorian city, was perhaps the first demonstration of the potential of the mass media and the closest verbal and graphic equivalent which we have of Victorian urbanism." See Michael Wolff and Celina Fox, "Pictures from the Magazines," in *The Victorian City: Images and Realities*, ed. H. J. Dyos and Michael Wolff (London: Routledge and Kegan Paul, 1973), 2:559.

[11] Donald J. Gray, "Early Victorian Scandalous Journalism: Renton Nicholson's *The Town* (1837–42)," in *The Victorian Press: Samplings and Soundings*, ed. Joanne Shattock and Michael Wolff (Leicester: Leicester University Press, 1982), p. 318.

[12] Ibid., p. 329.

[13] Ibid., p. 346.

middle class, and this fluidity helped to shape new urban images and identities.

Contemporary reviews of Dickens's *Sketches* tended to strike one of two notes, both of which speak to the same characteristics of Boz's urban vision and may seem perplexing to the modern reader. Either they made much of the absolute verisimilitude of the sketches (the *Morning Post* reviewer praised their "pleasing *vraisemblement*"), or they took Boz to task for elevating the "commonplace," for dwelling on subjects and incidents that were not worthy of his prodigious talents.[14] Both of these critical observations would seem to point to the same fact: Dickens's sketches featured the middle- and lower-middle classes in ways that were unfamiliar to readers, and in ways that delighted those who experienced the sketches as powerfully real but dismayed those who regarded them as vulgar. When reviewer and popular reader alike reported that they found the sketches accurate or mimetic of reality, they no doubt meant that the sketches were about them and not solely about the slumming young aristocrats and gin-sodden beggars of Pierce Egan. What was recognizable to Boz's readers seemed, therefore, persuasively real.

Those characters who populate Boz's sketches are the very people who read *The Town*; they are also the same aspiring young men (and just a few women) who populated what Duane DeVries calls the "world of [Dickens's] early initiation into manhood—the London of lawyers' chambers, law courts, newspaper offices, the reporters' gallery in Parliament, public dinners, theaters, concert halls."[15] Clerks, apprentices, shop assistants, carpenters, bonnet makers, milliners, and shoe binders are the protagonists of Boz's London, whereas the street folk and dandies of the metropolis generally appear only as extras dotting the scene.[16] Boz himself makes a point of his own class identity: although he is a walker of the streets, a perambulator, and man of a

---

[14] See Dexter, "The Reception of Dickens's First Book," pp. 48, 50. J. Hillis Miller argues against the notion that Boz is, above all, faithful to reality as the starting point for his deconstructive reading of the *Sketches*, in which he emphasizes their fictionality. J. Hillis Miller and David Borowitz, *Charles Dickens and George Cruikshank* (Los Angeles: William Andrews Clark Memorial Library, University of California, 1971).

[15] Duane DeVries, *Dickens's Apprentice Years: The Making of a Novelist* (New York: Barnes and Noble, 1976), p. 61.

[16] Virgil Grillo points out that in 1833–34, when Dickens was beginning to publish the short stories that would later make up the tales of *Sketches by Boz*, British periodicals featured few if any stories about middle-class people living in contemporary London. See Grillo, *Dickens' "Sketches by Boz,"* p. 15.

certain kind of leisure, he is not one of those blasé strollers in search of sensation who cannot genuinely enjoy the city or learn from it. He begins the sketch "Shops and Their Tenants" with this declaration:

> We have not the slightest commiseration for the man who can take up his hat and stick, and walk from Covent-garden to St. Paul's churchyard, and back into the bargain, without deriving some amusement—we had almost said instruction—from his perambulation. And yet there are such beings: we meet them every day. Large black stocks and light waistcoats, jet canes and discontented countenances, are the characteristics of the race. . . . Nothing seems to make an impression on their minds: nothing short of being knocked down by a porter, or run over by a cab, will disturb their equanimity.[17]

Boz then goes on to identify himself as a different kind of rambler, one whose "principal amusement" is to watch the rise and fall of shops, to learn the archaeology of the city and observe its layers of change. Similarly, he prefers the swagger of apprentices on a Sunday outing to the "precocious puppyism of the Quadrant, the whiskered dandyism of Regent-street and Pall-mall" (p. 233). He defends the "foolery" of the apprentice, no matter how ridiculous, and in so doing makes it clear that the streets now belong to the rising classes rather than to the already jaded. In a number of his tales—"The Tuggs's at Ramsgate" and "Horatio Sparkins" among them—Boz satirizes the pretensions of the newly rich who try to hide their petit bourgeois origins, signaling his middle-class audience that he rejects pseudoaristocratic behavior but understands the nature of social climbing and aspiration.

Dickens's identification with a middle-class sense of opportunity and mobility accounts for a number of the differences between his sketches and those in a more traditional mode. One crucial difference—his fascination with the processes of urban change—can best be understood by comparing the *Sketches* with the work of two other essayists and sketch writers, Charles Lamb in his "Elia" persona and Leigh Hunt. Lamb, whose essays Dickens read and greatly admired, perceives the city's past in its present and performs archaeological operations on the sites of London, very much as Dickens would do after him.[18] But Elia's real interest is in what is gone, irretrievable, submerged; his love is for

---

[17] [Charles Dickens], *Sketches by Boz, Illustrative of Every-day Life and Every-day People* (London: Chapman and Hall, 1867), p. 67; subsequently cited in the text.

[18] For Dickens's reading of Lamb and others, see Philip Collins, "Dickens's Reading," *The Dickensian* 60 (September 1964): 140.

the past, and the tone of his backward glance is nostalgic, regretful, even sad. He remembers the South Sea House of forty years past and savors its moribund qualities, preferring this "magnificent relic" to the "fret and fever of speculation" that now abound in the City. Addressing the trading house, he writes: "With what reverence have I paced thy great bare rooms and courts at eventide! They spoke of the past:—the shade of some dead accountant, with visionary pen in ear, would flit by me, stiff as in life. Living accounts and accountants puzzle me. . . . But thy great dead tomes . . . are very agreeable and edifying spectacles."[19] It is the ghostly that attracts him, the dead who speak to him; and although he is aware of the layers of history that the city contains, it is the process of recovery, of stripping away layers of time, rather than of transformation or accretion that inspires him. In matters of urban change, as in matters of his own life, Elia declares himself one of the "half-Januses" who "cannot look forward with the same idolatry with which we forever revert!"[20]

Leigh Hunt, whose "Townsman" essays were appearing in the *Weekly True Sun* as Dickens began to publish his sketches, resembles Lamb in his interest in the past, but his voice is that of the historian or tour guide, not the mourner for the urban dead. On his rambles and walking tours of various neighborhoods, the contemporary city becomes nearly transparent as he focuses on the past. Witnessing the city of the present is a way to conjure up what went before. "Dear 1833," he writes, recalling the Marylebone of his youth, "fall back awhile, and be as if thou had'st never been!"[21] Unlike Lamb, for whom urban history emerges as a highly personal memory, Hunt delights in the public, collective history of the nation and is particularly taken with the "great men" who have inhabited London's neighborhoods: Benjamin West in Marylebone; Thomas More, Jonathan Swift, and John Arbuthnot in Chelsea; Richard Steele in Cheyne Walk. In fact, he wonders why the English do not name their streets for great men as the French do. Why not call the street in Chelsea on which Mozart lived during his stay in England "Mozart-street"? For the citizen who utters such a street name the present will dissolve, and distant thoughts of music,

---

[19] Charles Lamb, "The South-Sea House," in *The Essays of Elia and Eliana* (London: George Bell and Sons, 1883), p. 3.

[20] Charles Lamb, "Oxford in the Vacation," in *Essays*, p. 12.

[21] Leigh Hunt, "The Townsman, No. V," in *Leigh Hunt's Political and Occasional Essays*, ed. Lawrence Huston Houtchens and Carolyn Washburn Houtchens (New York: Columbia University Press, 1962), p. 299.

poetry, and love will prevail. "From such dull thraldoms as Eaton-street and Ebury-street he is utterly delivered," writes Hunt. "He remembers nothing about them. He does not see even the dull houses on each side of him, —nor the dull weather, —nor the potato-shop, —nor the butcher's, nor the fine insipid houses."[22]

It is, of course, precisely the potato shop that Boz notices and wants us to notice. The present captures his interest as powerfully as the past, and he savors the quotidian and the ordinary in ways that Hunt cannot. When he plumbs the past of a neighborhood or building, he does so not to efface the present but to reveal it, to make it comprehensible and give it depth and dimension. When he sees a set of clothes in a secondhand shop in "Meditations in Monmouth Street," he conjures up their former owner's life history from the appearance of the garments: "There was the man's whole life written as legibly on those clothes, as if we had his autobiography engrossed on parchment before us" (p. 83). In "Hackney-Coach Stands" he muses on the potential interest of the "autobiography" of a broken-down coach, finding in all the objects and edifices of the streets the record of the city's past. Boz uses that past to animate the present, to bring it to life, just as he animates the rows of clothing hanging on Monmouth Street by imagining the histories of its wearers.

Boz's view of urban history is dynamic, more invested in the present than Hunt's, more welcoming of change than Lamb's. But Dickens learned much from Lamb, and there are moments in the *Sketches* when his nostalgia for the irretrievable past closely resembles Lamb's. In "Scotland-Yard" he laments the destruction of an ancient neighborhood after the rebuilding of London Bridge: "We marked the advance of civilisation, and beheld it with a sigh" (p. 75). He regrets that the "antiquary of another generation" will not be able to find the old Scotland Yard or observe the remembered landmarks. The spirit of the antiquary surfaces in the *Sketches* only occasionally, however; for the most part Boz delights in the juxtaposition of past and present and celebrates change as process rather than as loss.

This interest in process distinguishes Boz's sketches from those of most of his predecessors and contemporaries, and his descriptions of the city unfold and exist in time in a way that breaks the static mold of the traditional sketch form. Although both Lamb and Hunt look backward, their object, as I have said, is to bring the past into relief

---

[22] Leigh Hunt, "The Townsman, No. XI," in *Essays*, pp. 311–12.

rather than to suggest an active, organic connection between past and present. Boz's representation of time gives his sketches a narrative quality that subverts the tableaulike image of the city we have seen in Egan and De Quincey. Writing about the *Sketches*, F. S. Schwarzbach notes that Dickens's unique contribution consists in the "unifying vision . . . of the urban milieu as an eternal here and now." Invoking Carl Schorske's notion that the modern city's essential characteristic is a permanent sense of transience, Schwarzbach writes that in Dickens we find an early version of this distinctly modern sensibility, and that unlike Hunt, for example, Dickens embraces the contemporary city and ignores or belittles the past.[23] In contrast to Hunt or Lamb, Dickens depicts an experience of the city that is indeed more powerfully rooted in the here and now; but he also works against this sense of transience in a formal way and breaks the boundaries of the moment by creating narrative continuity and movement.

The first of the street sketches or "Scenes," titled "The Streets—Morning," provides a brilliantly effective example of the injection of the passage of time into what might otherwise be a static set piece. Boz describes the awakening of the city on a summer's morning as witnessed by one who has been out all night, whether for business or pleasure (a man dressed in top hat and cape leans nonchalantly on a post in the background of Cruikshank's accompanying illustration; see figure 6). This sketch partakes of a longstanding tradition of representing one location at various times of day. The most apposite eighteenth-century example is Hogarth's series "The Four Times of the Day," which features London, in four separate prints, in the morning, at noon, in the evening, and at night.[24] Each scene corresponds to a season, and each takes place in a different location: "Morning" shows a wintry scene of beggars, hawkers, market girls, and whores warming themselves by a fire in Covent Garden; "Noon" is set in Hog Lane in springtime and features two sets of lovers, one chaste and one bawdy; "Evening" takes us to the outskirts of the city in high summer and depicts a wilted, unhappy family strolling in the heat; and "Night" is set beneath a barber-surgeon's window in September, with a collection

[23] F. S. Schwarzbach, *Dickens and the City* (London: Athlone Press, 1979), pp. 41–42; Carl E. Schorske, "The Idea of the City in European Thought," in *The Historian and the City*, ed. Oscar Handlin and John Burchard (Cambridge: MIT Press, 1963), pp. 109–10.

[24] On Hogarth's series, see Sean Shesgreen, *Hogarth and the Times-of-the-Day Tradition* (Ithaca: Cornell University Press, 1983); and Ronald Paulson, *Hogarth: His Life, Art, and Times* (New Haven: Yale University Press, 1971), 1:398–404.

Figure 6 George Cruikshank, "The Streets, Morning." Charles Dickens, *Sketches by Boz* (1839).

of vagrants, intoxicated Freemasons, and others huddled together. Although Hogarth's series displays an interest in seasonal change and in the passage of time in a very abstract sense, its primary mode seems to be allegorical rather than representational, and it is engaged in a satirical survey of the pictorial tradition out of which it grew.[25]

[25] Shesgreen, *Hogarth*, p. 22; and see pp. 109–12 for examples of allegorical figures in the series.

Dickens's version of this time-of-day approach differs from Hogarth's in ways that elucidate the nature of his contribution to the form of the urban sketch. Unlike Hogarth, he focuses on one place and represents it as it changes, indeed, in the very process of change. Dickens turns the camera on and keeps it running, hoping to capture movement, above all, and to show how a variety of types occupy the same urban space. Although the passage of time is also part of the story Hogarth tells, he gives us four separate tableaux. Interestingly, George Augustus Sala, a disciple of Dickens's, borrowed a page from this eighteenth-century convention to produce *Twice Round the Clock, or the Hours of the Day and Night in London* (1858), a collection of twenty-four sketches, one for each hour of the day.[26] Sala as narrator moves from place to place, from Billingsgate market to the docks to Regent Street to a charity dinner to Bow Street, choosing appropriate locales to illustrate a given hour (the fish market at four in the morning, the green-room of a theater at seven in the evening, and so on). Although Sala owes much to Dickens, and to *Sketches by Boz* in particular, his times-of-the-day sketches capture a variety of places each at a single moment, rather than a single place or vantage point over a period of time.

It is approximately half past four in the morning, an hour before sunrise, when Boz's "Streets—Morning" begins and high noon when it ends. At the outset the streets are deserted, and the night walker is in "solitary desolation" (p. 55); at half-past five tables for street breakfasts are set up and market carts roll toward Covent Garden; at half-past six servants arrive at work and mail is loaded on the coaches; after another half hour or so clerks approach Chancery Lane and the Inns of Court from their homes in Camden and Islington, and apprentices take up their stations in milliners' and stay-makers' shops; by eleven all the work that has gone into preparing the city for business has subsided into invisibility, and customers and clients fill the streets. The description reaches a veritable climax as at midday the streets are "thronged

[26] The story of the genesis of Sala's sketches offers in microcosm a literary and biographical background to the nineteenth-century urban sketch. According to Philip Collins, Sala, a successful journalist and "bachelor of bohemian habits," expressed to his colleagues an interest in writing a book on Hogarth. Dickens lent him an eighteenth-century book that Thackeray had given *him* because it contained a long dedication to Hogarth. It was called *Low Life: or, One Half of the World knows not how the Other Half Lives* (1752), and from it Sala got the idea for his twenty-four-hour tour of the metropolis. He eventually came back to the book on Hogarth and published it in installments in Thackeray's *Cornhill Magazine.* See Philip Collins's rich and informative introduction to George Augustus Sala, *Twice Round the Clock, or the Hours of the Day and Night in London* (Leicester: Leicester University Press, 1971).

with a vast concourse of people, gay and shabby, rich and poor, idle and industrious; and we come to the heat, bustle, and activity of *Noon*" (p. 60). The sketch is written entirely in the present tense, and a sense of immediacy is maintained throughout. But rather than observing a tableau or catching a glimpse, we experience the movement, the unfolding and progression, of city life. Boz reveals what is not ordinarily visible to the casual observer: he offers a privileged glance behind the scenes at a world of activity and transformation that, for many of his middle-class readers, did not exist.

Boz transforms the sketch, then, by mining the past, catching the city in the process of change, and giving depth to the superficial encounters with urban life that characterized the form in earlier decades. This development emerges quite clearly in the third and fourth sections of the *Sketches*: "Characters" and "Tales." Not satisfied with physical descriptions or physiognomies of the street people who populate his scenes of London, Boz creates a kind of sketch that enables him to evoke character, indeed, the circumstances and full story of an individual life. The milliners and carpenters, dancing masters and "parlour orators" who come and go in sketches such as "The Streets—Morning" are given personal histories and dramas.

In "Shabby-Genteel People" the depressed and impoverished but still dignified Londoners of his description cease to be mere types and become individuals with observable identities. Boz achieves this by following one "shabby-genteel" man who used to "haunt" him in the reading room of the British Museum. A more traditional sketch might capture the man's appearance from across the reading room table, describe his books—as Boz does as well—and perhaps offer a bit of speculation on the man's place in the moral universe (think of Wordsworth's blind beggar or Lamb's chimneysweeps). But Boz, who himself inhabits the city and does not merely observe and record it, traces the man's progress over a period of weeks. The man suddenly disappears after regularly occupying the same seat every morning at ten. Boz worries that he has perhaps hanged himself or jumped off a bridge. Then the man reappears with all his clothing freshly dyed a shiny black; but after a week of incessant rain his suit fades to its former reddish-brown tint.

What distinguishes this kind of sketch is the urban observer's involvement over time with the types that come into view and his concern not just for classifying them but for reconstructing the details of their lives. In "The Hospital Patient," another of the sketches in the "Characters" section of the book to which I will return later, Boz begins as the rambler walking through the streets of the city in the evening and pausing beneath the windows of a public hospital to "picture to ourself the gloomy and mournful scenes that are passing within" (p. 255). But soon he leaves his rambler's vantage point and becomes the investigator or reporter. He follows an arrested pickpocket to the police station, hears him questioned about his role in the beating of the young woman with whom he lives, and then trails the police and the criminal to the hospital to hear the woman's deposition. Boz's entry into the hospital changes the rambler's role, taking him behind the facades of edifice and character alike.

In the final tale of the *Sketches*, "The Drunkard's Death," Boz again signals the change in his role as walker of the streets by making an encounter in a crowd the springboard for a story. J. Hillis Miller has observed that Boz's tales are "often the temporal unfolding of what is initially affirmed pictorially, in the instant of juxtaposition within a Sketch."[27] An image or vignette becomes or implies the progress of a character, and Boz thus unfolds what appears frozen and static. What Miller calls this "metonymic basis of realistic narrative" underlies Dickens's transformation of the urban observer's role and his innovations as a sketch writer.[28] "The Drunkard's Death" begins unremarkably for a street sketch:

> We will be bold to say, that there is scarcely a man in the constant habit of walking, day after day, through any of the crowded thoroughfares of London, who cannot recollect among the people whom he "knows by sight," to use a familiar phrase, some being of abject and wretched appearance whom he remembers to have seen in a very different condition, whom he has observed sinking lower and lower by almost imperceptible degrees, and the shabbiness and utter destitution of whose appearance, at last, strike forcibly and painfully upon him, as he passes by. (p. 515)

But what starts out as the quintessential experience of the crowd, of anonymity and momentary encounter, metamorphoses into the story of a nameless, deteriorating man. Boz follows him to his dying wife's bedside, through vile courts and alleyways, into brickfields and under arches where he sleeps, and finally to Waterloo Bridge. The unknowability of the urban passerby, on which the tradition of the urban sketch

---

[27] Miller and Borowitz, *Dickens and Cruikshank*, p. 18.
[28] Ibid., p. 19.

had largely been based, is undermined by this sketch-made-tale as Boz turns the objects of observation into subjects, into characters in their own stories.

Intimately related to Boz's commitment to the knowability of the city and his refusal to glorify an irretrievable past is the process of demystification that runs throughout so many of the sketches. Whereas for Lamb's Elia, for instance, the reality of the past remains forever unchallenged within the haze of nostalgia, the city of Boz's childhood emerges as a place of now exploded myths and artifice, where sweeps were said to be the sons of lords and the performers at Astley's circus were "beings of light and elegance . . . who flitted on sleek cream-coloured horses before our eyes at night" (p. 119). Although he relishes memories of London's entertainments and festivals, he readily admits their unreality, their distance from the experiences he tries without success to repeat as an adult. The players at Astley's reappear outside the ring as "dirty shabby-genteel men in checked neckerchiefs, and sallow linen, lounging about, and carrying, perhaps, under one arm, a pair of stage shoes badly wrapped in a piece of old newspaper" (p. 119); and when he visits Vauxhall Gardens, now open during the day as well as at night, he admits that sunlight has "rudely and harshly disturb[ed] the veil of mystery which had hung about the property" (p. 137). Now the child sweeps, once rumored to be the kidnapped scions of nobility, are revealed as the sons of other sweeps, and May Day dancers as scavengers, brickmakers, and costermongers merely dressed as sweeps (p. 186).[29] Whereas the urban observers of the 1820s converted the everyday scene to theater, Boz transforms theater into the ordinary and unremarkable. Spectacle itself is demystified and the distance between spectator and the city diminished.[30]

It is not only in the arena of the spectacular that Boz eschews the sensational in pursuit of the prosaic. In "A Visit to Newgate" Boz the rambler again becomes Boz the investigator, coaxing those who daily "pass and repass this gloomy depository of the guilt and misery of Lon-

[29] It is interesting to compare Dickens's sketch "The First of May" with Lamb's "Praise of Chimney-Sweepers," which the former must certainly have known. Although both essays combine a certain sentimental nostalgia with an ironic glance at the plight of the child sweep, Elia clings to the myths of bygone May Days while Boz explodes them directly, if with regret.

[30] For a related discussion of theater and disillusionment in *Sketches by Boz*, see Miller and Borowitz, *Dickens and Cruikshank*, pp. 20–26. Miller writes: "The theatrical metaphor expresses perfectly the process whereby Boz sees behind the scenes and leads his readers to see behind them too" (p. 26).

don" (p. 213) to enter its doors and see what lies within. One of the striking things about this sketch is that, somber as its tone may be, it offers no overt, angry critique either of the treatment of prisoners or of the social circumstances that land a boy of fourteen in the "condemned" section of the prison.[31] The aim here seems rather to reveal an ordinary world of men and women in an extraordinary place. His tone verging on the deadpan, Boz takes us through the women's quarters, the "school" for boys under fourteen, the prison chapel, and the cells of the condemned as if on a mission of instruction, with little sentimentality and less sensationalism. His description of the apartments of the condemned provides a notable example:

> In the first apartment into which we were conducted ... were five-and-twenty or thirty prisoners, all under sentence of death, awaiting the result of the recorder's report—men of all ages and appearances, from a hardened old offender with swarthy face and grizzly beard of three day's growth, to a handsome boy, not fourteen years old, of singularly youthful appearance even for that age, who had been condemned for burglary. There was nothing remarkable in the appearance of these prisoners. (p. 222)

Few of these men, he tells us, will be executed, and so their ordinariness of appearance should not surprise us; but eventually he turns his attention to one man who is scheduled to hang the next day. Here Boz stresses the irreducible humanity of the criminal. In a passage that rehearses Fagin's last meditations in *Oliver Twist*, Boz imagines the condemned man's final thoughts and reveries: he dreams that he is strolling with his wife in a "pleasant field, with a bright blue sky above them," that he begs her forgiveness for his crimes, and that he ultimately escapes the prison walls to freedom (p. 226). The simplicity of this man's desires and the other prisoners' unremarkable appearance do not stimulate pity on the readers' part but rather evoke the recognition of their own likeness in the prisoners' faces and souls. The unsensational quality of Dickens's approach in this essay differs markedly from Pierce Egan's look at Newgate in *Life in London*, in which Tom and Jerry—and the readers along with them—avert their gaze from the condemned yard of the prison.

---

[31] Philip Collins remarks that, compared with Dickens's later prison descriptions, "A Visit to Newgate" seems distinctly lacking in "penological point of view" and is for the most part noncommittal in tone. See Philip Collins, *Dickens and Crime* (London: Macmillan, 1964), p. 33.

"A Visit to Newgate" raises a central question about the *Sketches*: To what extent does Dickens insist on the connections *between* classes, and especially between the middle class and the outlaws and outcasts of the city? It is clear from the discussion thus far that Boz's audience is encouraged to see itself even in the "shabby genteel" and in the pretentious newly rich, but what about the slum dwellers, the criminals, the beggars of the city? In the Newgate sketch Boz hints at cross-class connections by desensationalizing the inmates, almost by stripping them of their criminality, of their difference. But what of those aspects of London life to which a middle-class bridge cannot easily be found or invented? What of the "dangerous" classes that put middle-class invulnerability at risk? It is one thing to make the outcasts of the city into mirrors of the middle-class self, but how to transform the unregenerate few who themselves threaten to transform, indeed contaminate, the secure and rising middle class? Dickens's own uncertainty about representing the most marginal members of urban society reflects this anxiety of the middle class about its own relation to the lower classes.

Virtually the only description of slum life to be found in the *Sketches* is in "Seven Dials," which enters a part of London not likely frequented by most of Boz's readers. In this sketch Boz refers to the hypothetical observer, part alter ego, part representative of the uninitiated reader, as "the stranger who finds himself in 'The Dials' for the first time." He continues:

> From the irregular square into which he has plunged, the streets and courts dart in all directions, until they are lost in the unwholesome vapour which hangs over the house-tops, and renders the dirty perspective, uncertain and confined; and lounging at every corner, as if they came there to take a few gasps of such fresh air as has found its way so far, . . . are groups of people, whose appearance and dwellings would fill any mind but a regular Londoner's with astonishment. (p. 78)

Despite the implied claim that a "regular Londoner" would not be astonished by the labyrinthine form and fetid atmosphere of Seven Dials, this part of London, unlike those represented in almost all the other sketches in the collection, is terra incognita to most readers. And presumably because it is unknown and unsafe territory, Boz alternates between an effort to expose its real nature—as he does in his initial description—and a retreat into the language of theatricality and artifice as a way of avoiding the harshness of his subject.

From the very outset Boz's treatment of the notorious slum seems exaggeratedly literary: he apostrophizes it as the "region of song and poetry" and alludes to the legendary figures—the criminals and those who made them famous—associated with Seven Dials. After taking his readers through the "gordian knot" of these slum streets, he zeroes in on a crowd gathered before two women who are quarreling viciously about what he euphemistically calls a "point of domestic arrangement." One woman's husband has abandoned her and their five children for the other's bed. Both women are drunk, and they are about to come to blows. What verges on turning into a shocking and ugly scene, a scene that introduces material strikingly out of place in the world of Boz's sketches, is suddenly converted into theater and thereby tamed: "The scuffle became general, and terminates, in minor play-bill phraseology, with 'arrival of the policemen, interior of the station-house, and impressive *denouement*' " (p. 79).

This gesture, reminiscent of Egan's departing flourishes and strategies for distancing himself and his readers from unpleasant truths, signals some ambivalence on Dickens's part about how real and unsettling he wants to make Seven Dials. A page later he again falters in his un-adorned description of the mean streets, the "dirty, straggling houses," the "half-naked children," the "long rows of broken and patched windows," and, by sleight of hand, makes the scene into what he calls a "still life [of] reeking pipes, bad fruit, more than doubtful oysters, attenuated cats, depressed dogs, and anatomical fowls" (p. 80). Having turned the quarreling women into characters in a melodrama, he now transforms the slum scene into a painting, choosing to soften the blow of reality by seeing it as art, or as artifice, and by using adjectives that establish a comic rather than a grim tone. Far from convincing his readers that this, like Newgate, is a real place, he offers them a benign stage performance and the entertaining world of squalor, which Cruikshank captures in his accompanying illustration of scrapping slum women.

In Cruikshank's sketch two sets of women go at each other while a crowd gathers to watch the proceedings (figure 7). Three male spectators at the right are drawn particularly distinctly; the expressions on their faces betray a kind of blasé amusement. One, dressed in white apron and cap, appears to be delivering crates of beer to a pub, and the other two are of the post-leaning class Boz describes in his sketch.

Figure 7 George Cruikshank, "Seven Dials." Charles Dickens, *Sketches by Boz* (1839).

These two, who look particularly smug, represent the working-class version of the idle rambler, the urban spectator without purpose. And, like their upper-class counterparts, they are also representative of the male gaze of urban observation. The women they watch figure not only as objectified females of the urban scene but also as isolated victims and markers of urban deprivation. Here, in Cruikshank's rendering, they are comic figures, their misery—only hinted at by Boz—obscured totally by their Punch-and-Judy poses. But elsewhere in the *Sketches*, as we shall see, women appear as emblems of suffering and social pain, as the sole casualties of a usually buoyant urban world.

In "The Pawnbroker's Shop" Boz brings together three sets of women in different stages of social distress in the same Drury Lane shop: a middle-class mother and daughter pawning an item of costly jewelry; a poor but gaudily attired young woman, in all likelihood a prostitute, who weeps as the "respectable" women in the shop shrink from her; and a destitute old woman who can anticipate only two more stages in her descent, the hospital and the grave. Boz juxtaposes these women not as a means of savoring variety, as Pierce Egan might have done, but as a way of impressing on his readers an awareness of the fundamental ties between apparently unrelated segments of society. The Cruikshank illustration that accompanies the sketch makes clear that the readers themselves are encouraged to do the work of perceiving connections: the ordinary poor folk pawning their possessions stand in a group in the main part of the shop, while those wishing privacy and anonymity (the mother and daughter, for example) stand in small compartments which they have entered through separate doors and can be seen only by the brokers—and by the viewer, whose vantage point is that of the brokers behind the desk (figure 8). So although the socially disparate clients cannot see one another and note their common plight, the reader can.

Readers are thus to some extent encouraged to recognize themselves in the middle-class mother and daughter, who form a bridge between the audience and the most destitute objects of urban observation. But Cruikshank's illustration again underscores for us one of the salient and unavoidable features of the sketch: the brokers, like the quintessential street observer and the hypothetical ideal reader of Boz's work, are male and the objects of their observation female. When Boz asks at the end of the sketch, "Who shall say how soon these women may change places?" he stops short of suggesting that "we," his readers, might change places with any of them, even though the respectable mother and daughter represent the female counterparts of his readers. "The Pawnbroker's Shop" perfectly illustrates Dickens's urge to represent the familiarity and closeness of social suffering while at the same time keeping it sufficiently remote and isolated so as not to threaten his audience's sense of their distance from social taint. In this case, as in others I shall consider, he uses the barrier of gender to introduce and yet quarantine urban misery.

Figure 8 George Cruikshank, "The Pawnbroker's Shop." Charles Dickens, *Sketches by Boz* (1839).

The world of Boz's London emerges largely, although not exclusively, as a masculine preserve. The author-stroller himself offers us a city that is available in its entirety only to men, and he writes, at least at the outset, for other men's eyes. The bachelor or man at liberty is present in the figure of the observer who, having been out all night, witnesses the opening of Covent Garden market in the early morning hours; he is present "promenading about, three abreast," through a tea garden on Sunday (p. 103); he is present in the persons of Mr. Thomas Potter and Mr. Robert Smithers, two clerks who "make a night of it" (p. 286); and he is present being ushered into a public dinner on behalf of the "Indigent Orphans' Friends' Benevolent Institution" (p. 176). Boz's London man is not the young swell or buck of Egan or the superannuated bachelor of Elia, though he shares their undomesticated condition. His peers and contemporaries are the bachelor members of the Pickwick Club in the novel that Dickens began to serialize in 1836, the same year the first collected *Sketches* appeared.

The overwhelmingly masculine world of *The Pickwick Papers* combines elements of the picaresque tradition that Dickens inherited from Cervantes by way of the eighteenth-century novel with an Edenic placidity that is not just prelapsarian but at times suggestive of a paradise before the creation of woman. Unlike the equally masculine world of Pierce Egan, which also stands behind at least the original plan for the novel, the Pickwickian universe is one in which women are almost entirely avoided, even as instruments of pleasure, and in which masculinity has been "gentled," as Steven Marcus puts it, to create a "vision of innocence and benignity."[32] Masculinity, in other words, has been desexualized, and women are consequently made superfluous and disruptive of bachelor serenity. The plot of *Pickwick*, such as it is, hinges on a moment when Mr. Pickwick is about to "propose" to Sam Weller, that is, to propose that Sam become his manservant and constant companion: "Do you think it a much greater expense," Mr. Pickwick asks his landlady, Mrs. Bardell, as he contemplates this major change in his life, "to keep two people, than to keep one?"[33] The naive Mrs. Bardell, hearing these words but assuming they come from quite a different script, assumes that Mr. Pickwick is proposing to *her*. When she later discovers that he has no intention of marrying her, she sues him for breach of promise and so brings about his eventual imprisonment in the Fleet. Thus, a woman's misunderstanding of and interference in peaceful homosocial relations leads to the bleakest episode in the novel.

The benign urban world of *Pickwick* transcends even that of *Sketches by Boz* in its cheerfulness, perhaps because the novel inhabits exclusively the London of Dickens's youth (the story is set in 1827) rather than straddling, as *Sketches* does, the immediate present and the recent past

[32] Steven Marcus, *Dickens from "Pickwick" to "Dombey"* (New York: Simon and Schuster, 1965), p. 38.

[33] Charles Dickens, *The Posthumous Papers of the Pickwick Club* (Harmondsworth: Penguin, 1972), p. 230; subsequently cited in the text.

that shaped it. The London character of the novel, which was not at all indicated by the publishers' original plans for the book, is firmly ensured by the centrality of Sam Weller, who emerges full-blown in chapter 10 out of the heart of an old coaching inn. Like many of the subjects and readers of *Sketches by Boz*, and like the author himself, Sam is a London man on the rise by virtue of his wit, talent, savvy, and mastery of language. He tells Mr. Pickwick that he has known nights under the dry arches of Waterloo Bridge along with the homeless creatures "as an't up to the twopenny rope," but that he is headed now for bigger things: "I was a carrier's boy at startin': then a vagginer's, then a helper, then a boots. Now I'm a gen'l'm'n's servant. I shall be a gen'l'm'n myself one of these days, perhaps, with a pipe in my mouth, and a summer house in the back garden. Who knows? *I* shouldn't be surprised, for one" (p. 290). Sam's London is a place in which his entry into the middle class is likely, in which even the bootblack or the boy who puts the labels on the blacking can prosper without foreseeable limit.

The harmonious world that Sam represents and Mr. Pickwick inhabits is marred, of course, by the machinations of the cynical lawyers Dodson and Fogg and by the consequent entry of virtually the entire significant population of the novel into Fleet Prison. The harmony is also interrupted, although hardly marred, by the interpolated tales sprinkled throughout the novel, many of which are gruesome, even horrifying, in tone and subject. As Steven Marcus—and before him Edmund Wilson—has noted, the tales indicate that "within the transcendent achievement of *Pickwick Papers*, encapsulated within its imagination of the possibility of innocent human relations, . . . is an imagination of an entirely opposite sort."[34] But as readers of *Pickwick* are aware, the grim imagination of the interpolated tales and even the sober realities of the Fleet do not penetrate—one might say do not contaminate—the rest of the novel.

Women are at best peripheral to and at worst destructive of the male bliss of the Pickwickian universe, but they have a distinctive role to play within the interpolated tales. Indeed, just as unhappy pairs of fathers and sons figure prominently in these episodes, so too do brutally victimized women. In three different stories—"The Stroller's Tale," "The Convict's Return," and "A Madman's Manuscript"—men assault or regularly beat their wives. In the first a dissipated and now delirious

[34] Marcus, *Dickens from "Pickwick" to "Dombey,"* p. 42.

husband has so mistreated his wife that he regards her with terror, convinced that *she* will murder *him* if he is left alone with her. The wife in "The Convict's Return" first suffers her husband's abuse for the sake of protecting her son only to witness the son's own deterioration and rejection of her. In "The Madman's Manuscript" a man who is convinced of his congenital madness determines to kill his wife before she can give birth to a child; in the aftermath of an aborted attack on her by her husband, the *wife* is diagnosed as mad and shortly thereafter dies. In these un-Pickwickian tales women do not merely suffer as victims of social and personal degeneration; they also emerge as objects of male rage and resentment, however deranged and misplaced it may be. In two of the stories the male assailant fears his victim, imbuing her with his own viciousness. These women are imagined as threats to an equally imaginary male equilibrium, and Mrs. Bardell is their comic analogue. The "possibility of innocent human relations" seems not to include relations between the sexes. What is benignly comic within the main narrative is cordoned off and represented bleakly within the tales.

There is a remarkable similarity between the appearance of such victimized women in *Pickwick* and their role in *Sketches by Boz.* In the companion sketch to "Streets—Morning," called "Streets—Night," Boz gives us a portrait of the city on a "dark, dull, murky" winter's evening (p. 61). All of the sights and figures he describes—the baked potato seller, the kidney pie stand, the cheesemonger's piles of colored cheeses—have lost their customary gaiety, and the streets have taken on a bleak and melancholy air. But one sole figure emerges not simply as a chilled and rain-soaked street character but as a victim of urban callousness and neglect:

> That wretched woman with the infant in her arms, round whose meagre form the remnant of her own scanty shawl is carefully wrapped, has been attempting to sing some popular ballad, in the hope of wringing a few pence from the compassionate passer-by. A brutal laugh at her weak voice is all she has gained. The tears fall thick and fast down her own pale face; the child is cold and hungry, and its low half-stifled wailing adds to the misery of its wretched mother, as she moans aloud, and sinks despairingly down, on a cold damp doorstep. (pp. 63–64)

Boz's stance then changes briefly from one of observation and sympathy to one of angry rhetorical scolding. Challenging his readers directly in a manner far more characteristic of the later Dickens than of the early Boz, he accuses them of indifference to this woman's anguish and charges them with ignoring the "fearful tale of want and famishing" that she sings (p. 64). A moment later he reverts to the urban street chronicler, describing the rowdy after-theater crowd feasting on oysters, chops, and kidneys. The song of the miserable woman is forgotten by revelers and narrator alike, and the city regains something of its former vibrancy as the feasting of gentlemen continues until three or four in the morning. The lone suffering woman gives way to a scene of buoyant masculine camaraderie as the normal flow of the *Sketches* is resumed. The late-night world of male revelry, familiar from Egan's *Life in London,* is here strikingly devoid of the lowlife but ebullient female counterparts an earlier literature would have featured. The "Cyprians" of Egan are absent, and in their place stands this solitary sufferer. Regency high life gives way to a proto-Victorian middle-class vision that overcomes an unsettling and threatening female sexuality by casting women as victims.[35]

In "The Hospital Patient," a sketch already mentioned, the image of woman as victim takes on a more dramatic and gruesome aspect. Boz the rambler follows a pickpocket and the magistrates who have arrested him to a public hospital, where a battered woman is expected to identify the prisoner as her companion and assailant. The woman, young and once beautiful, is chillingly described: "Her long black hair had been hastily cut from about the wounds on her head, and streamed over the pillow in jagged and matted locks. Her face bore frightful marks of the ill-usage she had received: her hand was pressed upon her side, as if her chief pain were there; her breathing was short and heavy; and it was plain to see that she was dying fast" (pp. 257–58). With a minimum of melodrama and a grim starkness that shocks the reader of these sketches, Dickens evokes a scene in which is concentrated the pain and ugliness of modern urban life ordinarily kept out of Boz's vision. The girl, who clearly prefigures Nancy in *Oliver Twist,* dies denying that the pickpocket, her lover and quite likely her pimp, has beaten her, and declares that she wishes she had died as a child, before her fall from respectability.

---

[35] See Lynda Nead, *Myths of Sexuality: Representations of Women in Victorian Britain* (Oxford: Basil Blackwell, 1988), chap. 5, "The Prostitute as Social Victim." Nead writes: "The implications of deviant femininity could be contained and controlled by constructing the prostitute as an object to be pitied, a victim in need of reclamation and charity" (p. 139).

Unlike "The Streets—Night" this sketch offers no cheering denouement and never shifts its focus away from the suffering woman. Although the (male) reader is not allowed to forget or repress her, he is
encouraged to see her as victim, as object, as embodiment of suffering
rather than as a like creature in whose place he can imagine himself.
Her death, like Nancy's, comes as a grotesque relief, the only imaginable end to an irrevocably sullied life. The murder of Nancy represents, in fact, a strange confluence, a place where the melodramatic
rendering of the compulsory pathos of the prostitute's life meets the
cathartic release of masculine rage. Dickens's compulsively repeated
public readings of the murder scene in *Oliver Twist* suggest at least the
possibility that he identified with Sikes's murderous rage as well as with
the tainted nobility of the trapped victim.[36]

That both the street singer in "Streets—Night" and the dying woman
in "The Hospital Patient" are sexually fallen or "ruined" women is
not surprising in light of the long tradition of the prostitute as stock
urban figure. The prostitute, unlike her "respectable" sisters, occupies
not domestic but public space and so functions as part of the visible
urban scene. She can also figure, as I suggested earlier, as an analogue
of the middle-class male observer's peripatetic self, a reflection of his
sense of otherness, as in De Quincey, or a partner in his urban sprees
and revelry, as in Pierce Egan. The prostitute can thus embody the
seemingly contradictory extremes of otherness and human connectedness. For Swift, for instance, in "A Beautiful Young Nymph Going to
Bed," she is a figure of radical otherness, a creature whose ultimate
humanity is grotesquely and convincingly masked beneath layers of artifice; whereas for Blake, in his "London" poem, she represents the
insidious yet inevitable link between otherwise separate social spheres.[37]

---

[36] There are numerous stories about Dickens's repetition of the Sikes and Nancy reading. Edgar Johnson recounts one involving Dickens's son Charley: "One warm afternoon
Charley was working in the library when he heard a sound of violent wrangling from
outside. At first he dismissed it as some tramp brawling with his wife, but as the noise
swelled into an alternation of brutal yells and dreadful screams Charley leaped to his feet,
convinced that he must intervene. He dashed out. There was his father—murdering an
imaginary Nancy with ferocious gestures." Johnson adds that by continuing to include
the reading in his repertoire, Dickens was "sentencing himself to death," confirming our
sense of the novelist as murderer and victim both. See Edgar Johnson, *Charles Dickens:
His Tragedy and Triumph* (Harmondsworth: Penguin, 1977), pp. 552–53.

[37] I am grateful to Ellen Pollak for reminding me of Swift's poem in this context and
for her insights on the ambiguities of its representation of the Covent Garden "toast."
Although Swift humanizes Corinna, the "Pride of *Drury-Lane*," he also depicts her as a
figure at the extreme limits of humanness. In her article "'Things, Which Must Not Be

The implied sexual taint of the street singer and the battered hospital patient becomes explicit in another of Boz's most startling sketches, "The Prisoner's Van." Here our street observer watches as two young prostitutes are taken from a police station and loaded into a van to be transported to prison for six weeks' hard labor. They are sisters, one no more than sixteen and the other not quite fourteen; the elder has a brassy and hardened appearance, though the younger, under arrest for the first time, weeps from shame. As in the "Seven Dials" sketch, a crowd gathers around the two women to watch and jeer. "The greater part of the crowd," Boz reports, "had been inexpressibly delighted with this little incident" (p. 294). Like the quarreling women of Seven Dials, these teenage prostitutes are objects of amusement and fascination; and they are viewed at a distance, with none of the inwardness that Dickens attempts on behalf of the Newgate prisoner who dreams of freedom on the eve of his execution. The egregiousness of these girls' circumstances is matched in *Sketches by Boz* only by the story of the dying woman who has been beaten by her lover. Their femaleness, their otherness, and their use as a means of representing and yet containing the extremes of urban life are inextricably linked.

But the containment of urban horrors and the implied remoteness of these prostitutes from ordinary experience is briefly but significantly undermined in this sketch by the implications of one sentence near its conclusion: "The progress of these girls in crime will be as rapid as the flight of a pestilence, resembling it too in its baneful influence and wide-spreading infection" (p. 294). Without explicitly invoking the "infection" of syphilis—as, for example, Blake does in his "London" poem—Dickens nonetheless alludes to the potential literal and metaphoric contamination that the prostitute represents. The paradoxical role of the streetwalker as both social outsider and social connector becomes a trope for the dangerous aspects of the urban condition.[38]

Expressed': Teaching Swift's Scatological Poems about Women," in *Teaching Eighteenth-Century Poetry*, ed. Christopher Fox (New York: AMS Press, 1990), pp. 177–86, Pollak compares Swift's representation of the prostitute to Lady Mary Wortley Montagu's in her parody of Swift's poem, "The Reasons that Induced Dr S[wift] to write a Poem call'd The Lady's Dressing room." Lady Mary's Betty, Pollak points out, is a "hard-nosed businesswoman—and a subject of retaliation, rather than an object of pity" (p. 183).

[38] In their book *The Politics and Poetics of Transgression* (Ithaca: Cornell University Press, 1986), Peter Stallybrass and Allon White include a fascinating chapter, "The City, the Sewer, the Gaze, and the Contaminating Touch," which also brings together the prostitute and the notion of contamination. They write, "It was above all around the figure of the prostitute that the gaze and touch, the desires and contaminations, of the bourgeois male were articulated" (p. 137).

She can be viewed as the isolated repository of social ills, assuring the middle and upper classes of their safety and protection within urban society, and she can be understood as the ineluctable destroyer of that safety, posing a threat to middle-class insulation. She promises containment and contamination both. Like the comic female figures of *Pickwick* and the pathetic women of that novel's interpolated tales, the prostitute is perceived as superfluous yet dangerous.

In trying to identify the transitional moment of the *Sketches* and the particular uses of gender and female sexuality that define it, we can look forward as well as backward for contrast. Just over a decade later William Makepeace Thackeray produced a series of sketches for *Punch* called "Travels in London" (1847–50), and ten years after that George Sala published his *Twice Round the Clock*. Thackeray makes use of a persona named "Spec," who has been commissioned by "Mr. Punch" to travel in London and bring in "an account of your town." Spec, hoping for a more exotic assignment, resigns himself to reporting on the familiar and covers a round of sights and activities common to the tradition of Egan and Boz: city dinners, night pleasures, pantomimes, parties, clubs, pawnbrokers' and shoemakers' shops in poor neighborhoods.

The stance of Spec in these sketches is, however, complicated and shifting. Thackeray begins, for instance, by satirizing precisely the kind of urban investigation that Henry Mayhew had begun in 1849 as "metropolitan correspondent" for the *Morning Chronicle* (his contributions turned into *London Labour and the London Poor*) and ends in his final sketch, "Waiting at the Station," by endorsing Mayhew's project, writing: "Yes, and these wonders and terrors have been lying by your door and mine ever since we had a door of our own. We had but to go a hundred yards off and see for ourselves, but we never did. . . . You and I—were of the upper classes; we have had hitherto no community with the poor."[39] The satirist, man-about-town, and world traveler gains a social conscience and sheds his customary eighteenth-century sensibility in favor of what we recognize as (for want of a better term) a Victorian one. Consistent with this shift are Thackeray's taming of the urban spectator and his bowdlerization of the urban scene. Not only is Spec a married man, but "Mrs. Spec" is a character in her own right. One of the kinds of parties Spec frequents is a child's party, his own child's,

---

[39] William Makepeace Thackeray, "Waiting at the Station," in *Contributions to "Punch"* (London: Smith, Elder, 1911), 2:464.

and he acts the part of the reluctant paterfamilias to Mrs. Spec's domesticating wife:

> "Why," says she, with the spirit which becomes a woman and mother, "you go to your *man's* parties eagerly enough: what an unnatural wretch you must be to grudge your children their pleasures!" She looks round, sweeps all six of them into her arms, whilst the baby on her lap begins to bawl, and you are assailed by seven pairs of imploring eyes, against which there is no appeal. You must go. If you are dying of lumbago, if you are engaged to the best of dinners, if you are longing to stop at home and read Macaulay, you must give up all and go.[40]

Thackeray has made his urban spectator not merely a husband and father but a middle-class man. His nighttime sprees and travels into the demimonde are things of the past, as are his bachelor freedom and privileged marginality.

No prostitutes populate Spec's London. In their place we find in "The Curate's Walk" a saintly and resourceful girl of ten, a charwoman's daughter, whose father lies in a pauper's graveyard and who performs the role of mother to her younger siblings, and in "Waiting at the Station" a "homely bevy" of thirty-eight women about to emigrate to Australia to find husbands. Spec represents these emigrants as impoverished and unfortunate, inhabitants of the "poor man's country" described by Mayhew, rejected by their own homeland because of their poverty and plainness. There is no hint of sexual taint here, no suggestion that what might be the case in parallel scenes—that these women had been prostitutes or mothers of illegitimate children or simply "ruined"—applies here. Thackeray's urban female victims are not the sexually suspect figures of Boz's sketches, and for this reason their victimization at the hands of a callous society is unequivocal.

George Sala's *Twice Round the Clock* is similarly restrained about sexual matters and the rambler's customary delight in the pleasures of the demimonde. Sala himself observed that he merely wished to tell the truth in his London scenes, "so long as that truth could be told without offence to good manners and in household language."[41] The Podsnappian demands of the 1850s have come into play here, constraining even

---

[40] William Makepeace Thackeray, "Child's Parties," in *Contributions to "Punch,"* 2:440.

[41] Quoted in Philip Collins's introduction to Sala, *Twice Round the Clock,* p. 17, where Collins observes that "Sala's book under-represents the amount and the openness of metropolitan profligacy."

Figure 9 William M'Connell, "Two o'Clock A.M.: The Turnstile of Waterloo Bridge." George Augustus Sala, *Twice Round the Clock; or the Hours of the Day and Night in London* (1859).

a man with a well-known bohemian way of life from including either the sexual or the criminal underworlds that must have been visible in a number of the locales he visits in his twenty-four-hour tour of the city. In the penultimate sketch, "Two o'Clock A.M.—A Late Debate in the House of Commons, and the Turnstile of Waterloo Bridge," Sala offers the text's single example of a streetwalker, and he does so in a highly sentimental and allusive way (see figure 9 for an illustration of this scene). At the turnstile a woman, a "phantom in crinoline," lays her hand on his arm and asks him for a halfpenny so that she might pass through to the bridge. Without a direct word about her identity or her destiny, he quotes two lines from Thomas Hood's "Bridge of Sighs"—"Anywhere, anywhere, / Out of this world"—and follows them with a self-imposed injunction not to "linger on the mysteries of the Bridge of Sighs."[42] Hood's poem, published in 1844, about the discovery of a prostitute's body under Westminster Bridge, had become almost a shorthand for the pitiable narrative of a ruined woman's sui-

[42] Sala, *Twice Round the Clock*, p. 373.

cide.[43] The specter of the victimized if tainted woman, present in Boz's "Streets—Night" sketch and relegated to the footnotes of Egan's *Life in London,* now stands in for all the female waifs and strays of the city. Female sexuality provides neither an insulated locus of social pain nor the threat of insidious contamination.

For Dickens, who in the mid-1830s urged on his readers a new but not a radically disturbing vision of the metropolis, the use of the fallen woman as container of urban pain and vice seemed an appropriately benign gesture of social admonition. As I have discussed at length, Boz sought to create a city recognizable and knowable to his middle-class readers. If he meant to hint at other links and class connections, it was with hesitation and by indirection. Because the fallen woman doubled as threat and reassurance, she proved an ideal emblem of the unsettling aspects of an otherwise assimilable urban experience. For as responses to the first cholera epidemic suggest, the general middle-class public resisted the notion that it shared the same experience suffered by the working class and the impoverished. And just as the second cholera epidemic elicited a different, more engaged response, so too did the 1840s see the beginning of a wider and more serious interest in the "problem" of the fallen woman and of her status as connector and contaminator.[44]

Dickens, always taking the pulse of his audience and almost always coaxing them beyond the complacency of the moment, settled for the most part in *Sketches* on what he called at the end of *Pickwick* the "brief sunshine of the world" rather than on the "dark shadows." There is striking evidence, however, that his coaxing took a more certain turn when in 1837 he began to publish all of the sketches over again in twenty monthly installments in the order he was eventually to use for

[43] See Nead, *Myths of Sexuality,* pp. 168–70, for the role Hood's poem played in the mythology of fallen sexuality.

[44] For the best discussion of prostitution and the controversy over the Contagious Diseases Act, see Judith R. Walkowitz, *Prostitution and Victorian Society: Women, Class, and the State* (Cambridge: Cambridge University Press, 1980). Walkowitz discusses "early responses" to the problem of prostitution in the 1840s and the later works of W. R. Greg and William Acton in the 1850s (pp. 33–47). Many of these English works were modeled on Alexandre Parent-Duchâtelet's study of Parisian prostitutes, *De la prostitution dans la ville de Paris,* published in 1836. In *Tainted Souls and Painted Faces* (Ithaca: Cornell University Press, 1993), Amanda Anderson discusses at some length the social commentary on prostitution in these decades and makes the interesting point that discourses on "the great social evil" at this time "insist on the irreducibly social aspects of what had hitherto been conceived as natural sin" (p. 48). Anderson explicitly challenges the notion that a moralistic bias necessarily informed Victorian discussions of prostitution.

the complete one-volume edition of 1839. The first section of the collected pieces, "Seven Sketches from Our Parish," ends with "Our Next-Door Neighbor," the story of a poor mother and her ailing son who come to London from the country. On his deathbed the son asks to be buried in the open fields, away from the "dreadful . . . close, crowded streets," which he says have killed him (p. 51). This sketch, written relatively late in the publishing history of the *Sketches* (December 1836), provides a jarring contrast with the other "Parish" sketches, which contain the most benign, idyllic, almost nonurban image of city life in the entire work. The next section of the newly arranged sketches, titled "Scenes," ends with "A Visit to Newgate" (also written in 1836); the "Characters" section finishes with "The Prisoners' Van"; and the final section, "Tales," concludes with "The Drunkard's Death," the last sketch that Dickens in fact wrote (December 1836).[45] By rehearsing this rearrangement of sketches I mean to suggest that as Dickens deliberately ordered the individual pieces which had begun to appear singly and in no particular order in 1833, he crafted a whole that repeatedly brought his audience down into the dark shadows of London and ultimately left them there. The city he thus created was not merely the province of the sometimes foolish and sometimes fading middle class but a place—if only momentarily—of the outcast, of "the flight of pestilence" and "wide-spreading infection."

[45] See Grillo, *Dickens's "Sketches by Boz,"* pp. 86–109, for the complicated publication history of this work.

THREE

"Vitiated Air":
The Polluted City and
Female Sexuality in
Dombey and Son and *Bleak House*

In the sketch "The Prisoner's Van," which records the arrest of two young prostitutes, Boz breaks his entertainer's stride to threaten his readers with the specter of pestilence and infection. In "The Pawnbroker's Shop" he suggests that the downward trajectory illustrated by three sets of women pawning their goods might soon be followed by any member of his comfortable middle-class audience. But for the most part Boz does not make good the threat of implicating his readers in the pattern of urban misery. Instead, as I have suggested, he creates a middle-class vision of the city which deploys fallen female sexuality as the container or sign of urban pain and degradation. In *Oliver Twist*, although the reputations of both Oliver's dead mother and Rose Maylie are marred by the hint of sexual stain, it is the street prostitute Nancy who embodies that stain and whose sacrifice purges the novel of danger and criminality. With *Dombey and Son* (1846–48) and *Bleak House* (1851–53), however, fallen female sexuality is introduced upward into the middle class. By now it can no longer be located solely in the lower classes and identified as separate from the realm of the bourgeois family. The distinction between the woman of the hearth and the woman of the streets no longer holds; the prostitute has now become a wife, and along with her urban pollution of all kinds has invaded the preserves of middle-class life.[1]

---

[1] Alexander Welsh, in *The City of Dickens* (Cambridge: Harvard University Press, 1986), writes suggestively about the connection between sexuality and the city in Dickens's novels. He outlines an opposition between the "heroines of the hearth," associated with the domestic sphere, and the fallen, sexualized woman, associated with the streets. The first

Raymond Williams writes of connection—the "consciousness . . . of recognitions and relationships"—as the mark of Dickens's vision of London and identifies this vision as the force that animates and gives form to his novels.[2] These connections, which determine the shape of urban existence and the structure of Dickens's novels alike, are "the necessary recognitions and avowals of society," and yet "they are of a kind that are obscured, complicated, mystified."[3] In *Dombey*, and more completely in *Bleak House*, those hidden connections that link apparently unrelated individuals, classes, and neighborhoods include not only moral and physical pestilence but tainted sexuality and its own accompanying legacy of disease. The prostitute, or even the sexually suspect woman of the "respectable" classes, embodies and enacts sexual connection and thereby threatens the separateness, health, and survival of the bourgeoisie.[4]

The image of the physically or morally infected woman made more personal and insidious the threat represented by the powerful symbol of Thomas Carlyle's Irish widow in *Past and Present* (1843). The widow, suffering from typhus and turned away by numerous charitable agencies, proves her "sisterhood" by infecting seventeen neighbors. Carlyle uses her as an emblem for the shortsighted callousness of those who will ultimately pay for their lack of humanity. Because the prostitute or sexually tainted woman is linked not just with sexuality but, potentially, with the private realm of family life as well, she embodies the possibility of an invisible and uncontrollable invasion of the middle-class home. She is associated in cultural imagery with what the French historian Alain Corbin has called a "process of degeneration that threatens to annihilate the bourgeoisie."[5]

---

appears as protector and savior, the latter as harbinger of death. Building on the kind of analysis Welsh offers, I suggest that in both *Dombey and Son* and *Bleak House* this safe distinction is powerfully threatened. See Welsh's chapter 9, "The Hearth."

[2] Raymond Williams, *The Country and the City* (London: Chatto and Windus, 1973), pp. 154–55.

[3] Ibid., p. 155.

[4] According to Lynda Nead, whose work on Victorian sexual mythology has been extremely useful and illuminating, prostitution constituted an "*invisible* danger." She writes: "The prostitute was the link between slum and suburb, dirt and cleanliness, ignorance and civilization, profligacy and morality; the prostitute made it impossible to keep these categories apart." See Lynda Nead, *Myths of Sexuality: Representations of Women in Victorian Britain* (London: Basil Blackwell, 1988), p. 121.

[5] Alain Corbin, "Commercial Sexuality in Nineteenth-Century France: A System of Images and Regulations," in *The Making of the Modern Body: Sexuality and Society in the Nineteenth Century*, ed. Catherine Gallagher and Thomas Laqueur (Berkeley: University of California Press, 1987), p. 212.

In these two novels, and in much of the social and sanitary reform literature of the mid-Victorian decades, the threat of disease from unsanitary urban conditions and spreading epidemics merges with the threat of disease and degeneration from exposure to infected female sexuality. In cultural imagery and scientific discourse, the prostitute was linked through metaphor and notions of contagion with the decay, contaminated waste, and insidious filth of the city. Corbin, in delineating the images associated with prostitution which fueled the demand for its regulation, finds the prostitute linked metaphorically with sewers, drains, stench, rotting corpses, and death.[6] Lynda Nead, in her work on Victorian myths of sexuality, shows how the "elements of sanitary debate . . . the tainted air and impure water, the miasma from metropolitan burial grounds" are marshaled in certain textual evocations of fallen women, among them Dickens's description of the prostitute Martha in *David Copperfield*.[7] In the works of the sanitary reformer James Kay and the venereologist William Acton, the language of contagious disease helps to create a particular notion of the noxious, epidemic nature of "vice" and prostitution. In the case of Kay, whose book on the "moral and physical condition" of the industrial working class begins as an investigation into the causes and spread of cholera, a carefully established discourse of physical contagion is deployed to indict the moral contagion of sin. In the very name of the laws that regulated prostitution—the Contagious Diseases Acts—venereal disease is euphemistically lost in and merged with a generic notion of contagion. Embedded in the vagueness of the language is an association of the prostitute with cholera, typhus, smallpox, and other frightening epidemic illnesses.

Reformers and artists alike sought to elicit the disgust, sympathy, anxiety, and indignation of their middle-class readers, to comfort them with notions of their superiority to the debased and diseased poor and sexually fallen, and yet to move them to social action by suggesting that they were not wholly safe from contamination from "below." Acton,

---

[6] Ibid., p. 211.

[7] Nead, *Myths of Sexuality*, p. 127. Nead emphasizes the degree to which the sentimentalization of the prostitute in literary and visual representation was a means for the middle class to control its fear of contamination. I believe that in *Dombey* and *Bleak House* something beyond sentimentalization, beyond seeing the "prostitute" as victim, is going on in the representation of Edith Dombey and Lady Dedlock. It is perhaps the case that the fallen woman of the lower classes can be safely sentimentalized, while her middle-class counterpart has already made inroads into the respectable domestic sphere and so cannot be managed merely with sentiment.

while depicting the prostitute herself as a "social pest, carrying contamination and foulness into every quarter," also took pains to argue that the majority of such women were transients in their work and were headed ultimately for reintegration into respectable society. He warned: "There is . . . never a one of them but may herself, when the shadow is past, become the wife of an Englishman and the mother of his offspring."[8] Kay warns of disease which, though presently confined to the dens of the poor, "threatens, with a stealthy step, to invade the sanctity of the domestic circle . . . unconsciously conveyed from those haunts of beggary where it is rife, into the most still and secluded retreat of refinement."[9] The disconcerting invisibility, the undetectability, of this process of invasion and infiltration might inspire the reformer's audience to attack the social problems at hand *before* they overran the boundaries of the netherworld. If the "conscientious parent" (read: father) would support the cause of regulating prostitution, argued Acton, "with what diminished anxiety would he not contemplate the progress of his boys from infancy to manhood?"[10]

In Dickens's novels the invasion has been achieved on all levels: disease, sexual sin, and moral corruption have made their way invisibly and momentously into the preserves of respectability. The mercantile London of *Dombey* and the litigious, labyrinthine, fog-ridden London of *Bleak House* connect the high and low through analogy, metaphor, and outright contagion. In my discussion of these two London fictions, we shall see that various threats of moral and physical contamination are clustered around images of fallen female sexuality; that the danger to middle-class survival and renewal is posed in the form of debased womanhood; and that the redemption of chaste reproductive female sexuality is prescribed as the antidote to middle-class barrenness and moral bankruptcy. What begins in *Dombey* as a tenuous link between the conditions of poverty and prostituted sexuality becomes in *Bleak House* a tight interweaving of slum-bred pestilence and the inherited taint of illicit sexuality. Florence Dombey, who rescues the "house" of Dombey by ensuring a healthy and reinvigorated family line, serves as a rehearsal for Esther Summerson, whose centrality to the personal and social redemption even tentatively envisioned in *Bleak House* is signaled by her role as one of its narrators. Esther's powerful transcendence of

---

[8] William Acton, *Prostitution* (1857; rpt. London: MacGibbon and Kee, 1968), p. 756.
[9] James Phillips Kay, *The Moral and Physical Condition of the Working Classes Employed in the Cotton Manufacture in Manchester* (1832; rpt. Manchester: E. J. Morten, 1969), p. 12.
[10] Acton, *Prostitution*, p. 27.

the taint of inherited sin makes her the ideal female exemplar. To begin in sexual transgression and end by representing what Ellen Moers calls "Right Woman" is not just to enact the redemption of female sexuality but to offer a model for the salvation of society.[11]

In both novels the ascendancy of uncorrupted womanhood can only follow the expulsion of debased womanhood, and in both novels the real threat to chastity comes in the form of other women, especially women who are mothers. Like the "sordid and rapacious" mother of the teenage prostitutes in "The Prisoner's Van," who had thrown them onto the streets at an early age, the mothers of Alice Brown, lower-class thief and whore, and Edith Granger, her middle-class cousin and counterpart, are responsible for their daughters' debasement. Florence must be kept not only from Edith's mother but ultimately from Edith herself, and Esther Summerson, in a much more complicated process of acceptance and distancing, must free herself from the maternal heritage of guilt. Victorian notions of the source of sexual defilement inform and corroborate Dickens's seemingly symbolic rendering of the threat to female chastity. Discussions of the Contagious Diseases Acts reveal that the site of danger and contamination was imagined to be the woman, the prostitute; it was her body that was the pollutant and that needed to be regulated.[12] According to Sander Gilman, after the Enlightenment, woman replaced man as the exemplary syphilitic patient in European iconography, "with the female as the image of the source of infection."[13] If women were imagined as the polluters of men, they were also seen as a danger to other women, most particularly to their own daughters. Lynda Nead has pointed out that in some Victorian medical and legal discussions of adultery, female infidelity is defined as "a congenital disorder [that] may be inherited by the female offspring."[14] But if in Dickens, as elsewhere, chaste womanhood is threatened by womanhood already defiled, it is also the case that only another woman can absolve, reclaim, and expiate the sins of one who has fallen.

In both novels a vigorous and moral bourgeois ethos is under siege and in need of defense: not the smarmy, hypocritical middle-class com-

---

[11] Ellen Moers, "*Bleak House*: The Agitating Women," *The Dickensian* 69 (January 1973): 14.

[12] See Judith Walkowitz, *Prostitution and Victorian Society* (Cambridge: Cambridge University Press, 1980), p. 146.

[13] Sander Gilman, *Disease and Representation: Images of Illness from Madness to AIDS* (Ithaca: Cornell University Press, 1988), pp. 252–54.

[14] Nead, *Myths of Sexuality*, p. 50.

placency pointedly exemplified by Mr. Vholes, who blathers about his
devotion to respectability and to his father and three daughters while
ruthlessly taking advantage of the weakness and dwindling fortune of
Chancery supplicants, but the energetic, efficacious, and generative
spirit of the Bagnets, symbolic of good family, of healthy sexuality, even
of sane and hearty Empire.[15] Social and economic changes, including
changes in class relations and technology, promise improvement and
simultaneously unsettle social equilibrium. The railroads, the new en-
trepreneurship, the obsolescence of old ways of measuring time and
distance and of doing business in *Dombey;* the new power of industry,
the political ascendancy of the industrialist, the fading of the aristocracy
in *Bleak House*—all are viewed with both hope and suspicion. At the
same time, within this nexus of change, progress and loss, contagion
and tainted inheritance—both moral and physical—threaten to mire
in the past a society that must go forward toward renewal. It is here
that the role of woman and of female sexuality is crucial: woman stands
either to destroy or to re-create, to foster sterility or to make fertile, to
cure pestilence or to be the agent of its circulation.

The London of *Dombey and Son* hovers between a bygone but exotic
world of exploration and trade, represented by the antiquated nautical
instruments of Sol Gills's Wooden Midshipman, and the new world of
the powerful, demonic railroad. It is a world changing with ruthless
speed as a result of what Gills calls "competition, competition—new
invention, new invention—alteration, alteration."[16] Needing to negotiate but more often neglecting the economic implications of this
change, Mr. Dombey doggedly pursues the production of a male heir
and the continuance of his name according to an ethic better suited
to a would-be aristocrat than to a businessman of the upper bourgeoisie. Just as he ignores the insidious results of his manager Carker's

[15] In *Bleak House* the Bagnet family is constructed as a direct contrast to the Jellybys,
even in the matter of their respective attitudes toward Empire. The Bagnet children, born
into a military family that has roamed the earth and now lives modestly, happily, and
musically in London, are named for "the places of their birth in barracks": Malta, Wool-
wich, and Quebec (p. 440). Mrs. Jellyby, who of course ignores her children while devoting her life to the settlement of English families and the education of the natives in
Borrioboola-Gha, lacks the strong, nurturing, commonsense maternality and healthy ad-
venturousness of Mrs. Bagnet.

[16] Charles Dickens, *Dombey and Son: Wholesale, Retail and for Exportation* (Harmondsworth:
Penguin, 1970), p. 93; subsequently cited in the text. In *Dickens from "Pickwick" to "Dombey"*
(London: Chatto and Windus, 1965), Steven Marcus calls his chapter on *Dombey* "The
Changing World."

"extending and extending his influence, until the business and his owner were his football" (p. 840), Mr. Dombey remains oblivious to the economic and spiritual value of his female progeny. As a consequence he is impotent in business, in his overweening will, in his second marriage, in his attempt to produce his own future. He must learn that a daughter, who had been to him "a piece of base coin that couldn't be invested" (p. 51), can indeed offer a return on his investment and redeem the moral and physical health of the family and the firm, and by extension the life of the middle class.[17]

As a result of his failure to understand the power and place of redemptive femininity and the true nature of inheritance, Mr. Dombey unleashes on his own family the treachery of debased (female) sexuality. After the death of Paul, son of Mr. Dombey's sickly and discarded first wife, he must find a suitable woman to produce another male child. Edith Granger, procured for him by the tumescent pander Joey Bagstock ("swollen and inflamed about the head" [p. 347]), promises to fit the bill: she has no money but does have aristocratic connections, "blood," and beauty, and she has proven herself capable of producing a son, though she is no longer encumbered with the child, who has drowned. She also promises to make no demands on Mr. Dombey's blocked and tightly restrained emotions, for her air of "exquisite indifference" gives his pride and coldness free rein (p. 367). Because she has been bred by her mother to be bought on the open market— "hawked and vended here and there, until the last grain of self-respect is dead within" (p. 473)—she regards marriage as a business transaction in which she is the commodity rather than the buyer or seller. She expects and asks from it no psychic sustenance for herself.

Mr. Dombey thus makes the error not only of valuing his offspring according to an outmoded economic calculus but of relying on the cash nexus to determine the realm of sexuality as well. He buys the maternal sexuality of Polly Toodles in an effort to preserve his son's life and then buys the reproductive sexuality of Edith Granger so that he can replace that son. Edith herself is from the first remarkably clear-eyed about her role in this process of buying and selling. She confesses: "I have been offered and rejected, put up and appraised, until my very

---

[17] For a fascinating analysis of the relationship between lines of descent and business in *Dombey*, see Robert Clark, "Riddling the Family Firm: The Sexual Economy in *Dombey and Son*," *ELH* 51 (Spring 1984): 69–84. It is interesting to note that in the end Dombey is bailed out by Harriet and John Carker, inheritors of the fortune of James Carker, in whose family the order of inheritance has also been subverted.

soul has sickened. I have not had an accomplishment or grace that might have been a resource to me, but it has been paraded and vended, to enhance my value, as if the common crier had called it through the streets" (p. 845). The novel is equally direct about the analogy between middle-class marriage and prostitution which is exemplified by Edith and her cousin Alice Brown, who explains that her mother, "covetous and poor, . . . thought to make a property of me" (p. 847).

The novel, however, proposes more than a relationship of analogy or parallelism in its representation of these two women and of prostituted sexuality in two different classes. The women are linked to each other directly by blood, by the same seducer, and by traits of debasement that make them both, however victimized themselves, a threat to the purity of individuals and society. Their fathers, we learn quite late in the narrative, were brothers, "the gayest gentlemen and the best liked" that Good Mrs. Brown had ever encountered—two rakes, one of whom married Edith's upper-class mother and the other of whom dallied with Alice's mother, a "fresh country wench," leaving her with a child (p. 92). The taint the women share is not merely a parallel one created by grasping, corrupt mothers who act as bawds for their own daughters; it is in fact the identical one, inherited, congenital, and physiologically borne (see figure 10 for an illustration of the two mother-daughter pairs as reflections of each other). The stain on Alice's character is deepened by poverty and illegitimacy, and part of the novel's point is to suggest the unfairness of Alice's suffering as compared with Edith's prosperous, albeit exiled, survival. But the novel also points in another direction: both of these women are indelibly, dangerously marked—and in the same manner—so that to save the Dombey family, and above all Florence, from contamination, Edith, like Alice, must be removed.[18]

Florence, although apparently incorruptible and unchangeable, is repeatedly exposed to women who threaten to infect her with their own depravity, whether intentionally or by means beyond their control. The brief and seemingly purposeless kidnapping of Florence by Good Mrs. Brown early in the novel is paradigmatic of this ongoing threat to the

---

[18] Amanda Anderson, in *Tainted Souls and Painted Faces* (Ithaca: Cornell University Press, 1993), also stresses Dickens's need to "dispel" both Alice and Edith, but though she acknowledges the contaminating powers of these women, she focuses instead on the teleological nature of fallenness which determines their inevitable downward trajectory: once fallen, neither Alice nor Edith has the ability to recover (p. 82). Indeed, Anderson's compelling thesis is that the fallen woman represents something like the radical absence of agency or autonomy within Victorian discourses of social reform.

Figure 10 Hablot K. Browne, "A Chance Meeting." Charles Dickens, *Dombey and Son* (1848). Department of Rare Books and Special Collections, Princeton University Libraries.

child's purity.[19] The hag snatches Florence from her two good mothers, Polly Toodles and Susan Nipper, in Stagg's Gardens and takes her through a wasteland of brickfields and tile yards to a hovel surrounded by mud and blackened by cinders. There she removes the child's clothes and shoes and replaces them with rags and the "crushed remains of a bonnet that had probably been picked up from some ditch or dunghill" (p. 130). She threatens to cut off Florence's long curls but spares her this indignity because of the daughter far away who had been proud of her beautiful hair. Mrs. Brown's ostensible motive for terrorizing Florence is the desire for indirect revenge on Mr. Dombey's manager, Carker, the man responsible for ruining her daughter, Alice; and she takes the girl's clothes—and would have taken her hair—for their marketable value. But on a more powerful symbolic and affective level, Mrs. Brown threatens to turn Florence into what her daughter

[19] For a more fully developed exploration of the centrality of the episode with Mrs. Brown, and for a fascinating discussion of its connection to *Fanny Hill,* see Joss Lutz Marsh, "Good Mrs. Brown's Connections: Sexuality and Story-Telling in *Dealings with the Firm of Dombey and Son,*" *ELH* 58 (Summer 1991): 409–414.

has become, and she enacts this transformation in just a very few moments. Her fairy-tale identity as the *bad* Mrs. Brown, the witch who might kill or devour the innocent princess, only heightens the sense that what she is threatening is an emblematic defloration of the child: "Florence was so relieved to find that it was only her hair and not her head which Mrs. Brown coveted" (pp. 130–31).[20]

Florence continues throughout the novel to be exposed to predatory or dangerously polluted mothers. Just as Edith Granger is about to marry Mr. Dombey, Florence must be protected from Mrs. Skewton, Edith's mother, who threatens her in precisely the same way Mrs. Brown had done. Mrs. Skewton wants to claim possession of the girl and remarks, too, on Florence's resemblance to her own daughter when young. Edith, assessing the situation correctly, orders her mother to return Florence to her home. "It is enough," she admonishes her mother, "that we are what we are. I will have no youth and truth dragged down to my level. I will have no guileless nature undermined, corrupted, and perverted, to amuse the leisure of a world of mothers" (p. 514). Finally, it is Edith herself from whom Florence must be protected. As Carker begins to dominate and threaten Edith, she starts to withdraw from her stepdaughter, and as she is about to run off with him, she warns the girl not to come near her or speak to her or touch her. Like "some lower animal" (p. 754), Edith crouches against the wall so Florence cannot reach her, and then she springs up and flees, as if her touch would defile the girl (see figure 11 for an illustration of this scene). Even at their final meeting, when Edith assures Florence that she has not in fact committed adultery, she nevertheless acknowledges a guilt that must "separate [her] through the whole remainder of [her] life, from purity and innocence" (p. 965). The novel suggests that, though not set on corrupting Florence in the way that her mother and her aunt had been, Edith would ultimately have the same effect by her very presence. Although as her stepdaughter Florence is in danger of contracting the infection Edith cannot help but embody, she is not Edith's daughter and so does not automatically inherit a taint that must be actively purged.

All of these women threaten Florence with the "unnaturalness" that the narrative keeps circling back to in a variety of ways. Mrs. Skewton's affected devotion to "Nature" coupled with her absolute artificiality

[20] For more on the uses of fairy tale in *Dombey*, especially in Florence's story, see Louise Yelin, "Strategies for Survival: Florence and Edith in *Dombey and Son*," *Victorian Studies* 22 (Spring 1979): 297–319.

Figure 11 Hablot K. Browne, "Florence and Edith on the Stairs." Charles Dickens, *Dombey and Son* (1848). Department of Rare Books and Special Collections, Princeton University Libraries.

introduces the theme of connection between the commodification of sexuality and its perversion. Both Alice and Edith display characteristics that mark them as unnatural, if not demonic. When Alice weeps at Harriet Carker's kindness to her, she is described as "not like a woman, but like a stern man surprised into that weakness" (p. 564). Her hair, once her pride, as her mother told Florence, is now the object of her rage, and she seizes it "as if she would have torn it out," then flings it back "as though it were a heap of serpents" (p. 565). Edith, too, is evoked as a gorgon when, after her marriage to Dombey, she is likened to a "beautiful Medusa" who would strike dead an unnamed "him" had she the charm (p. 741).

Although the text suggests Alice's unnatural mannishness (like Miss Blimber she is unsexed, albeit in a radically different way), it need not indicate the debased nature of her sexual relationships, for such relationships in the life of a prostitute are by definition perverse.[21] As for Edith, however, a careful case is constructed to signal the frigidity of her relations with Dombey on the one hand and the sadomasochistic qualities of her strange tie to Carker on the other.[22] When Dombey and his second wife return from their Continental honeymoon, the question of whether Edith will produce an heir is all but answered by the news that they both had found Paris cold and dull (p. 583). Repeated references to Edith's bosom, which throbs and swells, causing her diamonds to rise and fall, bespeak a passion that is thwarted, locked in, the source of no pleasure to herself and out of reach to her husband (pp. 650–51). The marriage is sterile in its failure to produce a child and in its sexual as well as its emotional coldness.

And yet the sexual passion that lies stifled and restrained but still discernible beneath the diamond necklaces erupts in Edith's response to Carker's sadistic advances and takes the form of pain inflicted on herself. As her husband speaks of Carker's growing role in the marriage, Edith turns a bracelet "round and round upon her arm; not winding it about with a light, womanly touch, but pressing and dragging it over the smooth skin, until the white limb showed a bar of red" (p. 653). The jewelry that plays such an important role in the representation of Edith's sexuality suggests in a graphic and literal way the symbolic effect Mr. Dombey's wealth has had on his wife. In addition, the emphasis on the *unwomanliness* of Edith's gesture again underscores the distortion of "natural" sexuality that his wealth and its uses have engendered. Still unable to unleash her loathing for Carker at him directly, she continues to cause herself pain, striking the hand he has just kissed against a marble chimney-piece rather than against his "fair face" and causing the hand to bleed (p. 692). Carker the predator, the wolf, smells blood with pleasure and associates the "mystery of [her] gloved hand" with the promise of sexual passion (p. 735). What might be dismissed as melodramatic excess in the depiction of these relationships seems rather Dickens's careful portrayal of a sexual pa-

---

[21] Paul Dombey wonders why Miss Blimber's hair does not grow long like Florence's and "why she was like a boy" (*Dombey and Son*, p. 216). Throughout the novel Dickens signals unnaturalness in women by marking them as masculine. See Nina Auerbach, "Dickens and Dombey: A Daughter after All," in *Dickens Studies Annual*, vol. 5, ed. Robert B. Partlow, Jr. (Carbondale: Southern Illinois University Press, 1976), pp. 95–114, for a discussion of the masculinity of Edith and Alice.

[22] See Marcus, *Dickens from "Pickwick" to "Dombey,"* pp. 346–51, for a fascinating discussion of Carker as Dombey's double and of the two men as two sides of the author himself.

thology that is specifically the result of buying and selling what he believes ought to be naturally given.[23] He creates a nexus of unnatural
desires and responses that are not simply symbolic of but organically
and profoundly tied to making people into property. The organic nature of these disturbances further establishes Edith Dombey's influence
as unalterably insidious.

The novel's theme of the unnatural culminates in a long, meditative
passage in chapter 47, just before Edith flees with Carker and before
Dombey, in angry and vicious response, strikes his daughter. The passage evokes a world in which unnatural humanity has become the "natural" result of the cruel conditions, "enforced distortions," and
imprisoning monomanias of modern life. But the unnaturalness that
Dickens's narrative voice addresses here goes beyond the perverseness
at the heart of the Dombey–Edith–Carker triangle; it also (and in a way
that is implicitly linked with the unnaturalness of the rich) refers to
the unnaturalness of the poor, the sick, the slum dweller, the convict.
The movement from Dombey's "master-vice" to the "Vice and Fever"
of dark haunts and "wicked cities" might seem almost gratuitous, a
lengthy and artificial digression to strike a blow for sanitary reform, but
it serves as a point of connection for the social, psychological, moral,
and physical pestilence that runs through society like a blight. The
allusions shift from moral taint to physical—the "noxious particles that
rise from vitiated air"—and back to moral:

> But if the moral pestilence that rises with them [the noxious particles], and
> in the eternal laws of outraged Nature, is inseparable from them, could be
> made discernible too, how terrible the revelation! Then should we see de-
> pravity, impiety, drunkenness, theft, murder, and a long train of nameless
> sins ... overhanging the devoted spots, and creeping on, to blight the in-
> nocent and spread contagion among the pure. . . . Then should we stand
> appalled to know, that where we generate disease to strike our children down
> and entail itself on unborn generations, there also we breed, *by the same
> certain process*, infancy that knows no innocence, youth without modesty or
> shame, maturity that is mature in nothing but in suffering and guilt, blasted
> old age that is a scandal on the form we bear. (p. 738; emphasis added)[24]

[23] Amanda Anderson, in *Tainted Souls and Painted Faces*, reads Edith's melodramatic
moments as suggestive of her status as commodity and of her alienation from her own
passions and feelings (p. 85).

[24] Norris Pope writes of this passage from *Dombey* that it was "conscious propaganda
for the sanitary movement," written in the aftermath of a warning in the *Times* of the
likelihood of a new cholera epidemic. See Norris Pope, *Dickens and Charity* (London:

These shifts between the moral, or the metaphoric, and the physical ultimately cancel one another out, for in the end there can be no sustainable separation between spiritual and bodily taint or, for that matter, between the spread of cholera and the spread of evil.[25] The city breeds "Vice *and* Fever"; and the innocent are struck down by both inheritance and contagion. The passage alludes to Mrs. Brown's urban wasteland dwelling where Florence's purity was threatened, to the "convict-ships" that took Alice across the sea, to the sexual taint—both physical and psychic—that infects Dombey's second marriage, and to the feebleness of body that Mr. Dombey passed on to his son and the feebleness of both body and soul that Mrs. Granger and Mrs. Brown passed on to and nurtured in their daughters. The "disease" that entails itself on unborn children appears as a conflation of poverty-bred and sexually transmitted illnesses. The covert reference to syphilis here serves to connect the taint of the slums with the taint of the middle-class family in a way that recalls Blake's culminating vision of the blighted "Marriage hearse" in his "London" poem.[26] Although never explicitly mentioned elsewhere in the text, syphilis haunts the plot because of its association with the prostitute and her death on the one hand and the ᴧarrenness of middle-class marriage on the other.[27] This passage makes clear that the middle class is endangered not only by virtue of its willful ignorance of the miasmic haunts that breed pestilence but also because it has already assimilated into its ranks "perversions of nature" of all kinds.

Macmillan, 1978), pp. 221–22. Indeed it was after the predicted epidemic, which occurred in 1848–49, that Dickens used lar age very close to that of the *Dombey* passage in an address to the Metropolitan Sanitary Association in February 1850. See *The Speeches of Charles Dickens*, ed. K. J. Fielding (London: Harvester, 1988), p. 106.

[25] See F. S. Schwarzbach's suggestive essay, "*Bleak House*: The Social Pathology of Urban Life," in *Literature and Medicine*, vol. 9, *Fictive Ills: Literary Perspectives on Wounds and Diseases* (Baltimore: Johns Hopkins University Press, 1990), pp. 93–104. Schwarzbach makes the important point that social reform movements of the period "treated the social, political, physical, and moral problems of urban England as symptoms of one underlying disease" (p. 95).

[26] "But most thro' midnight streets I hear / How the youthful Harlot's curse / Blasts the new born Infant's tear, / And blights with plagues the Marriage hearse." William Blake, *Songs of Experience* (1789).

[27] Gail Savage, in her essay "'The Wilful Communication of a Loathsome Disease': Marital Conflict and Venereal Disease in Victorian England," *Victorian Studies* 34 (Autumn 1990): 39, emphasizes the association of venereal disease with sterility in establishing syphilis as grounds for divorce. As to the absence of any overt reference to syphilis in the novel, William Acton reminds us at the beginning of *Prostitution* that as late as the 1850s the "subject of prostitution and the 'secret diseases' could hardly be mentioned outside the pages of the medical press" (p. 7).

The novel's carefully developed commentary on social sterility and disease, then, places sexuality at its center. But this is not sexuality conceived in a general way, touching on male and female alike, but sexuality as it resides in woman. Although Carker is in some important sense the cause of both Edith's and Alice's sexual fall, a creature of monstrous and predatory appetites who, like Bill Sikes, must be brutally destroyed, he merely exploits the weaknesses these women inherited from their mothers. In the world of *Dombey*, as in certain strains of Victorian sexual mythology, men like Carker take advantage of what is already set in motion by maternal inheritance.

The clearest indication of the need to root out dangerous female sexuality and replace it with its redemptive, reproductive form is, of course, the expulsion of Edith from England as well as from the narrative and the reformation of Mr. Dombey—far guiltier of inhumanity than his wife—through the integration of Florence into his psychic and familial life. Given the discourse of contamination that pervades the narrative, Edith cannot be redeemed; the only partial rehabilitation she is allowed comes through Florence's ability to soften her stepmother, to make her weep and ask for forgiveness. Likewise, it is asking forgiveness of her father, the guilty party in their relationship, that marks Florence's Christlike transcendence of the ordinary human need to understand justice as revenge. She must take her father's sins upon herself. And she must marry a brotherly figure, thus ensuring the chastity of their bond, as well as a man of the lower classes. Walter Gay offers Mr. Dombey's family and class not precisely the proto-Lawrencian energies of Mr. Toodles but rather the ancient mythic power of a Dick Whittington. Though chaste, the marriage of Walter and Florence is, significantly, reproductive, and it breaks the cycle of death and impotence that had plagued the Dombey line. They present Mr. Dombey with two grandchildren, a girl he "hoards in his heart" and a boy to continue, in reinvigorated form, the house of Dombey. Through the daughter, then, as Mr. Toots explains, "Dombey and Son will ascend ... triumphant!" (p. 974). In order that patriarchy might flourish, a particular kind of womanhood must be recognized, celebrated, and absorbed.

On the "woman question" the novel appears to take a stand unapologetically opposed to the powerful anger and bitterness of those women who have been society's victims. Edith Dombey and Alice Brown can serve as the means to mount a powerful critique of a proud and mercenary patriarchy, but the indelible stain they bear makes their continued presence in the narrative not only expendable but untenable. This enmeshes the novel in the tensions, not to say the contradictions, associated with a vision of women as dangerous if not culpable victims. The text wavers between the desire to marshal the spirit of reform and the urge to protect the sanctity of middle-class life. That Dickens appears to be fully aware of the varieties of women's opposition to patriarchal order and to have chosen carefully which sort to rescue and which to reject can be confirmed in the person of Susan Nipper, the sharp-tongued mother of three daughters. "If ever the Rights of Women, and all that kind of thing, are properly attended to," declares her husband, the addled Mr. Toots, "it will be through her powerful intellect" (p. 946). The novel can absorb Susan Nipper and her barbs, aimed repeatedly against the hierarchy of the sexes; but it keeps her securely on the margins, a bit player whose class position and comic presence make her particular kind of rebelliousness instructive yet benign, no real threat to the ultimate health of the middle-class family. When Dickens next creates a female character explicitly devoted to the rights and emancipation of women, it will be Mrs. Jellyby, whose position as a disastrous middle-class mother makes her not just a comic figure but a malignant one.

What is merely suggested about the connections between urban blight and sexual contamination in *Dombey and Son* becomes the very machinery that drives *Bleak House*. The tainted sexual legacy of Lady Dedlock and the fever that spreads from the pauper's graveyard in London by way of Jo, the crossing sweeper, to the protected middle-class preserve of John Jarndyce's home near St. Alban's determine the novel's plot and governing images. The opening paragraphs of the text establish the inseparability of urban pollution and social sin. At "the very heart" of the fog that "rolls defiled among the tiers of shipping, and the waterside pollutions of a great (and dirty) city" sits the Lord High Chancellor, "most pestilent of hoary sinners."[28] Just as fog, mud, and gas invade London and its environs, so does the Chancery suit of Jarndyce and Jarndyce taint all of its wards and supplicants, and so too does

---

[28] Charles Dickens, *Bleak House* (Harmondsworth: Penguin, 1985), pp. 49–50; subsequently cited in the text. Schwarzbach makes the point that the fog of the opening chapter of the novel is a *literal*, not simply metaphorical, bearer of disease ("*Bleak House*: The Social Pathology of Urban Life," p. 95).

Lady Dedlock's past defile Esther's life and the life of the aristocratic family into which she has married.[29]

The unexpected connections between classes that in *Dombey and Son* are centered on the relationship of Alice Brown to Edith Dombey here become pandemic: identity, kinship, affinity, and correspondence can be said to define the very condition of social and spiritual life in this novel. In answer to the narrator's question, "What connexion can there have been between many people in the innumerable histories of this world, who, from opposite sides of great gulfs, have, nevertheless, been very curiously brought together" (p. 272), the novel answers: every kind. Chancery is but the most obvious connector of lives; it serves, as many have commented, as an analogy to the condition of society itself. But there are also apparently insignificant blood relationships (Sir Leicester Dedlock, for example, is related to John Jarndyce, Ada, and Richard) and nearly gratuitous connections from the distant past (Mr. Jarndyce and Miss Barbary—now Mrs. Chadband, Boythorn and Lady Dedlock). The novel abounds in emblems of connection that reproduce and reinforce one another: the fever that spreads via Jo; the handkerchief that links Esther to the brickmaker's dead baby and ultimately to her own mother (also the mother of a supposedly dead baby); the clothing these two mothers—Jenny and Lady Dedlock—ultimately exchange; the veils worn variously by Lady Dedlock, Hortense, and Esther; and the "starry circle" of which Esther yearns not to be a part in her fever-induced delirium (p. 544). As has also often been observed, the slum of Tom-all-Alone's is prominent among the novel's points of intersection. It signals a correspondence between the pestilential haunt that nurtures Jo and the case of Tom Jarndyce, for whom the slum may have been named. It is part of the property of the Jarndyce estate and is linked to the house—Bleak House—where Tom's descendants now live. And it is also connected, the narrator tells us, to the "place in Lincolnshire, the house in town, the Mercury in powder," that is, to the Dedlocks and their own family secrets and inheritance (p. 272).

Less obvious to readers of *Bleak House* is that Tom-all-Alone's also serves as a point of intersection for society's crimes against the poor and the inheritance of sexual taint. In a passage that personifies "Tom" and makes him a moving agent of contamination, the trope of marriage makes this hidden connection clear:

---

[29] Richard Carstone, referring to the case and all that accompanies it, declares to Esther that "it taints everybody" (*Bleak House*, p. 581).

There is not a drop of Tom's corrupted blood but propagates infection and contagion somewhere. It shall pollute, this very night, the choice stream (in which chemists on analysis would find the genuine nobility) of a Norman house, and his Grace shall not be able to say Nay to the infamous alliance. There is not an atom of Tom's slime, not a cubic inch of any pestillential gas in which he lives, not one obscenity or degradation about him, not an ignorance, not a wickedness, not a brutality of his committing, but shall work its retribution, through every order of society, up to the proudest of the proud, and to the highest of the high. (p. 683)

Like the long set piece in *Dombey* that joins the pestilence of disease to moral pestilence, this passage collapses the distinction between real infection—like Jo's fever—and all the invisible corruptions for which disease ordinarily figures as metaphor. But it also collapses the distinction between the contagion of disease and the transmission of sexual taint: the "blood" of a Norman house will be polluted through an alliance that cannot be prevented. The aristocracy—particularly those families that are, like the Dedlocks, "as old as the hills"—stand to lose their purity, their health, their fecundity as a result of exposure to the contaminated blood of "Tom," who is imagined as the carrier of all manner of disease. Inheritance and contagion know no separation either in the realm of epidemic disease or in that of sexual corruption. Lady Dedlock's dowry and legacy of sexual sin, then, have the same meaning, origin, and result as the plague transmitted to her daughter by Jo, inhabitant of Tom-all-Alone's.

I maintain that the various threats to social health represented by the slum of Tom-all-Alone's are ultimately resolved in the novel in the realm of female sexuality. Inheritance and contagion reinforce each other and merge in the text most forcefully in the person of Esther Summerson, whose role as narrator signals the centrality of her story to the working out of this double blight. Here Dickens creates and sustains a female narrative voice for the first and only time to illustrate *from the inside* and with considerable psychological complexity the trajectory of a threatened and ultimately efficacious female sexuality and to underscore the role of this trajectory in the creation of a (re)productive and efficacious middle class. Donning the mask of female self-effacement, Dickens is able to assert the value of a female sexuality that falters at first but then succeeds. Florence Dombey never overshadows her stepmother, even after Edith is banished from the scene; but Esther Summerson, in part because she has been granted the voice that Florence never has, dominates the novel with her over-worked modesty and supplants her mother's story of sin and pride with her own narrative of triumph. The argument has been made, most cogently by Virginia Blain, that even at the conclusion of her story Esther is sexually repressed, makes an asexual marriage, and pays for her mother's errors by remaining essentially virginal, without desire.[30] I would suggest, however, that Esther's narrative carefully charts the evolution of a woman who begins in radical repression and ends in a state of what Dickens and the culture he helped to create would have understood as healthy female sexuality. The problematic set out by the novel—how can society emerge from the corruption of tainted inher-itance—finds its solution in Esther's ability to marry the reforming phy-sician Allan Woodcourt, who promises to cure the ills of poverty and the infirmities of his own class as well.

At the outset of her narrative Esther is a reluctant storyteller and has difficulty representing herself as the subject of her own account: "It seems so curious to me to be obliged to write all this about myself! As if this narrative were the narrative of *my* life! But my little body will soon fall into the background now" (pp. 73–74). Her reluctance to narrate is bound up, of course, with the notion her aunt worked hard to establish: that she bears the mark of her mother's disgrace and in-deed embodies it. She has difficulty beginning, she says, because she is not clever and has known this since earliest childhood. To write is to claim the legitimacy of her existence, and this she has been taught never to do. In spite of her profound reluctance—or perhaps because of its defensive power—she finds herself "always writing about myself" when she "mean[s] all the time to write about other people" (p. 162). The "little body" not only will not fade out of the picture but will become the very focus of Esther's narrative when her illness and disfig-urement become central to her story.

Esther's wish that her body "fall into the background" also suggests discomfort with her femaleness and, ultimately, with her sexuality. The connection between her reluctance to narrate and her will to deny sexual desire expresses itself as a recurrent narrative tic in Esther's

[30] Virginia Blain, "Double Vision and the Double Standard in *Bleak House*: A Feminist Perspective," in *Charles Dickens's "Bleak House,"* ed. Harold Bloom (New York: Chelsea House, 1987), pp. 139–56. See Alex Zwerdling, "Esther Summerson Rehabilitated," *PMLA* 88 (1973): 429–39, for an analysis of the deft psychological portrait Dickens achieves in Esther's narrative. Ellen Moers, in *"Bleak House*: The Agitating Women," was the first to take seriously the degree to which this novel constitutes a commentary on the "woman question."

references to Allan Woodcourt. Her initial allusions to him are a maze of indirection: "There was someone else at the family dinner party. It was not a lady. It was a gentleman. . . . I thought him very sensible and agreeable. At least, Ada asked me if I did not, and I said yes" (p. 233). From a very early point in the narrative Esther starts to withhold information about Allan and, more specifically, about her feelings for him.[31] "I have omitted to mention . . . ," "I have forgotten to mention—at least I have not mentioned . . .": these are the phrases that invariably preface her codelike references to Allan, just as ellipses or dashes often conclude them (pp. 233, 255). Certain passages circle around her feelings of longing and leave a blank at the center: "I was wakeful and low-spirited. I don't know why. At least I don't think I know why. At least, perhaps I do, but I don't think it matters" (p. 288). The language of the narrative makes clear that Esther's interest in Allan is neither belated nor lukewarm, but it does so precisely by representing that interest, or desire, as an absence. And it represents the absence itself as a pathological inability to narrate the sexual self.

For much of the novel, then, Esther can narrate herself only as the bearer of instinctive maternal powers joined to a perpetual celibacy. When she arrives at the Jellybys for the first time, Caddy and Peepy are immediately drawn to her and recognize her as a source of the maternal comfort they have never found in their own mother. In a novelistic world populated by bad mothers, orphaned or neglected children and infantile, helpless men, Esther holds the keys to domestic peace. Equally apparent, however, is that Esther is fated to mother children not her own: to care for Caddy and Peepy, to shop for Caddy's trousseau, to tend Caddy's ailing baby, to participate in Richard and Ada's courtship as a maidenly observer. The nicknames given her by the inhabitants of Bleak House—"Little Old Woman," "Old Woman," "Mother Hubbard"—underscore a maternal yet sexually superannuated identity. Like the type of the Victorian spinster sister-in-law, who figured so prominently in Dickens's own experience, Esther is sexually out of the running. That maternal inheritance and its psychic scars have made Esther's biological maternity impossible is borne out by her response to Mr. Guppy's proposal. Although she does not want Guppy for a husband, his proposal nevertheless arouses deep sorrow in her as

---

[31] In a more sustained and complicated manner Charlotte Brontë creates a heroine with the same habit of obfuscation and suppression in *Villette* (1853). It would be interesting to speculate on Esther as a rewriting of Jane Eyre and Lucy Snowe as a revision of Esther.

well as the feeling that "an old chord had been more coarsely touched than it had ever been since the days of the dear old doll, long buried in the garden" (p. 178). Esther's long-discarded hope of living the life of a "normal" woman makes marriage even to the law clerk impossible and ultimately renders a truly asexual and, in all likelihood, sterile marriage to the fatherly Jarndyce her only imaginable course.

Lady Dedlock's legacy to her daughter does not end with illegitimacy and the inheritance of guilt; she also passes on to Esther the blight of barrenness that here, as in *Dombey*, follows upon the taint of unlicensed sexuality.[32] Lady Dedlock herself is described at her first appearance in the novel as "childless." Although this identification is meant to resonate with irony later in the text and to establish the mystery of her past, she has indeed become, as a result of that past, a barren woman. Her marriage to Sir Leicester, like Edith Granger's to Mr. Dombey, is sterile, and, also like Edith, she is icy and anesthetic: "Having conquered *her* world, [Lady Dedlock] fell, not into the melting, but rather into the freezing mood" (p. 57).[33] She is indeed the reincarnation and fulfillment of Sir Morbury Dedlock's wife, the ghost of Ghost Walk, who had neither children nor a drop of "the family blood in her veins" (p. 140).

The "family blood" of the Dedlocks, understood as an undefiled male line, includes the legacy of gout, a condition passed down through the men and worn like a badge of honor by Sir Leicester. Unlike contagious diseases that suggest exposure to the poor or to tainted female sexuality, and unlike inherited venereal disease or an illness common among the masses, gout bespeaks class privilege and masculinity. We read: "Other men's fathers may have died of the rheumatism, or may have taken base contagion from the tainted blood of the sick vulgar, but the Dedlock family have communicated something exclusive" (p.

[32] See Thomas Laqueur, *Making Sex: Body and Gender from the Greeks to Freud* (Cambridge: Harvard University Press, 1990), for a discussion of the presumed sterility of prostitutes and other "fallen" women during the nineteenth century. Laqueur stresses the economic meaning of the barrenness Victorian culture attributed to prostitutes, who were considered an "unproductive commodity" as contrasted with a "household economy of sex, which is quintessentially social and productive" (pp. 230–32).

[33] In *Bleak House* Dickens enlists an anesthetic response to Paris to suggest the sterility of the Dedlock marriage just as he had done in *Dombey*. Like the Dombeys, who find Paris, the site of their honeymoon, cold and dull, Lady Dedlock in particular is so terribly bored in the French capital that she cannot get away too quickly (p. 204). The narrative of the Dedlock sojourn abroad suggests that observers of Lord and Lady Dedlock on tour think "he might be her amiable father," signaling that Jarndyce's paternal relationship to Esther replicates in an important way her mother's marriage to Sir Leicester (p. 206).

271). Women who marry into the family—Sir Morbury's wife, the current Lady Dedlock—are cast as the bearers of corruption, polluters of the "choice stream," and agents of sterility. Even Esther, the child to whom the "childless" Lady Dedlock gave birth, has a stillborn shadow self that is identified with the brickmaker's dead baby through Esther's handkerchief, Lady Dedlock's assumption that her baby had died, and the clothing Lady Dedlock wears as her final disguise. Esther must also bear the mark of "base contagion," a communicable disease that, in its disfiguring and blinding effects, recalls syphilis.

Among Esther's many alter egos in the novel, the one who connects her most definitively with the conditions of urban poverty and decay is Jo, the crossing sweeper. But Jo is linked to Esther through more than just the fever he brings to her home from the paupers' graveyard in London. He also signals her relationship to her father, Captain Hawdon, and the other half of her genealogy. Jo, the child of no one, is the spiritual child of Hawdon/Nemo and thereby stands as a kind of sibling to Esther. Like Nemo, Jo has no legal identity, no origins, no inheritance, apparently no last name. The legal copyist had been good to the boy, and, as a result, Jo remains loyal, sweeps the passage and steps to the paupers' graveyard where Nemo's body has been thrown, and asks to be buried near him there, a "place of abomination" though it may be (p. 278).[34] When Jo becomes infected with the fever and then contaminates Esther, he thus passes on to her her father's legacy. If the origin of the disease is not actually Nemo's corpse, it is at least the burial ground where he lies (see figure 12 for an illustration of the paupers' cemetery).[35] The fever, then, is emblematic both of the urban blight centered in the foulness and inhumanity of the paupers' graveyard and of the illegitimacy and guilt surrounding Esther's birth. The fever thus joins the social and the personal plots, and not only as an agent of connection.

A number of interesting investigations into the identity of the fever of *Bleak House* have focused on Dickens's choice of an illness—in all

[34] Edwin Chadwick, in his *Report on the Sanitary Condition of the Labouring Population and on the Means of Improvement*, ed. M. W. Flinn (1842; rpt. Edinburgh: University of Edinburgh Press, 1965), remarks on the large numbers of parentless children living in poverty. There are, he writes, "a thousand children who have no names, or only nicknames, like dogs" (p. 199).

[35] It is significant that Lady Dedlock does not fall ill after her visit to the paupers' graveyard to see her former lover's place of burial. Perhaps she is immune from contagion because she is already tainted by sexual sin, the interchangeable analogue to contagious disease in the novel.

Figure 12 Hablot K. Browne, "Consecrated Ground." Charles Dickens, *Bleak House* (1853). Department of Rare Books and Special Collections, Princeton University Libraries.

likelihood smallpox—that was known to be contagious and not, as was believed of cholera, "miasmic," or environmentally caused. Although the communicable nature of the fever is essential to both the plot and the symbolism of the novel, the connection between the disease and the hideous sanitary conditions of the lives—and deaths—of the poor seems equally important.[36] Just as Jo is a victim of both the conditions into which he is born and his exposure to the diseased corpses in the graveyard, so is Esther a victim of both heritage and contagion.

[36] See Schwarzbach, *"Bleak House*: The Social Pathology of Urban Life"; and Michael S. Gurney, "Disease as Device: The Role of Smallpox in *Bleak House*," in *Literature and Medicine*, 9: 79–92. Crucial to Dickens's use of smallpox as a stand-in for, among many other things, cholera was the general sense of the period that cholera was both contagious *and* miasmic, communicated through contact with other people and also caused by exposure to a polluted environment.

Syphilis, alluded to through the smallpox from which Esther suffers, is also a disease that can be inherited as well as contracted.

When Esther falls ill, then, she bears the full weight of the social crimes the novel wants to expose and the hereditary taint her own private story reveals. The onset of her illness also marks Esther's initiation into a more penetrating vision of London, a vision more akin to that of the other narrator of *Bleak House* than to her own initial enthusiasm for the "wonderful city" she views on an early morning walk with Ada, Richard, and Caddy Jellyby early in the novel. On that morning she had "admired the long succession and varieties of streets, the quantity of people . . . the number of vehicles . . . the busy preparations . . . the extraordinary creatures" (p. 97). Now, just before she makes her fateful visit to the brickmaker's cottage, where the fever-racked Jo is staying, Esther looks toward London, where "a lurid glare overhung the whole dark waste." At that moment, unaware of what will soon happen to her, she nevertheless feels "an undefinable impression of myself as being something different from what I then was." Her face covered by a veil, she then enters the cottage and is greeted by a look of "surprise and terror" from Jo, who thinks her to be the veiled woman (Lady Dedlock dressed in Hortense's clothes) he had led to Nemo's grave (pp. 484–85).

Into this moment the narrative compresses all the elements that will come together in Esther's illness: the city as place of origin for the fever and all it represents; the transformation in identity Esther will undergo as a result of physical trauma and the shock of learning about her parentage; the link with her mother the illness will bring about and symbolically reinforce; the suggestion of unregulated passion that Hortense, her mother's and now her own alter ego, embodies throughout the text.[37] Esther's illness and subsequent discovery of her history are part of the same process of deepening self-abnegation. She takes on the full burden of her inheritance of sin and wears it, as it were, unveiled on her face. She couples them in her thoughts: "my disfigurement, and my inheritance of shame," "the deep traces of my illness,

---

[37] See Virginia Blain in "Double Vision and the Double Standard in *Bleak House*," on Hortense as Lady Dedlock's alter ego, an embodiment of "the fiendish powers of violent female sexuality" (p. 149). Hortense's nationality is, as many have remarked, significant. In *Myths of Sexuality* Lynda Nead points to the iconographic importance of a Balzac novel in Augustus Egg's 1858 triptych *Past and Present*, the pictorial narrative of a middle-class wife's sexual fall: the woman's two young daughters build a literal house of cards on top of the novel, an allusion to the instability inherent in the sexual danger of French culture (p. 73).

and the circumstances of my birth" (pp. 667, 668). It is as if she takes
her mother's sin upon herself and wears it as a physical manifestation,
a stigma. At this moment the barrenness of Esther's future seems to be
assured and her woman's body definitively desexualized, or so it appears to her. When John Jarndyce then proposes and she agrees to
marry him, she acts on the belief that no sexual future can come out
of her sexually tainted and now physically marked past. In a paroxysm
of self-sacrifice Esther dedicates herself to becoming the mistress of
Bleak House, to a life of being "busy, busy, busy—useful, amiable, serv-
iceable" (p. 668). What might be read as heroic devotion to duty on
Esther's part is, in the context of the narrative's inquiry into her evolving psychic condition, a mark of her nearly pathological will to self-
suppression.

It is not only this radical self-abnegation that results from Esther's
double trauma. Her crisis also initiates a process of reintegration in
which the pieces of her past, as of a puzzle, start to come together, and
long-suppressed feelings are allowed to surface. As soon as she permits
herself to look at her altered appearance in the mirror—something she
does at her mother's home, Chesney Wold, rather than her own—she
acknowledges for the first time in her narrative what the alert reader
already knows: that she loves Allan Woodcourt. In a gesture that combines self-denial with a new narrative candor, she considers throwing
away the flowers he had once given her because she wishes to be "generous" to the man she "could have been devoted to." Deciding finally
to keep them only as a "remembrance of what irrevocably was past and
gone" (p. 559), she nevertheless incorporates the fact of her love for
Allan into her narrative in a way she had previously suppressed. The
"little body" Esther had tried to put in the "background" of her narrative now takes center stage by virtue of its stigmatization.[38]

Even before she discovers that Lady Dedlock is her mother, something in that woman's face enables Esther to begin to recover the parts
of herself that had been shed—or buried, like her doll—in the past.
In the church at Chesney Wold Lady Dedlock's gaze calls up in Esther

---

[38] On this and other related points, Helena Michie's superb essay, "'Who Is This in
Pain?': Scarring, Disfigurement, and Female Identity in *Bleak House* and *Our Mutual
Friend*," *Novel* 22 (Winter 1989): 199–212, is illuminating. Using feminist psychoanalytic
and Lacanian theory, Michie writes tellingly of the significance of mirrors in Esther's
rebirth: "In this configuration of mirrors, Esther's refusal to be identical to and identified
as her mother becomes the point in her text where a self begins to emerge. Like the
female self in Wittig, Esther must enter the text through the scarring of her body; she
moves from figure to body through disfigurement" (p. 202).

a string of associations and memories that bring back to her her childhood self. She first recalls dressing before a mirror at her godmother's, then wonders why the beautiful woman's face should be "like a broken glass" to her. Finally, the abandoned self of childhood appears to her: "*I—I*, little Esther Summerson, the child who lived a life apart . . . seemed to arise before my eyes, evoked out of the past by some power in this fashionable lady" (pp. 304–5). It is Lady Dedlock's face (and indeed its resemblance to Esther's godmother's) that initiates Esther's process of self-recovery rather than the knowledge that Lady Dedlock is her mother. Esther's ability to look at herself in the mirror, destroyed by her godmother's regimen of guilt and self-punishment, begins to be restored to her when she sees a face that so forcefully recalls the past and mirrors, even in a fragmented way, her own.

Esther's transformed appearance both registers her tie to her mother and enables her to begin to exorcise her mother's ghost. Like Edith Dombey, Lady Dedlock must be purged from the text she haunts so that a chaste but truly (re)productive female sexuality may prevail. Esther's pursuit of Lady Dedlock in and out of London with Inspector Bucket is both a journey toward union with her mother and a flight toward freedom from her.[39] Lady Dedlock enters the nighttime labyrinth of the city on her own, "need[ing] no further escort" (p. 718), and risking identification with the homeless women, the women by the river, the women who have drowned themselves in the Thames.[40] Esther, by contrast, goes in the protective company of Inspector Bucket, holder of secrets, who can traverse the city without danger. Tracking Lady Dedlock back to the city's fetid and polluted center—the paupers' graveyard, the source of Esther's illness and the home in death of Esther's father—Bucket and Esther follow her to her compulsory end. Now dressed as Jenny, the brickmaker's wife, she appears to Esther to be "the mother of the dead child" (p. 868). Her death marks the end

[39] Virginia Blain sees the pursuit of Lady Dedlock solely as Esther's definitive casting off of her mother through an alliance with her "father," Jarndyce, and with Bucket ("Double Vision and the Double Standard in *Bleak House*," p. 153).

[40] As Esther and Bucket traverse waterside neighborhoods in search of Lady Dedlock, they come across a bill posted on a moldering wall that reads "FOUND DROWNED" (*Bleak House*, p. 827). Bucket, fearing the bill might refer to Lady Dedlock's corpse, goes to inspect the body that has been dragged from the river. Although, as we know from the early chapters of *Our Mutual Friend*, such postings were routine and referred to all unidentified corpses found in the Thames, the words "found drowned" would have been associated with the iconography of fallen women who had thrown themselves into the river, at least in part by connection with the G. W. Watts painting of that title (1848–50) depicting the corpse of a presumably ruined woman.

of that other dead child, Esther's shadow self (see figure 13 for an illustration of Lady Dedlock at the paupers' graveyard).

With her mother's death Esther "dies" into life. The text—and in particular Esther's narrative—is startlingly silent on the subject of Lady Dedlock after the discovery of her corpse. Even in Esther's final chapter, in which she sums up the fate of the major players in her story, no further mention of the dead mother is made. Esther's own maternity takes its place. The fact that she is able not only to have Allan but to have children—two daughters—as well suggests that the taint inherited through the female line has been expunged. By careful contrast Caddy Jellyby's little daughter, at the conclusion of the novel "deaf and dumb," suffers the blighted maternal legacy handed down by her grandmother. At birth, we read, the child had curious dark marks under her eyes, "like faint remembrances of poor Caddy's inky days" (p. 736). The healthy maternal body of Esther has replaced the "little body" that promised to absent itself at the beginning of her narrative. Esther's text ends quite literally with her halting admission of the possibility of her own beauty, suggesting that to be able to acknowledge but not necessarily to articulate her attractiveness is the sign of healthy sexuality in a woman. The "domestic mission," which Mrs. Jellyby and her friends revile, concludes—and takes the place of—the narrative mission that for Esther had proved so problematic.

Directly contradicting the proto-feminist ravings of Miss Wisk at Caddy Jellyby's wedding, then, the novel prescribes for middle-class women the "domestic mission . . . in the narrow sphere of Home" (p. 478). When Mr. Jarndyce presents Esther with the second Bleak House, he gives her a home and a husband—Allan, not himself—as the final step in his creation of Esther as the maternal solution to social evils. The reconstituted Bleak House is free from the taint of the Jarndyce inheritance, from the legacy of stunted middle-class life, from the need for a growlery (the wind that blows there is never from the East),[41]

---

[41] A passage from a speech Dickens gave before the Metropolitan Sanitary Association in May 1851 suggests that the wind from the East that disrupts Jarndyce's equanimity may be a reference to the polluting breezes that emanate from London's East End. The passage reads: "That no one can estimate the amount of mischief which is grown in dirt; that no one can say, here it stops, or there it stops, either in its physical or moral results, when both begin in the cradle and are not at rest in the obscene grave, is now as certain as it is that the air from Gin Lane will be carried, when the wind is Easterly, into May Fair, and that if you once have a vigorous pestilence raging furiously in Saint Giles's, no mortal list of Lady Patronesses can keep it out of Almack's." See *The Speeches of Charles Dickens*, ed. K. J. Fielding (London: Harvester, 1988), p. 128.

Figure 13 Hablot K. Browne, "The Morning." Charles Dickens, *Bleak House* (1853). Department of Rare Books and Special Collections, Princeton University Libraries.

from the shadow of London. Here in Yorkshire life undefiled will prosper, and the evils represented by Tom-all-Alone's will, as if by sleight of hand, resolve themselves in Esther and her doctor-husband's domestic happiness.

The unsettling middle-class romance of maternal sexuality that the novel offers as a resolution to deeply painful and problematic social suffering is linked to the enigmatic transformations that Sir Leicester Dedlock and Chesney Wold have undergone by the narrative's end. That aristocratic world has clearly become moribund, like the mausoleum that houses Lady Dedlock's remains. Yet Sir Leicester's image after his wife's death is radically sentimentalized, ennobled, and redeemed, especially by the devoted presence of Mr. George, who has chosen to remain as a companion to the broken aristocrat rather than to join his industrialist brother in the making of England's future. Earlier in the novel Sir Leicester's conviction that the ironmaster's candidacy for Parliament marked the decline of British civilization stood as an indictment of Sir Leicester's narrow-mindedness and class snobbery. Mr. George's decision to stay with Sir Leicester suggests a reversal of this earlier social vision and, at the very least, an unwillingness to abandon old England for new. It is as if Dickens's uneasiness about the philanthropic middle class—represented by Mrs. Jellyby—and the entrepreneurial middle class—represented by George's brother, the ironmaster—leads him to imagine Esther's modest but fecund femininity, her husband's humanitarian professionalism, and their escape from a polluted and disease-ridden London as the basis for a productive bourgeois life. But the replication of Bleak House in the provincial North has a double edge: it remakes the old Bleak House in a more salutary form, but it also marks both the present and the future of the house with an indelible connection to the legacies of the past, and especially to Tom-all-Alone's, the slum "in Chancery" that nurtured Jo and that breeds fever still.

In 1850, two years after the publication of the completed *Dombey* and three years before *Bleak House* appeared, W. R. Greg wrote a now much quoted article on prostitution for the *Westminster Review*.[42] After a measured discussion of poverty as the chief cause of prostitution and a call

---

[42] In his untitled piece on prostitution in *Westminster Review* 53 (1850): 448–506, W. R. Greg reviewed four works on the subject: Parent-Duchâtelet's *De la prostitution dans la ville de Paris,* James Talbot Beard's *Miseries of Prostitution,* Dr. Ryan's *Prostitution in London,* and Henry Mayhew's *Letters in the Morning Chronicle—Metropolitan Poor.*

110

Walking the Victorian Streets

for "more Christian feelings of grief, compassion, and desire to soothe and to save," Greg moves on to the subject of the prostitute as social contaminant. Two things are worth noting in Greg's account: first, that the spread of syphilis is for him a "sanitary matter," a question to be considered along with "quarantines against the plague" and "precautions against cholera," and second, that the ultimate toll the disease will take is incalculable because of its spread, through procreation, to "innocent individuals in private life." Nothing less than the "deterioration of public health and of the vigor of the race . . . in the course of a generation or two" is at stake.[43] Like many of his contemporaries who wrote on the subject, Greg saw in the prostitute a threat to public and private life, a destroyer of health—like cholera or the plague— and a silent and invisible corrupter of apparently respectable families.[44] Syphilis was the disease of the city, often alluded to in fiction by the substitution of other communicable diseases associated with urban life and, in particular, with the confluence of rich and poor. It raised the specter of a public threat that, like smallpox or cholera or typhus, might invade the private realm; it marked that point of convergence where the city streets and the middle-class drawing room might meet.

Not only, then, did female sexuality become imaginatively central to representations of the dangers of the city, but also the nature of the relationship between the woman of the streets and the woman of the hearth became a social and symbolic question worth pondering. The woman of the hearth might be innocent victim, heroic redeemer, or insidious reflection of her fallen counterpart. In Dickens's hands this relationship became a means for exposing social hypocrisy, as in the cousinly connection between Alice Marwood and Edith Dombey; for expressing anxieties about the moral and physical health of the middle and upper classes, as in the barrenness of the Dombey and Dedlock marriages; and for imagining social redemption, as in the purging of Edith and Lady Dedlock and the ascendancy of Florence Dombey and Esther Summerson.

In *Dombey and Son* the use of female sexuality as a fulcrum for social

[43] Ibid., pp. 467–77.

[44] Elaine Showalter has written that the culture of the fin de siècle imagined syphilis as a symbol of the disease of the family. Although Greg's and Acton's warnings about the incursion of the disease into the middle-class home suggest that this idea had its origin before the 1890s, I would argue that in the middle decades of the century syphilis symbolized the disease of the streets, of the city. See Elaine Showalter, "Syphilis, Sexuality, and the Fiction of the Fin de Siècle," in *Sex, Politics, and Science in the Nineteenth-Century Novel*, ed. Ruth Bernard Yeazell (Baltimore: Johns Hopkins University Press, 1990), p. 89.

criticism involves Dickens in a critique of patriarchal values which at
the same time sacrifices perhaps their most powerful, certainly their
most dramatic and compelling, critic: Edith. As readers of the novel
often note, although Edith is indeed punished and purged, she leaves
an indelible mark on the text. Dickens's investment in Edith—his use
of her to make the statement that middle-class marriage can also be a
form of prostitution; his endowing her with passion, clear vision, and
maternal tenderness—makes Dickens's sacrifice of her a gesture that
vexes and rankles until the narrative's end. Never again, and certainly
not with Lady Dedlock, did Dickens allow himself that overt identification with female rage and transgression.[45] In *Bleak House* it is the
chaste daughter who occupies the center, successfully eclipsing her
mother in the narrative in a way that Florence Dombey never manages
to do. But her chastity, because of the circumstances of her birth, is
ambiguous. In Esther Summerson Dickens can plot the entire progress
from taint to purity, from a blighted female sexuality to the promise of
nothing less than social regeneration. Contamination and foulness, as
Acton remarked, might indeed be carried to every quarter, but through
the transformation of female sexuality itself, the social body may be
restored to health.

---

[45] Laurie Langbauer writes of Dickens's identification with women, and especially with
Nancy in *Oliver Twist*, in terms of "his own identification with victimization but also of
his desire to elude it." She reminds us in this context that Dickens was himself a walker
of the streets. See Laurie Langbauer, *Woman and Romance: The Consolations of Gender in the
English Novel* (Ithaca: Cornell University Press, 1990), p. 155.

PART TWO

Fallen Women

❧ FOUR ❧

The Female Pariah:
Flora Tristan's London *Promenades*

The first extensive nonfictional portrait of London produced by a woman in the nineteenth century was the work of a Frenchwoman, Flora Tristan, whose short life was even more remarkable than the text she published in 1840, *Promenades dans Londres*. The illegitimate daughter of a Peruvian and a Frenchwoman, herself an exile in Spain during the French Revolution, Tristan suffered the disadvantages of social marginality in a variety of ways throughout her lifetime, ultimately transmuting her status as "pariah" into a revolutionary stance on behalf of disenfranchised workers, displaced women, utopian socialists, and political exiles.[1] Denied her inheritance after her father's death by his wealthy aristocratic family, and impoverished by her estrangement from an abusive husband, she struggled to overcome the economic and social stigma of independence. Her peripatetic life defied notions of female passivity and helplessness: she traveled to Peru alone in an attempt to claim her patrimony, visited England at least

[1] For an excellent brief introduction to Tristan's life, see Doris Beik and Paul Beik, eds., *Flora Tristan, Utopian Feminist: Her Travel Diaries and Personal Crusade* (Bloomington: Indiana University Press, 1993), pp. ix–xxi. Other useful biographical sources are Dominique Desanti, *A Woman in Revolt: A Biography of Flora Tristan,* trans. Elizabeth Zelvin (New York: Crown, 1976); and Laura S. Strumingher, *The Odyssey of Flora Tristan* (New York: Peter Lang, 1988). Tristan's parents were married in Spain by a refugee French priest, but they had no French marriage license, so their legal tie was not recognized in France. Nor did Tristan's father leave a will (Beik and Beik, *Flora Tristan,* p. x). Exile became a familial pattern: Tristan's daughter Aline married Clovis Gauguin, a journalist and revolutionary of 1848, who left France with his wife and two children in 1849 to seek asylum in Peru. One of those children, Paul Gauguin, thus began his life in exile in Peru, his great-grandfather's homeland, and ended it in exile in Tahiti.

four times to work for a living and investigate British society, embarked on a tour of provincial France to spread the word of her plan for a workers' union, and produced during her lifetime five volumes of fiction, polemic, travel writing, and autobiography.[2]

The tension between Tristan's intrepid, defiant nature and her horror of social ostracism pervades her written work and gives particular force to her London journal. Only a woman with Tristan's sense of personal and political mission would have taken on the project of urban observation in the 1820s and 1830s, when respectable women had no place as spectators on the city streets; and only the experience of *flânerie*—or of its attempt—could have crystallized for Tristan in quite so dramatic a way the pangs of economic and sexual marginality. By the time she published her first piece of work, a tract urging support for foreign women in the French capital, she was able to write: "For a long time we have traveled *alone* and as a *stranger*, we know, therefore, all the unhappiness of that cruel situation. We have been a stranger in Paris, in provincial cities, in villages, in watering-places. We have also traveled in several parts of England and its immense capital. We have visited a large section of [South] America, and what we report will come from the heart."[3]

As a female traveler Tristan knew poverty, loneliness, fear, humiliation, and shame; she faced mistrust, suspicion, and the general inability of strangers to place her in the social scheme of things. The fundamental ambiguities of her class position were intensified by travel and dislocation, and her unsettled marital state also gave rise to misunderstandings and confusion in foreign settings.[4] But it was in exploring and writing about London that Tristan had to confront the reality of her debased double, the most extreme type of sexually and economically vulnerable woman, the ultimate female pariah, the woman whose very name declared her estrangement from the private realm of domesticity: the streetwalker, or *fille publique*.

Flora Tristan's *Promenades dans Londres* affords us the opportunity of

---

[2] Flora Tristan's major works are, in order of publication, *Nécessité de faire un bon accueil aux femmes étrangères* (1835); *Pérégrination d'une paria* (1833–34); *Méphis* (1838); *Promenades dans Londres* (1840, 1842); *Union ouvrière* (1843); and *Le tour de France: état actuel de la classe ouvrière sous l'aspect moral, intellectuel, matériel* (1975), a posthumously collected and published series of accounts of her final tour.

[3] "Women Travelers," from *Nécessité de faire un bon accueil aux femmes étrangères*, trans. in Beik and Beik, *Flora Tristan*, p. 2.

[4] Divorce had effectively been abolished by the Restoration in France. See Desanti, *A Woman in Revolt*, p. 13.

asking what happens when a woman tries to take the role of urban spectator. What does the text reveal about her existential struggle to ramble, to stroll, to promenade? And what happens to the text itself as a result of her efforts to occupy a male role and a masculine space? One critic of Tristan's work has commented that the title of her London book has a banal ring given the trenchant social criticism the work contains, and argues that the activity it invokes—promenading—would have been restricted to the leisured rich.[5] The title can sound frivolous, but only if the *promeneur* is masculine. Once a *promeneuse* takes his place, the title suggests something disruptive and disorienting: the insertion of a female subject into a cultural and literary tradition that habitually relegates her to the position of object, symbol, and marker. Furthermore, a woman's occupation of public space does more than unsettle her domestic and private identity; it threatens her respectability, her chastity, her very femininity.

In her analysis of the spaces of masculinity and femininity in impressionist painting, Griselda Pollock addresses the relationship between the places that defined the experiences of masculine modernity (bars, brothels, backstage, cafés, the streets) and the formal qualities of the paintings produced by male impressionists, who celebrated them, and female impressionists, who were excluded from them. These particular public spaces, so frequently the subjects of impressionist painting, signified for men "losing oneself in the crowd away from [the] demands of domesticity," whereas for women they meant "losing one's virtue, dirtying oneself, . . . the idea of disgrace."[6] Respectable women could not frequent the bars and brothels of Paris and so could not paint them in anything like a realistic mode. But, perhaps more significantly, their paintings of those spaces they could enter—whether on the border between domestic and public life, such as a garden or a balcony, or in the "safe" public places provided for decorous display, such as parks or theater loges—represented in formal ways the conditions of confinement and of vulnerability.

For female impressionists such as Berthe Morisot and Mary Cassatt, Pollock argues, the very circumstance of being looked at, of being on display, becomes the subject of painting.[7] For male impressionists, how-

---

[5] Sandra Dijkstra, *Flora Tristan: Feminism in the Age of George Sand* (London: Pluto Press, 1992), p. 124.

[6] Griselda Pollock, *Vision and Difference: Femininity, Feminism, and the Histories of Art* (London: Routledge, 1988), p. 69.

[7] Ibid., p. 76.

ever, the subject of the demimonde looms large, and the modern artist, like the flaneur, is defined by his access not only to a public realm but to a sexual one in which the body of the nonbourgeois woman can be purchased.[8] In effect, then, Pollock's analysis suggests a triangle of male artist, bourgeois female, and commodified female which determines the dynamics of a modern and an *urban* art. When, as in the case of Tristan, the ostensibly respectable woman assumes the role of urban spectator, she pushes the boundaries of those spaces of femininity which she can navigate with equanimity. Trespassing into those spaces of masculinity in which the male artist holds sway and in which she finds no conceivable niche, she is unwittingly thrust into the position of whore. The existential and rhetorical struggles of the female subject to take the part of urban spectator come together with Tristan's habitual stance as peripatetic and pariah in her efforts to represent and ultimately resolve her interchangeability with the woman of the streets. The threat to her respectability that inevitably results from her urban explorations also calls into question her femininity, a cultural trait dependent on caste and gentility. We read in the *Promenades* a rhetorical effort to recover that femininity as a means of resisting debasement. This recovery or reinvention of femininity, as we shall see, informs Tristan's ultimate political philosophy as well as the rhetoric of her London text.

Crucial to Tristan's project of urban observation and to her efforts to occupy spaces prohibited to her sex was the resource of disguise, a phenomenon that figured in the lives of a number of nineteenth- and even twentieth-century women who sought to escape the geographic and social boundaries assigned to their sex. For George Sand the thought of donning men's clothing originated with her desire to navigate the streets of Paris, attend the theater, and soak up the atmosphere of the bohemian world of letters. After experimenting tentatively with a man's greatcoat (*redingote-guérite*) she became enchanted with the freedom and anonymity that masculine garb afforded her. She writes: "I flew from one end of Paris to the other. It seemed to me that I could go round the world. . . . My clothes feared nothing. I ran

---

[8] Pollock writes: "This other world of encounter between bourgeois men and women of another class was a no-go area for bourgeois women. It is the place where female sexuality or rather female bodies are bought and sold, where woman becomes both an exchangeable commodity and a seller of flesh, entering the economic domain through her direct exchanges with men" (ibid., p. 78).

out in every kind of weather, I came home at every sort of hour, I sat in the pit at the theater. No one paid attention to me, and no one guessed at my disguise. . . . I was no longer a *lady*, but I wasn't a *gentleman* either. . . . No one knew me, no one looked at me, no one found fault with me; I was an atom lost in that immense crowd."[9] That sense of invisibility and invulnerability was attainable for women on the streets only by altering their external identity. As important as the inability of others to recognize them was their own experience of transformation, not necessarily into a convincing other but into a disguised form of themselves.

Tristan understood the uses of incognito for female travelers as well as for women on their home soil. When she visited Peru in 1833, she was struck by the garb of Liman women. The loose and baggy *saya* and *manto*, or veil, enabled women of all classes to go out in public alone whenever they wished and be virtually unrecognizable—or so she believed: "They remain free and independent in the midst of the crowd."[10] Like Lady Mary Wortley Montagu, who herself donned Turkish dress as a form of camouflage during her sojourn in Adrianople in 1717–18, Tristan associated this freedom of movement with unusual opportunities for female independence. " 'Tis very easy to see," Lady Mary wrote to her sister, that Turkish women "have more liberty than we have. . . . No man dare either touch or follow a woman in the street. This perpetual masquerade gives them entire liberty of following their inclinations without danger or discovery."[11] In a gesture reminiscent of Sand's forays to the opera, Tristan once went unescorted to a Parisian ball in her Liman *saya* and *manto* in the hope that she would be unrecognizable.[12] So seductive was the possibility of camouflage for these European women that they romanticized what, from another perspective, could be understood as a repressive regime of dress for the women of Turkey and Peru.

[9] I use Ellen Moers's translation of Sand's memoirs in *Literary Women: The Great Writers* (Garden City, N.Y.: Doubleday, 1976), p. 9. For the original, see George Sand, *Histoire de ma vie* (Paris: Calmann-Lévy, 1926), 4:81, 102.

[10] Flora Tristan, *Peregrinations of a Pariah, 1833–1834*, trans. Jean Hawks (London: Virago, 1986), p. 274.

[11] *The Letters and Works of Lady Mary Wortley Montagu* (London: George Bell and Sons, 1887), 1:175. It is interesting to note that Lady Mary wrote from Paris the following year that the city was like a "puppet-show" in which everyone stares: "Staring is à la mode" (1:274). Both Lady Mary and Tristan commented on the freedom with which the women they observed in Turkey and Peru evidently conducted extramarital affairs as a result of their disguising costumes.

[12] Desanti, *A Woman in Revolt*, p. 144.

In London Tristan employed a variety of disguises, some more overt than others, in order to explore the city unimpeded. In chapter 6 of the *Promenades*, "A Visit to the Houses of Parliament," she records with bravado her efforts to disguise herself as a man in order to observe the making of English law in a period before women were admitted, even as spectators, to Parliament.[13] Indignant at a nation that would, as she put it, sell women in the marketplace but refuse them entry into its legislative assembly, she is determined to "insinuate her[self] into the sanctuary of male power." "The will of woman," she proclaims right-eously, "is the will of God" (p. 58). But the will of this woman holds no sway over any of the English, French, German, or Spanish men of her acquaintance from whom she seeks to borrow clothing. Her solu-tion once again suggests the interesting connection between gender disguise and cross-cultural disguise, for it is a Turkish gentleman who finally obliges her. To her delight, and in confirmation of the coward-ice of his European peers, he offers her a complete set of clothes, his admission card, his carriage, and his company.

Through a kind of mystification of the Oriental, Tristan welcomes the robes' accentuation of her otherness and senses that they lend her a kind of serenity and control: "My heart was beating violently and I blushed despite myself; I was in agonies. . . . However, my appearance inspired respect. I overcame my agitation and preserved a calm de-meanour, for such is the influence of costume that, in donning the Turkish turban, I had acquired the serious gravity habitual to the Mos-lem" (pp. 59–60). The sustenance that Tristan usually derives from her marginality and dislocation is heightened here: she is now more foreign, more exotic, more mysterious than before, and her feelings of virtuous indignation increase accordingly. As soon as she enters the Parliament chamber, she hears murmurings to the effect that the "young Turk appears to be a woman," and she never deludes herself that she has fooled these English gentlemen about her sex. It is *as a woman* that she comes among them, though a woman protected and ennobled by the garb of an "Oriental" man. Indeed, she regards the men's rudeness as an affront to her femaleness: "Without the slightest respect for my status as a woman and a foreigner, or for the fact that

---

[13] See Flora Tristan, *The London Journal of Flora Tristan, 1842*, trans. Jean Hawks (Lon-don: Virago, 1982); subsequently cited in the text. For the French text, see *Promenades dans Londres* (Paris: Maspero, 1983). Tristan visited England in 1826, 1831, 1835 (on her way home from South America), and 1839. She attempted to visit Parliament on her second trip to England, in 1831; women were not allowed even as spectators until 1835.

I was there in disguise, all these so-called gentlemen passed in front of me, staring at me boldly through their lorgnettes" (p. 60). The camouflage is thus meant not to conceal her identity but to furnish her with a sense of invulnerability by inhibiting the responses of others. She ends the chapter with an apparently confounding remark that in the House of Lords, which she later visited in the same incognito, the true urbanity and *politesse* of the aristocrats (as opposed to the "overlords of finance" in the Commons) enabled them to be "tolerant of a lady's whims" (p. 63). They too recognized that she was a woman, but because she was a woman in disguise, they felt constrained from remarking on her anomalous presence.

Tristan's presumption of immunity from the derision of those around her, both in Parliament and outside it, originates in her status as a foreigner. Her foreignness gives her license to observe English society and to criticize it aggressively throughout her text; and it also gives her the expectation that she can trespass with impunity into areas of the city an Englishwoman would instinctively avoid. Her exoticism, another form of disguise, protects her—or so she imagines. Indeed, she remarks in her chapter titled "Foreigners in London" that others like her can re-create themselves and their identities in the English capital because of the shrewdness of the French and the credulity of the English. "Frenchwomen are no fools," she writes, gently mocking her hosts, "and living in a country which is the traditional home of advertisement and exaggeration, they are quick to pick up the forms. You will hear Englishmen say of some lady of the streets, 'Oh, she comes from a very good family; she is a niece of the comte de La Rochefoucauld,' or 'she is related to M de Broglie,' and so on. Nobody but the English could be taken in by such humbug" (p. 31). She notes that "kept women and even prostitutes" masquerade as baronesses and countesses, that women of the streets who dress as noblewomen and invent titles for themselves are able to make their mark, and sometimes their fortune. If only, she muses, the English could come to know the French better, they would be able to distinguish "the duke from his valet and the duchess from her maid" (p. 31).

The bluster of these passages hints at Tristan's confidence that she too can carry off an incognito in the English context, but it also betrays an anxiety associated with the ambiguity of her position. The reader knows little more about the identity of Tristan as narrator than the ignorant English know of those masquerading prostitutes she describes, and she deliberately shrouds that identity in obscurity. Tristan's part in the confusion between duchess and lady's maid was more complex than she would admit here, or anywhere else. Suppressed from the *Promenades* and from other records of her life is the fact that between 1826 and 1828, in order to support herself after giving birth to her three children and leaving her husband, Tristan served as a lady's maid and companion to a number of Englishwomen traveling on the Continent and in Britain. Her first trip to London, in 1826, was almost certainly taken in the company of one of her employers, and she, like those French maids parading as duchesses, sought to conceal her social status, at least in written accounts of her London sojourn.[14] Suppressing any sign of her true economic status, Tristan depended on her critical stance and her foreignness to disguise her dependence and vulnerability and to secure her moral authority.

The disguises of foreignness, exoticism, and androgyny that appear to buoy Tristan on her journeys through the streets and institutions of London are of no use to her in her encounters with the subject of her chapter on prostitutes, or *filles publiques*. In fact, something like the obverse of disguise occurs in Tristan's earnest attempts to observe and analyze the practice of prostitution. Her foreignness, her class, her respectability, her critical stance, even her adoption of the spectator's role all fall away, leaving only her femaleness. She falters when confronting the women of the streets, in large part because she is linked to them by sex and, as we shall see, by their common participation in the world of commercial exchange. The chapter reveals her inability to interpret, even to her own satisfaction, the social phenomenon of prostitution or to situate herself in relation to these women. Despite her proclaimed sympathy for the oppressed, the most immediate and vexing question for Tristan is that of her existential relationship to these women whom she calls "un impénétrable mystère":

> I can understand the brigand who robs travellers on the highway and forfeits his life on the guillotine, the soldier who gambles with death every day in return for a few pence, the sailor who exposes his life to the fury of the sea, for all three find a sombre and terrible poetry in their calling. But I cannot understand the prostitute. To surrender all rights over herself, annihilate her will and feelings, deliver her body to brutality and suffering, her soul to contempt! The prostitute is an impenetrable mystery to me. . . . I see prosti-

[14] See Strumingher, *Odyssey of Flora Tristan*, p. 69; and Beik and Beik, *Flora Tristan*, p. xi.

tution as either an appalling madness or an act so sublime that my mortal understanding cannot comprehend it. . . . She is wedded to sorrow and doomed to degradation: physical torture . . . , moral death every moment, and—worst of all—*boundless self-disgust!* (p. 81)

Understanding the brigand, the soldier, and the sailor poses no threat to her integrity because she cannot be taken for one of them; the prostitute, by contrast, unsettles Tristan's sense of her own identity.

The female social investigator or reformer finds the prostitute a particular challenge to her sympathetic eye.[15] This is especially true for the urban spectator, the female rambler, whose street walking cannot necessarily be distinguished from that of other "public" women; but it is true as well for women such as Harriet Martineau, who encountered a similar challenge to her efforts at objectivity in visits to "hareems" in Cairo and Damascus.[16] Martineau strives for a relativist perspective, as friends counseled her to do in her travels, but her conclusion, quite simply, is that "if we are to look for a hell on earth, it is where polygamy exists."[17] Like Tristan, who claims she can understand other forms of criminality but not prostitution, Martineau must separate the debasement of harem life from that of even the poorest London slum. She writes: "I feel that a visit to the worst room in St. Giles' would have affected me less painfully. There are there at least the elements of a rational life, however perverted; while here humanity is wholly and hopelessly baulked."[18]

Although it is the moral and existential nature of concubinage and polygamy, not of prostitution, that Martineau contemplates, her disgust, much like Tristan's, arises from the link of femaleness that binds the observer to women whose lives appear to be defined by unlicensed sexuality, and it is this bond that makes objectivity or relativism unthinkable. Martineau's own femininity is revealed as a subject of interest to the women of the harem; they advise her and her companion on the proper wearing of their veils, try on the Englishwomen's bonnets

[15] For an uncharacteristic response to prostitution on the part of middle-class women, see Judith R. Walkowitz, *Prostitution and Victorian Society: Women, Class, and the State* (Cambridge: Cambridge University Press, 1980). Walkowitz recounts the story of the campaign of Josephine Butler and other activists to repeal the Contagious Diseases Acts in an implicit recognition of the inviolable rights and bodily integrity of the prostitute.

[16] Harriet Martineau described her reaction to the "ʻareems" in *Eastern Life, Present and Past* (1848). See Gayle Graham Yates, ed., *Harriet Martineau on Women* (New Brunswick, N.J.: Rutgers University Press, 1985), pp. 173–84.

[17] Yates, *Harriet Martineau on Women*, p. 174.

[18] Ibid., p. 178.

and gloves, and ask questions about their living arrangements. Indeed, this moment of camaraderie ends with the women of the harem wishing that Martineau and her friend could "stay always." Unable to understand how a woman might take care of herself or to imagine what it means for Martineau to write books and live in her own house, they see the Englishwomen as potential new recruits to their ranks. The uncomfortable lack of distance between the traveler and her investigative subjects which is implicit in this admittedly fleeting intimacy inhibits Martineau's dispassionate scrutiny of the harem. That is, because she is a woman, the boundary between her identity and that of the women she studies cannot easily be drawn.

Similarly, in Tristan's chapter on prostitution she searches for some way to approach a subject that vexes and confuses her. She wants to uncover the abuses at the heart of a cruel society, but she cannot muster the wished-for sympathetic identification with these particular victims. After the introductory confession that she cannot fathom the prostitute's way of life, she alternates between turning away from the women themselves toward other forms of analysis and trying, without success, to confront head on the ostensible subjects of her investigation. In this chapter she experiments with a number of the discourses available to social observers of the urban underworld. Her inability to settle on any one is a symptom of the anxiety this enterprise arouses in her.

After repeating that prostitution is "either sublime, or it is madness," she shifts her focus to the unequal distribution of wealth and the sexual double standard which are the causes of this "revolting degradation." Her prose takes on some of the indignation characteristic of her other outcries against the oppression of women, but hers is also the tone of someone determined to convince herself that the blame is wholly on the side of men. Men impose chastity on women and then abandon them to the streets if they transgress; men deprive women of education and access to the professions so that poverty is inevitable; men abuse women in marriage and force them to choose between "oppression and dishonour." By the time she has finished cataloguing the very real social injustices under which women labor, she is able to argue that women cannot possibly have any moral sense because they are afforded no freedom to choose between good and evil: a woman "cannot call her soul her own," so "let [her] be exonerated" (pp. 81–82). She thus divests women of all agency, empties them of judgment, and renders them passive—and morally vacuous—victims. Tristan has been praised by critics for her economic analysis of prostitution. It seems important to add to this praise recognition of the fact that she cannot accept prostitutes as moral beings or allow herself to imagine what the economic realities of a given female life might entail. Despite her intimate knowledge of the difficulty of making a living in a "respectable" manner, she avoids articulating the conclusion that prostitution might, in fact, be a choice wholly motivated by economic necessity. Her attention shifts repeatedly to the male villain who robs women of their choice and will. If women could exercise any will at all, this vision implies, they would not, could not, sell their bodies.

Not content, however, to ignore entirely the experience of the prostitute, Tristan next tries to enter her world. Accompanied by two male friends armed with canes, she embarks on an evening's exploration of a streetwalkers' enclave off of Waterloo Road. Knowing "it is courting danger to go there alone at night," she expects to be protected by her companions. Here, in a gesture reminiscent of her perilous journey to Peru, Tristan exposes herself to danger as a challenge both to herself and to the social order. What occurs, however, brings her closer to the prostitute's experience than she can bear, and deepens rather than moderates her feelings of repugnance. She observes the "revolting sight" of women—some naked to the waist—walking with their pimps, men of "criminal, cynical expressions." Before long she and her companions are accosted by one such pimp, who asks them if they would like a room. When they decline, the man adopts "a threatening tone" and demands, "What are you doing here then, if you don't want a room for you and your lady friend?" (p. 84). In this world it is understood that any woman is for sale and any man is in search of a woman to buy. The place makes threateningly real Tristan's interchangeability with the woman of the streets. What had vexed her at the outset—the nature of her relationship to these women—finds no resolution off Waterloo Road.

She does make one last effort to conquer her anxiety, or, as she puts it, "to overcome my repugnance" (p. 85). With the same male companions Tristan determines to enter a "finish," one of the gin palaces frequented by fashionable gentlemen in search of drink, women, and amusement, hoping to learn if the stories she has heard about the treatment of women in these pleasure houses could possibly be true. She discovers that her worst expectations are confirmed. At first Tristan uses the occasion once again to condemn the British ruling class: "The finishes are the temples which English materialism raises to its gods," she writes. "The servants who minister in them are dressed in rich

liveries, and the capitalist owners reverently greet the male guests who
come to exchange their gold for debauchery" (p. 85). In this sexual
underworld aristocrat and capitalist collaborate in debasing women and
dehumanizing themselves. She describes the revelers, "honourable
members of Parliament," as they undress and "set up their private
boudoir in a public place" in preparation for an orgy (p. 86). So long
as the men of the ruling class are the object of her attention, her firm,
indignant tone does not waver; once she turns her attention to their
female partners and victims, however, she has difficulty finding her
critical bearings. In this exclusive space of masculinity, akin to the
haunts visited by Pierce Egan's swells and parallel to the brothels and
bars represented by the male impressionists, Tristan cannot locate her
rhetorical or existential place.[19]

As the orgy proceeds, Tristan's position as female spectator becomes
nearly untenable. She remarks on the difficulty of remaining in her
seat as the men urge women to drink to the point of insensibility, feed
them mixtures of vinegar, mustard, and pepper until they suffer convulsions, and pour wine and brandy all over their semicomatose bodies.
There is nothing in Tristan's text to suggest any direct engagement on
her part with these debased women: the bodies on the floor have no
identity, no life, indeed no speech or movement. The painfulness of
the scene makes the observer-narrator squirm; the indignity of the
women's position causes her to avert her eyes. Tristan's only moment
of overt identification with an individual woman is banished to a footnote. An "Irish girl of extraordinary beauty," causes a sensation upon
entering the "finish" and calls up in Tristan what appears at first glance
to be a sentimental response: "As for me, my eyes filled with tears at
the sight of such a beautiful creature" (p. 105). Her clothing appears
tasteful and charming, her feet are dainty, her pearls luminous. What,
Tristan seems to ask through her tears, is this creature who so resembles
me doing in this place? The woman is soon reduced to an unconscious
victim like all the others: three hours later she lies drunk, soaked with

---

[19] Sandra Dijkstra probes some of the complexities of Tristan's interest in prostitution,
suggesting that Tristan may even have prostituted herself in order to support herself and
her children after leaving her artist-husband, André Chazal (*Flora Tristan*, p. 159). Dijkstra
also comments on the scene in the "finish" and concludes that Tristan's "stance as the
'femme honnête' who rejects this debauchery permits [her] to appear undisguised. . . .
Her feminine clothes offer a protective device" (p. 159). It seems to me, however, that
Tristan's "disguise" of respectability fails her here and on the streets, leaving exposed
the common denominator of gender. I would add that her presence in the "finish" still
puzzles me.

wine, trampled underfoot by servers "as if she were a bundle of rub-
bish" (p. 105).

Tristan does not comment further on this scene, except to say that,
had she not actually witnessed this "shameful desecration," she would
never have believed it. The footnote on the Irish beauty inspires in the
text itself a brief passage on the short lives and grim deaths of prostitutes:
"The dying dog is favoured with a kind look from his master, but the
prostitute dies alone in the gutter with nobody to spare her a pitying
glance" (p. 87). This comment constitutes virtually the last statement
that directly addresses the subject of prostitutes themselves in a chapter
that goes on for fourteen more pages. Whereas at first the narrator had
wavered between approaching and distancing herself from the subjects
of her inquiry, she now turns away completely, enlisting the help of the
"authorities," through whose words she is able to establish the extent of
the problem as a purely statistical phenomenon. The discourses of social
science give weight to her critique of prostitution and act to insulate her
from the troubling issues she raises. Less unsettling, less threatening,
than a personal account is the testimony of experts.[20]

Having been rendered more or less speechless by the sight of adult
female prostitutes, Tristan concludes her chapter on a related but significantly different topic, that of child prostitution. Although she never
completely abandons her reliance on the evidence of acknowledged
authorities or resumes a tale of personal observation and exploration,
she does establish a comfortable and self-assured voice—the voice of
the indignant mother—in excoriating a society that sexually exploits
its young. Children are kidnapped, trapped, purchased from destitute
parents, snatched from the street as they look in shop windows. They
are, in short, unwilling victims whose participation in the exchange of
sex for money never raises the question of their culpability. The vexing

[20] Tristan inserts twenty-nine footnotes in this chapter, a number not approached in
any other chapter save that on prisons. (The average in most other chapters is around
ten). The authorities she cites are, not surprisingly, all men: Parent-Duchâtelet, James
Beard Talbot, and Dr. Michael Ryan. In his book *Engels, Manchester, and the Working Class*
(New York: Random House, 1974), Steven Marcus discusses in a way that is wholly rele-
vant to the case of Tristan the struggle to represent in language the new and profoundly
disturbing realities of industrialization. He writes: "In these scenes of early industrial life
. . . something new had happened. In part that newness consisted in the actual conditions
that were being created and disclosed; in part it had to do with human consciousness
struggling to make, and often to resist, the radical alterations and accommodations within
itself that these conditions required. . . . Men were abruptly discovering that . . . masses of
human beings were now constrained to live under conditions of unimaginable extremity"
(p. 45).

problem of the adult prostitute's moral nature does not impose itself here. The guilt of a society that demands and devours the lives of young people is indisputable; so, too, is the essential innocence of those young people. Tristan's shock and indignation rest on firmer ground here, and she finishes her chapter with the kind of Swiftian irony that failed her in the face of the degradation of her own kind: "Evidently the annual consumption of between eight and ten thousand children by the moneyed classes fits neatly into the Malthusian system for decreasing the surplus population; and from this point of view, the keeper of a brothel is a *pillar of respectability* and a useful citizen of his country!" (p. 102). She is now a long way from confessing her inability to comprehend the prostitute, or from trying to do so. She flees from her own disgust—and from the "self-disgust" she attributes to the streetwalkers—by finding an analogous crime that never presents the problem of the victim's agency or subjecthood and that allows her to don the cloak of maternal femininity.

Tristan's footnote on the comatose Irish beauty in the "finish" does not merely mark the romanticization of female beauty; it is an episode of painful self-recognition. Separate from the body of the text, it represents a suppressed moment of realization that, having started as spectator, she cannot help but fall into the role of debased spectacle. The repetition of this moment in the "Prisons" chapter which follows carries a similar narrative weight, but it ends in a resolution rather than an impasse. In Newgate Prison, on a tour of the women's quarters, Tristan begins by summarily dismissing the prisoners as ignorant, lowerclass, and in some cases exceptionally depraved. Their presence behind bars does not surprise her. But then she comes upon one woman who interests and unsettles her:

> Picture a young woman of twenty-four, small, well-made and tastefully dressed, standing with head held high to reveal a perfect profile, graceful neck, delicate well-formed ear, and hair a model of neatness and cleanliness. . . . My eyes filled with tears. . . . There was such dignity in this beauty . . . that I was overwhelmed with emotion and could not believe for one moment that she was wicked. Her soul was pure: I could tell it from her expression, the set of her head, her whole person. (pp. 115–16)

The threat to Tristan is clear: if this woman is indeed a criminal, if she appears to be other than she is, then so too might Tristan be something other than the refined, well-bred lady she presents to the world. The cover of respectable femininity may be exposed for what it is, a form of disguise to protect the woman who wanders into prohibited spaces.

This apprehension of a corrupt double begins, then, much as it did in the episode in the "finish." But Tristan's distress dissolves into a kind of elation when the wardress explains that the woman is in prison for stealing in order to feed her three children after having been abandoned by her drunkard husband. The parallels with her own situation increase, and now confirm her suspicions. "I had guessed right," Tristan triumphantly proclaims. "Such a woman could never be a prostitute or a professional thief! She was a *mother* who had felt the pangs of hunger devouring her unhappy children" (p. 116). Although Tristan herself had repeatedly left her own children behind in France, in part so she could make a living and support them and in part to re-create herself as a single woman, she bolsters her self-esteem through this distinction between prostitute or professional thief and mother. Transported by this vindication of an idealized self, she muses on the redemptive powers of motherhood. Whatever this woman had done to incriminate herself in the eyes of society, she is inherently innocent and above reproach; whatever Tristan herself has had to do to make a living and protect herself from an abusive husband, she maintains her essential purity and innate nobility. The final confirmation of Tristan's redeemed femininity comes in the form of words she imagines the prisoner to utter: "A halo seemed to encircle her head; her eyes veiled with tears, her quivering features and trembling lips were all so eloquent that I almost heard her say, 'Oh, you are a mother! Can you understand my anguish? *You* would have stolen; your children's hunger would have given you the courage! You know what strength I needed to act as I did. Thank you for understanding me' " (p. 117). The maternal figure, guilty but noble, in whom Tristan has perceived her mirror image in turn recognizes Tristan as her double.

The discovery of a kindred other, one who also appears in a context that defines her erroneously, confirms the woman traveler's identity as distinct from the debased culture she observes and lifts her out of the suspect economic or social position in which others might place her. For the nineteenth-century woman whose travels had an economic motive and whose journey ended up as a text to be sold, the implicit advertisement of genteel poverty, of the need to earn a living, required some kind of public self-exoneration. The unaccompanied woman traveler who wrote about her experiences for publication was called upon to answer for her economic need, her independence of male protection, and her distance from home and the maternal role. Tristan's moment in Newgate Prison, when she sees her own reflection in the ostracized but finally beatific woman prisoner, is a kind of epiphany, a focal point for all the anxiety and pride of the dislocated woman.

Another such moment is to be found in Frances Trollope's *Domestic Manners of the Americans* (1832), published just eight years before Tristan's *Promenades*. Trollope records an experience in a public square in Philadelphia where she sat to wait for touring friends. Under a catalpa tree on a bench sits a young woman watching a small boy. "There was something in her manner of looking at me," she writes, "and exchanging a smile when her young charge performed some extraordinary feat . . . that persuaded me she was not an American."[21] Trollope discovers that the woman is in fact German and that she longs to return home after a year spent among a people she finds cold and dour. After describing the woman's beauty of expression and animating smile, she uses the occasion to conclude that American women, however handsome, are universally uninteresting and fundamentally unattractive. This woman, who, like Tristan's Newgate prisoner, is marked as a maternal figure, functions as the writer's double. She confirms the writer's superiority not only to the foreign culture she describes (Tristan's England victimizes women; Trollope's Americans are crass and insensitive) but ultimately to her readers, on whose patronage she is dependent for her livelihood. Both Tristan and Trollope made bad marriages; both needed to support their families and traveled widely in search of a means to make a living; and both successfully published and sold accounts of their travels. But both women also felt the need to account in some way for their suspect role in the marketplace and to deny any wound to their femininity that it might signify.

Anna Jameson, another woman traveler of the generation of Tristan and Trollope, also suppressed the conditions of the journey she described and, to some degree, fictionalized in her *Diary of an Ennuyée* (1826). The daughter of a miniaturist, she worked as a governess to help support her family, both before she was engaged to her future husband and after the engagement was temporarily broken. It was as a governess that she toured France and Italy for the first time in the

---

[21] Frances Trollope, *Domestic Manners of the Americans* (New York: Dodd, Mead, 1839), p. 26.

1820s, but it is as a respectable woman of leisure making a grand tour that she represents herself in the *Diary*. The record of her travels, which Ellen Moers has called "a hybrid work, part novel, part diary, part guidebook," adopts a tone of melancholy and hypochondriacal suffering, and inserts along the way bits of art criticism that indicate where Jameson's talents really lay.[22]

Although the *Diary* lapses into frequent accounts of physical and emotional pain and near-paralysis, it never touches on the biographical details of the *ennuyée's* life. Indeed, it features few encounters with other people and focuses almost exclusively on sights, some of them suffused with a Wertheresque emotion. But here, too, the female traveler represents herself indirectly through the evocation of singular others, except that in Jameson's case the others are paintings of women, not women themselves. Two paintings in particular emerge from all those she describes as having some highly charged significance for her: the first is one of Hagar that hangs in the Brera in Milan and the second is of Beatrice Cenci at the Barberini in Rome. Hagar, Abraham's Canaanite concubine who went into exile in the desert to avoid the wrath of Sarah and the supplanting of her son by Sarah's offspring, inspires in the *ennuyée* a sustained and rapturous response: "The affecting—the inimitable Hagar! what agony, what upbraiding, what love, what helpless desolation of heart in that countenance! . . . The face of Hagar has haunted me sleeping and waking ever since I beheld it."[23] The Beatrice Cenci portrait, an engraving of which she uses as the frontispiece to her book, moves her both for its representation of "dying beauty" and for the extraordinary fame of its subject. Said to have been painted in the interval between its heroine's "torture and her execution," the work depicts a story "as familiar in the mouths of every class, as if instead of two centuries, she had lived two days ago."[24] Found guilty of helping to murder the father who had raped her, Cenci publicly accused her assailant before being put to death. For Jameson these two tormented figures—one exiled and the other horribly victimized but still heroic—serve as images of herself, as reflections of emotions she

[22] Moers, *Literary Women*, p. 188. Jameson later became well known for her many books on art, especially the art of the Italian Renaissance. She also produced volumes on travel in Canada and Germany, on Shakespeare's heroines, and on celebrated female characters in poetry.

[23] Anna Jameson, *The Diary of an Ennuyée* (Boston: Ticknor and Fields, 1860), p. 46.

[24] Ibid., p. 140. In *Mary Barton* Elizabeth Gaskell alludes to this same painting in describing Mary's tortured demeanor when she testifies in court (see my discussion in chapter 5).

can hint at but never articulate. They mirror her suffering and outcast state and suggest, even in their heroism, the taint of public disgrace.

If the London prostitute is Tristan's debased, feared, and disavowed double, her idealized counterpart is to be found not only in the woman prisoner in Newgate who stole to feed her children but also in the domestic female saviors of the working class. Maternal and heroic femininity becomes for her a redemptive personal image as well as a part of her political vision. In a chapter on factory workers which anticipates Marx and echoes Carlyle, Tristan describes in horror the labor of stokers at a gasworks in Westminster. As the men leave work, she waits to see if their womenfolk will appear to offer them comfort. She writes: "Dear God! I thought, have these men no mother, sister, wife or daughter waiting at the door as they emerge from that hell, to wash them in warm water, to wrap them in shirts of flannel; to give them something nourishing to drink; to greet them with friendly words that would give them heart and help them to endure their cruel lot?" (*London Journal*, p. 75) In her *Union ouvrière*, published in 1843, she envisions the role of the working-class woman as the pillar of the home: "In the life of the workers, woman is everything. She is their sole providence. If she is gone, they lack everything. So they say, 'It is woman who makes or unmakes the home.' "[25] The working-class woman—or, more precisely, the working-class wife and mother—is (potentially) all-powerful and, consequently, all to blame. Through education she will gain the means to redeem herself and her family. But in her current, often brutalized state, she is responsible for the defection of her husband and the degradation of their children. "Among the poor girls in houses of prostitution and the poor men moaning in jails," Tristan asks, "how many can say, 'If we had a *mother able to raise us*, then we would not be here.' "[26] Like the beatified woman in Newgate and those stokers' wives sought in vain, the working-class women imagined in the *Union ouvrière*, who will redeem their class by virtue of their transcendent maternality, embody the gifts of nurturing, tending, and healing. But, as Tristan's rhetoric more than implies, maternal femininity is both heroic and deficient.

Tristan tended either to idealize or to censure the omnipotent and often apparently guilty mother, and she became entangled in the prob-

---

[25] Flora Tristan, *The Workers' Union*, trans. Beverly Livingston (Urbana: University of Illinois Press, 1983), p. 79.
[26] Ibid., p. 82.

lem of maintaining a clear distinction between rapacious mothers and innocent daughters.[27] It was mothers who sent their daughters into the streets (Tristan accused her own mother of forcing her into the "legitimate prostitution" of marriage) and, as she herself had done, abandoned their children out of economic necessity.[28] Her own guilt and ambivalence about the maternal role complicated her celebration of it and her desire to cloak herself in it as a redemptive mantle. She sought ultimately to adopt the role in theory while abandoning it in practice. She understood herself as distinct from others of her sex in that she loved humanity, not hearth, children, or spouse.[29] Although all women had a moralizing mission, *she* would assume her place in a complex female hierarchy as a guide and apostle. Her own conviction that she was one of the elect, separate from other women, reflects something of her belief in the authority of the natural aristocrat, but it also represents a solution to the problem of marginality and debasement.[30]

Tristan saw herself not as the housewife on the hearth but as a visionary mother-guide leading the working class to emancipation and union. No "daughter of the people," as one historian comments, she assumed a relationship to the workers that was maternal.[31] Women like

[27] Tristan's ambivalent identification with her own sex can be detected in her only novel, *Méphis* (1838). Here she casts herself partly as the male worker-hero, Méphis, who regards women as apostles of social regeneration. The women in the novel, including the idealized but fundamentally conservative heroine, Marequita (note the Spanish name), resist Méphis's revolutionary plans for them.

[28] Desanti, *A Woman in Revolt*, p. 12. Tristan left her son and daughter in France on her trips to England and Peru for reasons that were economic, legal, and psychological, and she never had an easy or close relationship with the child Aline (later Aline Gauguin, mother of Paul), whose custody a court granted her. Desanti writes of the "deep wound that marriage inflicted on [Tristan's] sexuality" (p. 64). It seems likely that giving birth to three children (one of whom did not survive infancy) in the space of three years, beginning when she was nineteen, and in the context of a distasteful marriage, inflicted its own wounds as well.

[29] S. Joan Moon, "Feminism and Socialism: The Utopian Synthesis of Flora Tristan," in *Socialist Women: European Socialist Feminism in the Nineteenth and Early Twentieth Centuries*, ed. Marilyn Boxer and Jean H. Quataert (New York: Elsevier, 1978), p. 30.

[30] "A very strange apostle of working-class unity," as G. D. H. Cole calls Tristan in his history of socialism, "she was imperious and, with all her sympathies for the workers, very conscious of her family connections." Tristan is the only woman, however, to whom Cole devotes an entire chapter of his two-volume history, and he credits her with the idea of a Workers' International. See chap. 27 of G. D. H. Cole, *A History of Socialist Thought* (London: Macmillan, 1955), 1:187. Tristan's biographer Dominique Desanti explains her "imperiousness" in this way: "The sense of error [Tristan] felt in breaking up her marriage is transformed into a consciousness of social privilege and a rejection of . . . inequities. But the attraction toward the aristocracy persists, constantly struggled against" (*A Woman in Revolt*, p. 199).

[31] Strumingher, *Odyssey of Flora Tristan*, p. 81.

herself belonged in the role of apostle. "Cast out of the Church, out of the law, out of society," she wrote, women were ideally situated to preach salvation to the workers.[32] She drew on the Saint-Simonian notion of the "female Messiah" and on Fourierist ideas of women's emancipation to create her own version of the *femme guide.*[33] The Christian source for her mission rings out emphatically in Tristan's rhetoric: "Well, as a woman who feels faith and force, why shouldn't I go, just like the apostles, from town to town announcing the good tidings and preaching fraternity and unity in humanity to the workers?" It was the responsibility of women like herself—"intelligent women who are God-loving and humanitarian"—to instruct and inspire the working class to unite in its own self-interest and, more immediately, to transform the condition of working-class women through education.[34]

In the final chapter of her *Promenades,* titled "English Women," Tristan makes it clear that she finds her heroic counterpart not only in the pariah-mother imprisoned in Newgate but in the unsung revolutionary Mary Wollstonecraft. "One woman's voice was heard in England half a century ago," she writes, "a voice which found its boundless energy in the truth which God implanted in our souls; a voice which was not afraid to attack every prejudice and expose the lies and iniquities of which they are made" (p. 253). Like Wollstonecraft she might appear to be a notorious woman, but Tristan is also like the English feminist in that her outward deviance conceals visionary heroism and real virtue. She casts as her opposites the young Englishwomen who are "instructed in the *appearance* of chastity and innocence and the *reality* of vice" (p. 248). She takes English hypocrisy as her target both because it oppresses the workers and poor of England and because it misreads women like her—and like Wollstonecraft—as outlaws.

Tristan's distance from the domestic realm, her economic vulnerability, and her social marginality are dramatized and heightened by her adoption of the role of urban spectator. In the prohibited masculine spaces of the city where she is confronted with her debased double, the prostitute, she cannot avoid her own conflation with the woman of the

[32] Tristan, *Workers' Union,* p. 76.

[33] For an excellent discussion of Tristan's brand of utopian socialism and its connection to her feminism, see Moon, "Feminism and Socialism," pp. 27–30. See also Claire Goldberg Moses, *French Feminism in the Nineteenth Century* (Albany: State University of New York Press, 1984), pp. 107–16, for Tristan's links to the ideas of Saint-Simon and Fourier.

[34] Tristan, *Workers' Union,* pp. 42, 14.

streets. A few decades later the South African novelist Olive Schreiner, another nineteenth-century woman making her way in a foreign metropolis, would also see her own image in the streetwalkers of London. "Sometimes," Schreiner wrote "when I have been walking in Gray's Inn Road and seen one of those terrible old women that are so common there, the sense of agonised *oneness* with her that I have felt that she was *myself* only under different circumstances, has stricken me almost mad."[35]

The *fille publique* is defined by her public existence, her symbolic opposition to domestic life, and her ability to subsist by her own labor. Tristan embraces her status as pariah so long as it does not wholly separate her from the ethical purity and spiritual nobility associated with woman's private, maternal identity. Just as the robes of the Turk shield her sexual vulnerability, so the woman in Newgate confirms her ethical superiority and maternal self-sacrifice. The London prostitutes, however, make crudely obvious to Tristan what she tacitly understood: that in the eyes of society all women who wander beyond the bounds of domestic or sanctioned public space bear the mark of sexual taint and suspect economic independence. Unable and unwilling to find her heroic arena in the home, Tristan seized the political realm as her own and made exile a feminine, maternal, and sacred space of self-redemption.

[35] Olive Schreiner, *Letters*, vol. 1: 1871–1899, ed. Richard Rive (Oxford: Oxford University Press, 1988), p. 116.

FIVE

Elbowed in the Streets: Exposure and Authority in Elizabeth Gaskell's Urban Fictions

Manchester, the cotton-manufacturing center of Lancashire that Asa Briggs called the "shock city" of the Victorian age, made Elizabeth Gaskell a novelist. Indeed, it helped to make her the only major woman novelist of the era to forge and bequeath her own distinctive literary vision of urban life.[1] Hers is a vision that places female vulnerability, sexual danger, and the anxiety of power at its center and that poses questions about the rightful and problematic place of middle-class women—both as activists and as writers—in the resolution of social strife. Given the weight of a literary tradition that allotted to men the privileged position of urban rambler and observer but assigned women on the city streets the role of sexual victim, temptress, or illicit partner, Gaskell's was a double labor: she set out to claim *as a woman* the authority of urban spectatorship and interpretation and to work through the taint of exposure that was traditionally and powerfully associated with woman's public role. In this chapter I explore the methods and effects of this labor, suggest the intimate links between the political and sexual plots of Gaskell's fiction, examine her various rewritings of the fallen woman's story, and look at the consequences for Gaskell and her fiction of the trauma of public exposure. In Gaskell's own case exposure on the city streets and at the site of industrial conflict provided the subject of her fiction and stood as a kind of parable for the female writer's exposed position in the literary marketplace.[2]

[1] Asa Briggs, *Victorian Cities* (New York: Harper and Row, 1963), p. 96.

[2] Hilary M. Schor, *Scheherezade in the Marketplace: Elizabeth Gaskell and the Victorian Novel* (Oxford: Oxford University Press, 1992), touches on a number of the same themes in

If we begin by asking how and why Manchester made Gaskell a novelist, we might choose to find the answer in the accidents of her matrimonial history. In 1832 Elizabeth Cleghorn Stevenson, of London and Knutsford in Cheshire, married William Gaskell, Unitarian minister of Cross Street Chapel in Manchester, and moved to the industrial North, where she bore four children, began to write fiction, and became a successful and celebrated novelist. But the more telling, if more speculative, answer lies elsewhere, in the nature of the city itself, the kinds of class relations it bred, the place it gave to middle-class women in the dynamics of those relations, the sexual politics of manufacturing, and the sheer physical and spatial configurations of the town, its neighborhoods, and its streets.

In *The Country and the City* Raymond Williams describes Manchester as a concentration or distillation of the class relations that were also, of course, present in London. In the metropolis, however, "social relations . . . were more complex, more mystified," less available to a stark understanding of the schisms and tensions within society.[3] Though hardly reducible to a system of "masters" and "men," the lines of power, privilege, and exploitation were nonetheless more simply drawn in Manchester, and more accessible to schematic representation in fiction, blue book, and social investigation in the middle decades of the century.[4] Not only was an industrial working class large, dominant, and easily identifiable in the northern manufacturing towns, but also middle-class authority of a variety of kinds held sway there without substantial competition from aristocratic sources of power. The industrial towns, and above all Manchester, provided what one historian has called "the 'theatre' for the expression and consolidation of middle-class power."[5] Power was not just economic but cultural, political, and

---

Gaskell's work and life that I discuss here. Her excellent chapter on *Mary Barton*, for example, focuses on issues of "authority and authorship," and she has interesting things to say about Gaskell's extreme reticence in taking on political material and about her fears of being exposed as the author of her own work (pp. 25–28).

[3] Raymond Williams, *The Country and the City* (London: Chatto and Windus, 1973), pp. 219–20.

[4] Raymond Williams and others have talked about the way in which east and west became organizing structures and metaphors for understanding late-century London. Not until the 1880s, Williams observes, did this physical contrast become "an interpretive image" (ibid., p. 220).

[5] Alan J. Kidd, "The Middle Class in Nineteenth-Century Manchester," in *City, Class, and Culture: Studies of Social Policy and Cultural Production in Victorian Manchester*, ed. Alan J. Kidd and K. W. Roberts (Manchester: Manchester University Press, 1985), p. 5. I endorse Kidd's suggestion that we "need to examine more closely (and in a broader theoretical perspective) the complex, and sometimes contradictory, matrix of values, practices and institutions which constituted Victorian middle class ideology" (p. 17).

religious, and it signified responsibility and opportunity as well as dominance. The middle class could be imagined as the opponent of working-class peace and well-being; it could also be understood as a battleground of competing and conflicting ideologies and a field into which the novelist or social reformer might venture to instruct, debate, and convert.

Throughout the decade preceding the publication of Gaskell's first industrial novel, *Mary Barton* (1848), middle-class women writers did not shy away from the subject of industrial labor and conflict, from writing about strikes, machines, unions, and wages. In fact, as literary historians such as Wanda Neff and Ellen Moers have observed, women in the 1830s and 1840s took issues of industrial life as their special province and entered into debates about class relations, the causes of poverty, and factory reform with a sense of woman's mission to instruct, explain, and comfort.[6] The tales, novels, and poems of Charlotte Tonna, Harriet Martineau, Frances Trollope, Caroline Norton, and Elizabeth Barrett—and before them Mrs. Jane Marcet in her *Conversations on Political Economy* (1816)—formed a tradition that was primarily didactic and, in part, a response by middle-class women to the ways in which industrial towns and factory labor had radically transformed the lives of working-class women and their families.

According to the census returns of 1841, the largest category of employment for women at the time was domestic service, with roughly 700,000 women working as servants; next, accounting for another 115,000 women, was cotton manufacture.[7] By the mid-1840s over half the workers employed in cotton mills and 70 percent of workers in woolen and silk mills were female.[8] Not only was the manufacturing of cotton and other textiles *women's* work, but it was, because it collected women into groups in the workplace, visibly so. Unlike domestic workers, who were dispersed and virtually invisible except within the private space of the home, women factory workers constituted a recognizable collectivity, not only to those middle-class observers who visited the factories but also to those who saw them on the streets and in public places, going to and from work in groups (figure 14 shows a group of

[6] Wanda Fraiken Neff, *Victorian Working Women: An Historical and Literary Study of Women in British Industries and Professions, 1820–1850* (New York: Columbia University Press, 1929); and Ellen Moers, *Literary Women: The Great Writers* (New York: Doubleday, 1976), esp. pp. 22–30.

[7] Ivy Pinchbeck, *Women Workers and the Industrial Revolution, 1750–1850* (1930; rpt. London: Virago, 1969), p. 317. The silk and wool industries accounted for another 50,000 women workers.

[8] Ibid., p. 197.

Figure 14 Eyre Crowe, "The Dinner Hour, Wigan" (1874). © Manchester City Art Galleries.

female factory workers taking an outdoor dinner break). Visitors, among them Disraeli and Engels, regularly remarked on the presence of women in the factories, and virtually all discussions of women's labor in textile manufacturing touched on its deleterious effects on the family, its damage to femininity, and its threats to masculinity.[9]

The largely middle-class rhetoric of opposition to women's work in factories revolved around two major concerns: the displacement of male workers and the disintegration of family life.[10] Underlying these concerns were anxieties about female chastity and the subversion of supposedly "natural" sexual differences. Léon Faucher, a Frenchman whose articles on Manchester for the *Revue des deux mondes* were widely

[9] See Steven Marcus, *Engels, Manchester, and the Working Class* (New York: Random House, 1974), pp. 42–43. As part of a series on manufacturing for *Household Words*, Harriet Martineau published an article on the first Evening School for Women, opened in the late 1840s in Birmingham to teach women factory workers a variety of domestic skills. Martineau believed that on the whole it was "a pleasant thing to see, in a very large manufacturing town, lofty and well-lighted rooms filled with women, busy at their work of burnishing, stamping, and punching, painting, or varnishing," but she also thought it lamentable how few of these women could boil a potato or make a shirt. She therefore applauded the Evening School's efforts to take women's labor as an established fact and to remedy whatever disabilities it might have caused. [Harriet Martineau], "The New School for Wives," *Household Words*, April 3, 1852, pp. 84–89.

[10] Pinchbeck, *Women Workers*, p. 196.

read in English translation, followed a passage on prostitution in the industrial city with a discussion of the factory system's inability to foster "regularity of conduct" among its workers.[11] "The factory girls are strangers to modesty," writes Faucher. "Their language is gross, and often obscene; and when they do not marry early, they form illicit connexions, which degrade them still more than premature marriage." He goes on to describe couples strolling in the back streets of town during their breaks from labor or entering the beer shop in a "double debauch."[12] For him the question of promiscuity among factory workers was inseparable from the question of prostitution. He ends by citing the example of a young woman who worked thirteen hours a day in a factory before retiring each evening to a brothel, where she found lodging and worked as a servant.[13] The apparent moral ignorance of this girl—her inability to distinguish between types of labor—convinced Faucher that the factory system itself mixed work and debauchery, virtue and vice, in insidious ways.

Faucher's contemporary Friedrich Engels also commented on the moral dangers of factory work for women, repeating the Frenchman's observations about indecent language, the promiscuous crowding together of male and female workers, and the ease with which factory girls drifted into prostitution. In the first of two chapters on "The Proletariat" in *The Condition of the Working Class in England* (1845), Engels reports that three quarters of women between the ages of fourteen and twenty working in factories were unchaste, that most of the prostitutes in Leicester "had factories to thank for their present degradation," and that at least one witness before a parliamentary commission declared he would rather see his daughter beg than work in a factory.[14] Engels reproduces Faucher's moral rather than his economic analysis but adds to it the dimension of class exploitation: the factory owner corrupts his female workers through coercion and threat of dismissal and makes of his factory a "harem" (p. 168).

For Engels, however, the threat to the family posed by the structure of factory labor is of a piece with its threat to female chastity. Young

[11] Leon Faucher, *Manchester in 1844*, trans. with notes by "A Member of the Manchester Athenaeum" (1844; rpt. London: Frank Cass, 1969), p. 45. See Marcus, *Engels*, p. 57, on Faucher and on Engels's response to his articles.

[12] Faucher, *Manchester in 1844*, p. 46.

[13] Ibid., p. 47.

[14] Friedrich Engels, *The Condition of the Working Class in England*, trans. W. O. Henderson and W. H. Chaloner (Stanford: Stanford University Press, 1958), pp. 166–67; subsequently cited in the text.

women who work never learn to care for babies or homes; mothers who work leave children unsupervised and unloved: "A married woman cannot really be regarded as a mother if she is unable to spare the time to look after her child. . . . Such a mother is inevitably indifferent to the welfare of the child, which she treats without love and without proper care as if it were a stranger" (p. 161). This disintegration leads to the "universal decadence" of family life and to the "reversal of the normal division of labour within the family" as women go out to work while men, unemployed and displaced in the economy, are left at home to tend to the house. Engels imagines the anger of these male workers as they are "virtually turned into eunuchs" (p. 162). Although he clearly asserts that the traditional dominance of the husband is not natural but based on property relations, he does not avoid using a highly charged language of sexual chaos and gender confusion. This system of labor, he concludes, "deprives the husband of his manhood and the wife of all womanly qualities. . . . It is a state of affairs shameful and degrading to the human attributes of the sexes" (p. 164). Engels's analysis makes clear that this particular desexing of working-class men and women shifted the balance of power between them and made women not just unchaste but dominant in the sphere of public life. The notion of "unwomanliness" conflated anxieties about woman's sexual deviance with those about her unnatural economic power.

Gaskell took up issues of women's labor that were a matter of public controversy and made them the subjects of her urban fictions. Responding to the sexual ideologies that inform Faucher's and Engels's accounts, she used her novels to ruminate on the linked potential for danger and power inherent in women's participation in the public domain of industrial life. In *Mary Barton* she focuses on the working-class woman's experience of sexual danger and the power of bearing witness, and in *North and South* she moves on to the middle-class woman's exposure as political actor and sexual outlaw, making use of the sexual discourses surrounding working women to talk about women like herself. In these novels women work outside the home, give public testimony, intervene in class strife, flout laws and social convention, venture opinions about politics and the management of business, and enter forbidden or restricted areas of the city. All such public gestures in Gaskell's fiction offer women satisfaction, even triumph, and yet they also expose women to trauma and nearly irreversible disgrace.

In the preface to *Mary Barton*, Gaskell establishes the origins of her first novel in terms of her public experience of Manchester's streets and the anxiety of a deeply personal loss. The death of her infant son in 1845, to which she only alludes in the preface, left her with the need to "employ" herself in the writing of fiction. At first her longing for the country from the confines of industrial Manchester suggested to her a nostalgic subject in a rural setting. But then present experience overtook memory and longing as she wondered "how deep might be the romance in the lives of some of those who elbowed me daily in the busy streets of the town in which I resided."[15] Detecting "romance" in the lives of the common people is a more or less conventional gesture. As Dickens would write in the preface to *Bleak House* just a few years later, he dwelt in that novel on "the romantic side of familiar things."[16] More idiosyncratic and noteworthy, however, is the way in which Gaskell writes into her observation of others their engagement with her and makes the impact of the crowd on her just as crucial to her role as novelist as her vision of them. On the busy streets where she notes the careworn faces of working people and reads in them stories of loss, hunger, and rage, she herself is "elbowed," made conscious of herself and her own exposed position. Unlike the traditional male spectator, who depends on his invisibility and immunity within the crowd, the female spectator must always be both observer and observed, privileged and vulnerable.

Gaskell's experience of being elbowed and exposed may be said to have been the starting point for her fiction.[17] In three separate places in her writing, beginning with the first story she published on her own, Gaskell includes a version of the formative moment she describes in the preface to *Mary Barton*. In "The Three Eras of Libbie Marsh," published in 1847 in *Howitt's Journal of Literature and Popular Progress*, she establishes the plainness of the heroine early in the story with a statement about the general condition of being a woman on Manchester's streets: "You can hardly live in Manchester without having some idea of your personal appearance. The factory lads and lasses take good care of that, and if you meet them at the hours when they are pouring out of the mills, you are sure to hear a good number of truths, some

[15] Elizabeth Gaskell, preface to *Mary Barton: A Tale of Manchester Life* (1848; rpt. Harmondsworth: Penguin, 1970), p. 37; subsequently cited in the text.

[16] Charles Dickens, preface to *Bleak House* (1853; rpt. Harmondsworth: Penguin, 1971), p. 43.

[17] Walter Benjamin distinguishes between the "pedestrian," who "wedged himself into the crowd," and the flaneur, "who demanded elbow room." See Walter Benjamin, *Charles Baudelaire: A Lyric Poet in the Era of High Capitalism*, trans. Harry Zohn (London: New Left Books, 1973), p. 54.

of them combined with such a spirit of impudent fun, that you can scarcely keep from laughing even at the joke against yourself."[18] This passage strikes the reader as a statement as much about its author as about Libbie Marsh, as much about Gaskell as her next version of it in the preface was intended to be. It also clearly prefigures two other passages in Gaskell's work in which the narrator connects the heroine's experience of the streets with her developing sexual self-consciousness. Mary Barton, the working-class heroine who courts danger by aspiring to be the wife of a gentleman, is "let into . . . the secret of her beauty" and its power to attract the attention of men by the "factory people as they poured from the mills, and in their freedom told the truth (whatever it might be) to every passer-by" (p. 62).

In *North and South* Margaret Hale, Mary's middle-class counterpart, falls in with factory workers as she tries to cross the side of town where they work, and finds herself the object of women's comments on her clothing and, what is more disturbing, men's comments on her looks. Margaret, a woman who had always regarded "the most refined remark on her personal appearance . . . an impertinence," reacts at first with fear, then with indignation, and finally with amusement.[19] These moments of exposure initiate for Margaret a dual process in which she will ultimately become a self-conscious sexual being and discover her vocation as advocate for the distressed workers of the town (one of the men who comments on her "bonny face" turns out to be Nicholas Higgins, the workingman who educates both Margaret and the factory owner Mr. Thornton about the nature of class conflict).

The repetition of this scene of exposure—of being looked at on the street and assessed as an object of sexual interest—and the variation on it Gaskell used to explain the genesis of *Mary Barton* suggest its importance in the creation of her identity as urban novelist, as public woman, and as social critic. Manchester's streets made her a novelist not only because of what they taught her about the working people she encountered but also because of what they suggested to her about herself, her potential cultural authority, and her sexual vulnerability.

Steven Marcus remarks of Engels that he "learned how to read a city in the company—or through the mediation—of an illiterate factory

---

[18] Elizabeth Gaskell, "The Three Eras of Libbie Marsh," in *Elizabeth Gaskell: Four Short Stories* (London: Pandora Press, 1981), p. 24. See Ana Walters's introduction to this edition for details of the publication of "Libbie Marsh" in *Howitt's Journal* (p. 2).

[19] Elizabeth Gaskell, *North and South* (1855; rpt. Harmondsworth: Penguin, 1970), p. 110; subsequently cited in the text.

girl," Mary Burns, who was also his mistress, and suggests that Engels's vocational and ideological story was also a sexual one.[20] Choosing to write about Manchester was, as Marcus points out, a choice to write about his own experience, "to contend with it, to exploit it, to clarify it, and in some literal sense to create it and thereby himself."[21] Of Gaskell we can say the same: she wrote about Manchester in order to write about the experience of becoming a writer, of needing and seeking "employment," of being "elbowed" in the streets by a class of people with whom she felt a troubling identification, and of claiming those subjects for her fiction that would associate her with scandal, sin, and unwomanliness. As Engels powerfully rewrote the relationship between middle class and proletariat generated by his personal history, so did Gaskell embark on rewriting the story of woman's sexual fall and its relationship to urban life. In *Mary Barton*, *North and South*, and *Ruth*, the "fallen woman" novel linked to Gaskell's two industrial fictions by its urban themes of disease and illicit sexuality, the novelist tries to come to terms with the trauma of public exposure and the anxieties of authority.

In his seminal work on the industrial novel in *Culture and Society*, Raymond Williams credits *Mary Barton* with offering "the most moving response in literature to the industrial suffering of the 1840s" and then goes on to make the critical point that has had the greatest influence on subsequent readings of the novel: after the early chapters, in which the narrative focuses on the agonies of the working man John Barton (the center of Gaskell's original plans for the novel), the "flow of sympathy" is redirected in the text to the "less compromising figure" of Mary. Furthermore, the murder of Harry Carson by John Barton irrevocably cripples the reader's identification with the working man and serves to dramatize the "fear of violence . . . widespread among the upper and middle classes."[22] Unable to sustain real sympathy for a man whose rage against "the masters" leads him to trade unionism, Chartism, and beyond, Williams suggests, Gaskell lets her class identification

---

[20] Marcus writes: "There should be nothing very disquieting about this coming together of young Engels' passage into the hidden regions and meanings of Manchester and the developing course of his first extended sexual relation. The erotic, the social, and the intellectual passions regularly reinforce one another, or mingle in common interanimation" (*Engels*, p. 99).

[21] Ibid., p. 145.

[22] Raymond Williams, *Culture and Society, 1780–1950* (Harmondsworth: Penguin, 1961), p. 102.

overwhelm her initial intentions, and she uses the murder—an unrepresentative action—to drive a wedge between herself and John Barton. But Williams's next comment on the murder complicates this reading: this "act of violence, a sudden aggression against a man contemptuous of the sufferings of the poor, looks very much like a projection, with which, in the end, [Gaskell] was unable to come to terms."[23] The murder, then, places Gaskell imaginatively in two conflicting positions: as fearful middle-class victim of working-class violence and as enraged perpetrator of that violence. Gaskell did indeed see herself and her novel as mediators between these two positions or visions, and she understood her task as one of translation. Just as her husband, because of his knowledge of etymology, was able to provide glosses for the Lancashire dialect in the text, so Gaskell believed herself particularly well placed to explain to her own class the sensibility and grievances of the Lancashire workers.[24]

Another version of the novel's origins—this one related by Gaskell to a journalist—suggests why she may have felt this way. The impulse to write *Mary Barton* came to her not on the street but in a laborer's cottage, she claimed, while she was trying to calm the anger of a hungry and bitter father. The man grabbed her arm and challenged her tearfully, "Ay, ma'am, but have ye ever seen a child clemmed to death?"[25] Although the anecdote ends there, with the clear implication that Gaskell had no retort and would take upon herself the amplification and dramatization of this query in fiction, we can imagine a slightly different, albeit unstated, conclusion. Gaskell's ten-month-old son had not starved to death, but her experience of loss and profound grieving— she wrote to a friend that this "wound will never heal on earth," that it had changed her beyond what anyone could imagine—corresponded in some way to the agony of this man.[26] Because she had seen her child die, she could write from both inside and outside his despair, expressing it as her own and rendering it coherent to readers of her own class.

[23] Ibid., p. 102.

[24] William Gaskell's notes on Lancashire dialect do not simply translate the words but very often locate them in passages from classic English works such as *Piers Plowman* and *The Canterbury Tales* in order to suggest their legitimacy. His wife's novel appears to share the same impulse and the same method.

[25] John Geoffrey Sharps, *Mrs. Gaskell's Observation and Invention: A Study of Her Non-Biographic Works* (Fontwell, Sussex: Linden Press, 1970), p. 56. If readers of Gaskell's novels retain just one word of Lancashire dialect, it is bound to be "clemmed," which means starved.

[26] *The Letters of Mrs. Gaskell*, ed. J. A. V. Chapple and Arthur Pollard (Manchester: Manchester University Press, 1966), pp. 56–57.

Indeed, she uses the death of a son as the primary healing link between Barton, the murderer, and Carson, the mill owner and father of his victim.[27]

Engels argued in *The Condition of the Working Class* that separation and invisibility were the geographic and social principles that governed relations between the proletariat and the bourgeoisie of Manchester. The town was unique in Engels's experience in "the systematic way in which the working classes have been barred from the main streets" and the "tender susceptibilities of the eyes and nerves of the middle classes" were thereby protected (p. 56).[28] A middle-class man might live in Manchester for years, he claimed, and travel daily to and from work in the center of town without ever seeing a slum or a slum dweller. For Gaskell, given her experience of the streets and the laborer's cottage as well as her Christian commitment to reconciliation, the primary principle that defines relations between classes in *Mary Barton* is not, of course, separation but connection.[29] The novel also makes clear, however, that connection itself can be invisible to a callous and uneducated middle class, and that a second, more insidious principle—contrast— can supplant it in the minds of the aggrieved working class.

Although Gaskell's aim is to replace the structure of contrast between rich and poor with a structure of encounters (like her own) and con-

---

[27] See Sharps, *Mrs. Gaskell's Observation and Invention*, p. 70, for his discussion of three incidents in the novel in which central characters' encounters with unknown children in the street interrupt their self-absorption.

[28] In relation to Engels's observations on the separation of classes in Manchester, Marcus quotes from John Stuart Mill's essay "Civilization": "One of the effects of civilization (not to say one of the ingredients in it) is, that the spectacle, and even the very idea of pain, is kept more and more out of the sight of those classes who enjoy in their fullness the benefits of civilization" (*Engels*, 174–75). Gaskell emphasizes the tormenting visibility of these "benefits" to those who are in pain.

[29] The precise nature and extent of Gaskell's personal observation of the poor in their homes, rather than on the streets, is difficult to establish. Sharps records that she was one of the first volunteer visitors for the Manchester and Salford District Provident Society (*Mrs. Gaskell's Observation and Invention*, pp. 56–57), and we know too that she was active in prison philanthropy and in teaching girls' Sunday school. See "A Manchester Correspondent" [Mat Hompes], "Mrs. Gaskell and Her Social Work among the Poor," *Inquirer and Christian Life* (London), October 8, 1910, p. 656. R. K. Webb, however, suggests that Gaskell's "immediate experience of the poor" has been exaggerated, and that "much of what she wrote to enlighten her ignorant and unfeeling audience she had to learn from reading." R. K. Webb, "The Gaskells as Unitarians," in *Dickens and Other Victorians: Essays in Honour of Philip Collins* (London: Macmillan, 1988), p. 159. I suspect that Webb is correct here; but Gaskell's sympathetic evocation of the lives of industrial workers nonetheless surpasses in power and verisimilitude those of other industrial novelists, for, whether she spent much time in workers' homes or not, she did indeed live in their midst.

nection, her narrative gives powerful emotional weight to the poor's perception of inequality and painful difference which in John Barton's case becomes a "monomania" (p. 218). As his son lies at home dying of scarlet fever and malnutrition, an out-of-work John Barton stands before a shop window filled with "haunches of venison, Stilton cheeses, moulds of jelly," and watches in amazement as his former master's wife emerges from the shop loaded down with delicacies. The narrator turns the screw of ironic contrast once more: "And Barton returned home with a bitter spirit of wrath in his heart, to see his only boy a corpse!" (p. 61).

Well-filled and brightly lit shop windows figure in a second, more extended use of contrast in the novel, when Barton and George Wilson, after visiting the fever-racked Davenports in their damp, dark, fetid cellar dwelling, attempt to buy medicine and obtain an infirmary order from Davenport's employer. As Barton searches for a druggist, the narrative insists on the difference between the middle-class reader's delighted and nostalgic response to the phantasmagoria of the gaslit streets and Barton's angry awareness that they merely provide a painful contrast to the Davenports' gloomy cellar (p. 101). Similarly, when Wilson enters the kitchen of Davenport's employer, Mr. Carson, the narrative exploits the contrast between the worker's typhus-ridden dwelling and the master's kitchen, where smells of coffee brewing and steaks broiling fill the air and comfort the soul. What the middle-class reader might take for granted, Gaskell repeatedly underlines, the poor have never known; and when the starving witness the bounty of the well fed, they feel betrayal and anger.

Gaskell's own anger about the contrasts she so skillfully evokes—and to which Williams seems to allude when he writes of her "projection"—seeps into the text even as she tries to enlighten her readers in a measured and nonpartisan way. Her efforts at being evenhanded are often disrupted by both the sense of injustice she feels on behalf of the poor and her anxiety over seeming to accuse the rich. In the novel's preface her prose gets twisted out of shape by defensiveness and denial. She observes straightforwardly that working people are sore and irritable toward the rich, but she then introduces the language of equivocation: "whether" their grievances are "well-founded or no" is not for her to judge; the workers' sense of "injustice and unkindness" is a "belief"; the belief might be erroneous; and, finally, since she knows nothing of "Political Economy or theories of trade," it is only by accident that her views match those of theorists and other systematic critics (pp. 37–38).

These disavowals are in turn undercut by parenthetical phrases that legitimate the workers' rage, such as reminders that the fortunes amassed by the rich were in fact produced by the poor.

A similar kind of equivocation characterizes the description of the depression of 1839–41 which prefaces a discussion of John Barton's Chartist activity. Here Gaskell oscillates between blaming her Christian readers for their indifference to suffering and excusing them by reason of their ignorance (p. 126). She manipulates her readers' arrogance, pride, and guilt and, in so doing, tries to camouflage and control the sense of injustice she feels on behalf of the poor. Ostensibly she wants to explain the resentment that fueled Chartism without justifying it, but her own declaration of the guilty ignorance or callousness of the middle class establishes a justification nonetheless.

The murder of Harry Carson, then, constitutes a gesture that gives full vent to Gaskell's anger and seemingly closes her off from an identification with the deed. But the murder is not simply an act of vengeance against a man who is, as Williams observes, contemptuous of the sufferings of the poor. It is also an act of aggression against the man who threatens the chastity and future of Mary Barton. Thus, the "projection" of which Williams speaks expresses an overdetermined need to punish Carson for his crimes against worker and woman alike. The murderer is, of course, Mary's father, who, although he does not know of her secret relationship with Carson, is anxious about her chastity. In addition, Carson's arrogant indifference to Mary's well-being—an analogue of his extreme harshness toward the striking workers—functions as an important element in the novel by making it difficult for the reader to feel his murder as a loss or even as an unequivocal moral wrong. The narrative uses his caricatured upper-class lecherousness to mitigate, almost to cancel out, the horror of the crime against him. Here, as elsewhere, the novel conflates the story of threatened female virtue with that of the oppression of the poor. The murder is often identified by critics, however, as the turning point after which the novel's focus shifts from John Barton's working-class plot to the romantic plot involving his daughter.[30] As I hope to show, Gaskell's

---

[30] Raymond Williams is, I have said, foremost among those critics who have described this narrative shift. Catherine Gallagher treats the narrative inconsistencies in *Mary Barton* at some length in *The Industrial Reformation of English Fiction, 1832–1867* (Chicago: University of Chicago Press, 1985), chap. 3. Only after the murder, she argues, does Gaskell achieve "a kind of generic consistency by retreating into the domestic mentality of her heroine"; but this involves a "suppression of the tragic narrative" which seems to separate the novel into "mutually exclusive stories" (p. 67). Rosemarie Bodenheimer, in her ex-

rewriting of the sexual plot is at all points inseparable from the plot of class antagonism and is in a real sense both the starting point and the dominant preoccupation of her text.

The novel opens on the scene of a group of factory girls walking in Green Heys Fields and soon thereafter enters into the debate about the liabilities of factory work for women which we have seen in the commentaries of Faucher and Engels. The "merry and loud-talking" girls, clad in inventively arranged shawls, introduce the novel's implicit concern with the dangers and delights of woman's public role (p. 40). Although John Barton will, in a matter of pages, articulate the view that factory work corrupts women and is in all likelihood the cause of his sister-in-law Esther's sexual fall and disappearance, we have before us in these opening pages an image of young women unremarkable in every respect save "an acuteness and intelligence of countenance" (p. 41). Although no one character in the novel fully articulates the argument against Barton's position, the narrative itself—beginning with its opening portrait of the energetic, healthy, and intelligent-looking factory girls—continually undercuts the connection he makes between women's factory work and their sexual corruption.[31] Barton, who would prefer that Mary take up domestic service or dressmaking—occupations associated with a more private, less exposed setting—remains ignorant of the circumstances under which Mary finds employment. When Barton tries to find a job for Mary as a dressmaker he fails, not realizing that if she had accompanied him, her beauty would have won her a position as a "show-woman" (p. 63). Ultimately, of course, Mary finds herself a job as an apprentice on her own. But far from sheltering Mary from exposure, the dressmaker's shop "in a respectable little street" provides the setting for her introduction to Harry Carson, who notices her while waiting for his sisters to make purchases (p. 121). Neither was the factory responsible for Esther's seduction into an illicit relationship: her lover, an army officer, had no connection to the world of industrial manufacture.

For John Barton it is the economic independence, the money to spend on finery, and the late hours that make factory work so danger-

---

cellent essay "Private Grief and Public Acts in *Mary Barton*," in *Dickens Studies Annual*, vol. 9 (New York: AMS Press, 1981), p. 207, argues that the plot of the novel "muffles" the connection between the stories of industrial and sexual exploitation, so that the two stories are split and never reconnected.

[31] Critics have often assumed that Gaskell essentially endorsed John Barton's position on factory work for women. See, for example, Aina Rubenius, *The Woman Question in Mrs. Gaskell's Life and Work* (Uppsala: Lundequistka Bokhanden, 1950), pp. 147–48.

ous to women's virtue. Mary's and Esther's experiences with men, however, have little or nothing to do with their work. This point is
underscored by Esther's conviction that dressmaking—"a bad life for
a girl"—puts Mary in danger by forcing her to return home late at
night and subjecting her to such tedium that she will search after "any
novelty that makes a little change" (pp. 211–12). The street does expose women to danger, Gaskell suggests, but it is the desire to escape
work rather than the work itself that imperils them. Before her disappearance Esther talks seductively to Mary of becoming a lady, and Mary,
too, in a subtle form of rebellion against her father's detestation of
"gentlefolk," aspires to marry out of her class. Gaskell endorses the
apparently traditional notion that hard work is the safe and moral
course to good fortune, but she insists that this precept should apply
to working-class women as well as men. We need only think of fictional
heroines from Richardson's Pamela to Brontë's Jane Eyre to Disraeli's
Sybil to appreciate the cultural power of the competing idea of marriage as the route to upward mobility for "women of the people."

The novel's challenge to the myth that work, and especially factory
work, corrupts women complements its undermining of a number of
myths surrounding the figure of the fallen woman. Esther's narrative
in chapter 14 contests the notion that sheer depravity determines the
prostitute's life; it is rather economic necessity that drives those decisions that appear sinful to the respectable world. Esther ran off with
her officer for love rather than for vanity's sake, and she took to the
streets only when, abandoned, impoverished, and unable to make a go
of her shop in Chester, she had no other way to provide for her small
daughter, by now starving and deathly ill.[32] By playing the card of the
dying child, Gaskell reclaims Esther from her status as pariah and sit-
uates her within the framework of parental devotion and bereavement
that weaves classes together in the novel and binds John Barton and
the elder Carson to the author herself.[33]

Although the novel represents Esther as beyond redemption—she is
treated as a leper, addicted to drink, allied with an urban underworld

[32] Amanda Anderson, in *Tainted Souls and Painted Faces* (Ithaca: Cornell University Press,
1993), remarks that Esther's seduction by her army officer has "a distinctly literary flavor"
(p. 118), unlike Mary's near-seduction by a manufacturer's son. Although Esther's narrative does have the "literary" character Anderson detects, the moment when Esther
goes out on the streets to prostitute herself has a crucial economic dimension.

[33] Esther is closely associated with her brother-in-law John Barton, who had shunned
her after she became a prostitute. They both end up outcasts or "wanderers," buried in
the same grave (*Mary Barton*, p. 465).

of beggars, thieves, and whores—it also suggests that hers is a role created by society, not decreed by nature or by some higher morality. The novel accomplishes this in the remarkable and chilling scene of Esther's visit to Mary after the murder of Harry Carson. Wishing to place in her niece's hands the incriminating evidence she had found at the scene of the murder and yet hoping to spare her the knowledge that her aunt is "a prostitute; an outcast," Esther disguises herself as a respectable laborer's wife.[34] Reversing the usual downward trajectory associated with the theme of the pawnshop, Esther goes to a shop where she is well known and trades her gaudy streetwalker's clothes for "a black silk bonnet, a printed gown, a plaid shawl . . . the appropriate garb of that happy class to which she could never, never more belong" (p. 292). The disguise of respectability requires not merely clothing, however, but the "manners and character . . . of a mechanic's wife" (p. 293); and Esther plays the part so convincingly that she leaves the Barton home disappointed that she has not elicited from Mary the sympathy for her desperate situation she had silently craved. This scene raises the possibility that even "character" can be adopted, put on and taken off, played like a part, and that a woman like Esther is no more definable by the prostitute's finery that first announces her profession to John Barton than she is by the costume of a laborer's wife.

The scene also breaks the imagined circuit of influence into which some feared that Mary would be drawn by her aunt. Her father frets over the potential threat of Esther's legacy, worries about the foolish desire for wealth that Mary has in common with her aunt, and even, after Esther has gone, about the "very bodily likeness" between the two women which to him signals the possibility of "a similar likeness in their fate" (p. 172). Here the idea of an inherited taint affecting the female line, so crucial to Dickens's vision in *Dombey and Son* and *Bleak House*, is offered and then decisively rejected. Just as John Barton mistakenly believes that the factory itself would have a corrupting effect on his daughter, so too does he assign moral meaning to her physical resemblance to her aunt. But Esther's influence on Mary has not been indelible; and although the niece also attracts the attention of a man above her in station, she escapes sexual danger. She will, in fact, end

[34] See Hilary Schor's discussion of this scene, in which she treats Esther's appearance at Mary's door as the ghostly return of Mary's mother and also considers Esther's role as a "narratorial surrogate" (*Scheherezade in the Marketplace*, p. 30). Amanda Anderson reads Esther's disguise as a means of protecting Mary from contamination (*Tainted Souls and Painted Faces*, p. 123).

as a mechanic's wife, the very role that Esther chooses for her disguise. For this one moment at least, the two women's identities are suggestively interchangeable.

The connection between Barton's fear for his daughter's chastity and his murder of Harry Carson, the man who threatens that chastity, is one of the elements in the novel that fuses the plot of class antagonism with the sexual plot. Barton does not, of course, know of the relationship between Mary and the mill owner's son, but his intense psychic involvement from the very beginning of the narrative with the possibility of Mary's sexual fall suggests that his motives for murder are complex, multiple, and buried. And just as the picking of lots among the union men is meant to obscure and minimize the importance of the murderer's identity, so does the motive for murder float freely among many who know the victim. Jem, the prime suspect, knows about Mary's liaison with Carson, for Esther resorted to confiding in Jem about the danger to Mary's chastity when John Barton refused to listen. Barton is thus a surrogate both for Jem, the man who stands in for Barton in people's suspicions, and for his fellow workers.[35]

Moreover, the text underscores the parallel between Carson's treatment of Mary and his treatment of the striking workers. When Jem approaches Carson to try to reason with him about Mary, Carson treats him with disdain and mocks him as a meddling negotiator in their affairs: "Neither Mary nor I called you in as a mediator," he sneers (p. 229). Jem's "mediation" having failed, the interview ends in violence, with Carson striking the first blow and Jem's assault on the suddenly supine Carson—like Barton's fatal attack—elided from the text.[36] In the chapter that follows Carson reveals himself to be unyielding and punitive toward the strikers: he is identified as an extremist, "the head and voice of the violent party among the masters" (p. 234). He proposes that all communication between masters and union be suspended, that scabs be hired, and that no workers be employed in the future unless they swear independence from any trade union. Before the chapter ends, the aggrieved strikers, as if in direct and commensurate response to the kind of oath Carson wishes to extract from them, swear their own oath to murder him. They use for lots pieces of paper

---

[35] Rosemarie Bodenheimer refers to Jem and John Barton as "split doubles" in the murder plot ("Private Grief and Public Acts," p. 207).

[36] "The young man raised his slight cane, and smote the artizan across the face with a stinging stroke. An instant afterwards he lay stretched in the muddy road, Jem standing over him, panting with rage" (*Mary Barton*, p. 230).

torn from a caricature of themselves—"lank, ragged, dispirited, and famine-stricken"—which Carson had sketched earlier that day (p. 235). The upper-class rake and the mocking oppressor of the poor are joined in Harry Carson.

Although I would not disagree entirely with the critical view that after the murder the joint plot of industrial strife and sexual danger is sundered, I would describe this change in the narrative differently. As I have suggested, the novel concerns itself from the very first with the public role of women, especially but not exclusively Mary's role. After the murder, however, Mary is transformed from the passive subject of discussions of her sexual virtue and proper role to the active agent of her own fate. The efforts of those around her in the early part of the novel to keep her out of the public eye, to tie her safely to private domestic space, are totally defeated in the second half. Her ascendancy in the story marks an awakening of consciousness and purpose that reproduces the workers' earlier mobilization. Like them, she must go beyond even the public sphere of work and engage in the wider world of politics and law.[37] To the extent that she is the workers' double— that they are parallel victims of Carson's callousness and arrogance— she serves to vindicate them as she exonerates Jem and herself. The actual murderer, John Barton, never does come to trial, and the elder Carson's desire for revenge is severely criticized in the novel. As a result, the hearing in Liverpool takes the place of a public judgment of Barton and dispels the need to punish the perpetrator of an act whose criminality is represented with equivocation.[38] Mary succeeds, after all, not only in establishing Jem's innocence but also in protecting her father's guilt.

Mary's entry into public life is inaugurated dramatically by the novel experience of travel: she journeys to Liverpool on her first train ride and then searches for Will Wilson's ship at the Liverpool docks by going on a boat, also for the first time. The train ride places her definitively

---

[37] Rosemarie Bodenheimer's reading of the novel here, as elsewhere, is very close to mine. She writes: "In Mary's burst of heroism Gaskell imagined an even more direct image [than John Barton] of her own situation. For writing *Mary Barton* was her kind of 'bodily or mental action in time of distress,' and it leads, like Mary's journey, out of the domestic world and into a public one where one's deepest feelings are put on display for a curious crowd" ("Private Grief and Public Acts," p. 214).

[38] Commenting on Mr. Carson's passion for revenge, the narrator declares, "Oh! Orestes! you would have made a very tolerable Christian of the nineteenth century!" (*Mary Barton*, p. 266). Although the text evinces sympathy for Carson's loss, at no point does it sanction his desire to avenge his son's murder.

in a world cut off from the limitations and protection of home and also offers her the chance to understand her home as the city of Manchester itself. Facing backwards as the train leaves for Liverpool, Mary looks "towards the factory-chimneys, and the cloud of smoke which hovers over Manchester" (p. 343) and feels the new sensation of homesickness (Gaskell uses the German *Heimweh*). These sights, which the narrator concedes are unpleasant to most, evoke in Mary a yearning for the place she has never left before. Leaving gives her an identity in the wider world, and yet it gives her a civic identity too by tying her in a wholly new way to the city itself. The solitary train ride also, of course, exposes her to public scrutiny, and as she visits the docks and finally enters the courtroom, her vulnerability deepens. In the rowboat, alone with two "rough, hard-looking men," Mary is subjected to the curses and insults of sailors and captains, who assume that her pursuit of Will to supply an alibi for Jem masks some illicit purpose (p. 354). Even the wife of the old boatman who befriends Mary and takes her to his home wonders if she can actually be as virtuous as she seems. The woman muses, "Perhaps thou'rt a bad one; I almost misdoubt thee, thou'rt so pretty" (p. 377). It is in the courtroom, however, that Mary is most traumatically read and misread by a crowd that has, after all, gathered to hear her "heart's secrets" (p. 390).

Mary's extraordinary exertions on Jem's behalf, and her father's, culminate in the hearing on the Carson murder and in her testimony under the scrutiny of hundreds of onlookers. As in the riot scene in *North and South*, to which this is a companion piece, the heroine claims for herself a public role in order to bear witness to what is just, and in so doing struggles painfully with the sexually charged image she unwillingly creates. Her very appearance and the stories that have circulated about her place in a romantic triangle that has ended in murder mark her in the eyes of "the hundreds [who] were looking at her" as a woman sullied by sexual scandal (p. 389). To Mr. Carson she is "the fatal Helen" (p. 388); to an acquaintance of the narrator who was present that day, she resembles nothing so much as an engraving of Beatrice Cenci, the Renaissance heroine whose portrait, as we saw in chapter 4, had so captured the imagination of the diarist Anna Jameson.[39] It is the essential innocence and "mute imploring agony" of the young woman that this allusion to Beatrice Cenci is intended to evoke;

[39] The notes to the Penguin edition of *Mary Barton* indicate that an engraving of a portrait of Beatrice Cenci in the Barberini Gallery in Rome appeared with an article on her in vol. 12 of *Bentley's Miscellany* (1847).

but the image also calls up the stain of incest, the crime of parricide, and the heroic force of the victim who rises to accuse the powerful. Beatrice Cenci is, then, a woman whose heroism is inseparable from taint, and Gaskell's choice of this allusion implies a far more extreme and dramatic level of scandal and guilt than Mary's case would seem to suggest. Also striking in this passage is the degree of distance the narrator puts between herself and this image of Mary: "I was not there myself; but one who was, told me . . ." (p. 389). As the narrative moves outside Mary to describe the spectator's point of view, the narrator begins to disclaim the description. It is as if the objectification of Mary that automatically associates her with sin must be put in someone else's mouth, and yet it must also be included in the narrative because of its powerful ability to shape the condition and consciousness of the public woman.

The eager young barrister who questions Mary gives voice to the prurient curiosity of the spectators as he asks her which man—Jem Wilson or Harry Carson—had been her "favoured lover" (p. 390). Already implicitly accused of transgression, Mary feels compelled to explain her misguided interest in Carson in terms of moral ignorance, a result of having lost her mother when a girl.[40] She admits to foolishness, giddiness, and vanity, and she "confesses" twice to loving Jem Wilson. Not on trial for any crime, not guilty of any sexual sin, she must nevertheless make her confession. At this moment Mary's acceptance of sin and her consciousness of her *father's* guilt merge, reminding us again of the complex meaning of the murder as retribution for Carson's analogous crimes against worker and woman. The authentic accomplishment of Mary's presence at the hearing, the successful clearing of Jem's name, is eclipsed by the trauma of personal exposure and the overwhelming tension of knowing and suppressing her father's story. Devastated by assuming her father's guilt and by being cast as a scandalous woman—as Helen or Beatrice Cenci—by the gawking crowd, Mary collapses in convulsions. As if her subjective self had been crushed by this assault, she is reduced to a delirious, disintegrated consciousness.

The narrative of woman's public identity that began with the factory girls in Green Heys Field comes to a strange close in what can only be described as the rebirth of Mary Barton following her collapse in Liv-

---

[40] In *Ruth* Gaskell makes the same connection between the loss of motherly guidance and moral ignorance.

erpool. After a prolonged delirium Mary awakens, her mind "in the tender state of a lately-born infant's" (p. 415). Upon first opening her eyes she sees Jem, who has been watching by her bedside throughout her illness: "She smiled gently, as a baby does when it sees its mother tending its little cot; and continued her innocent, infantine gaze into his face as if the sight gave her much unconscious pleasure" (p. 416). After the trauma of public exposure Mary is thus reborn into innocence, purged of whatever intimations of sin had clung to her in the role of scandalous woman. Jem's maternal presence hovers over and protects her, a replacement for the mother whose absence Mary had blamed for her inability to make moral discriminations. This rebirth is stamped with the author's pained ambivalence toward women's experience beyond the domestic sphere. Although the value of public testimony is affirmed in the narrative, the dangers of exposure require the restorative of a radical cleansing. Even Mary's breakdown and revival are not quite sufficient to banish all remnants of the taint, and so, in a strange displacement, the task falls to Jem. No one in Manchester will employ the once suspect mechanic. "Too strong a taint was on his character," Jem fears, "for him ever to labour [there] again" (p. 417). Although a court has declared him innocent, he, like Mary, stands indelibly accused and seems still to carry the burden of John Barton's guilt. Jem even understands why the men shun him, for they have only their name and character on which to rely and so must "keep that free from soil and taint" (p. 430). Indistinguishable from the convicts and prostitutes who emigrate to the colonies at the conclusion of other nineteenth-century narratives, Jem and Mary must also leave England to make a life for themselves. It is as if once she had left home to take her place in the world, Mary could never quite go back.

The ambivalence toward her own entry into public life which Gaskell represented in the story of Mary Barton became more acute and anguished after the novel was published and reviewed. To begin with, she resented the public's demand to know the identity of the author (the novel had been published anonymously) and complained to her publisher Edward Chapman about the "impertinent and unjustifiable curiosity of people, who have tried to force one either into an absolute denial, or an acknowledgement of what they must have seen the writer wished to keep concealed."[41] In this case the writer "wished to keep

---

[41] Gaskell, *Letters*, p. 64; subsequently cited in the text. Hilary Schor points out that

concealed" not only her name but her belief that the manufacturers in whose midst she lived were in some way responsible for the poverty and misery she described in her novel. To articulate this belief in print in an anonymously-published novel and to have it identified with her not simply as an author but as an individual were two different things, or so she naively believed. Hostile reviews accused whoever had written *Mary Barton* of betraying the manufacturing class and blaming it for the faults of improvidence that were really the workers' own.[42] "The authoress of 'Mary Barton,' " wrote a critic for the *Edinburgh Review* in 1849, "has borne false witness against a whole class [and] flattered both the prejudices of the aristocracy and the passions of the populace."[43]

Her feelings of discomfort at having "borne witness" had much to do with her position, unique among the major cultural critics of industrial life, as the virtual neighbor of those she accused: they were her friends, her husband's congregants, members of her social and religious community. The defensiveness that can be detected in the novel's preface and its discussions of justifiable working-class anger were echoed in letters to friends who had discovered the secret of her authorship. She wrote to Miss Ewart, daughter of a Liberal M.P., "I can only say I wanted to represent the subject in the light in which some of the workmen certainly consider to be true, not that I dare to say it is the abstract absolute truth. . . . No one can feel more deeply than I how *wicked* it is to do anything to excite class against class; and the sin has been most unconscious if I have done so" (*Letters*, p. 67). Gaskell was to some degree unaware of what she had created, and amazed that her novel had "proved such a firebrand" (*Letters*, p. 68). In the passage just quoted she appears to be apologizing for a sin she feels she did not commit. But on another level she had indeed intended to stir up feelings of guilt in her middle-class readers by taking a stand, however defensively, on controversial issues of vital public importance. She resented terribly, however, the idea that people would take the liberty of identifying her as a private person with the sentiments she had unleashed in fiction. Later she would write to her daughter Marianne that she found it a "great impertinence" when people addressed remarks to her about her novels "in any way" (*Letters*, p. 209). In the aftermath of her first novel's publication, she complained to an unidentified cor-

---

Gaskell never mentioned *Mary Barton* in her letters while she was writing it, and apparently told no one when it was published (*Scheherezade in the Marketplace*, p. 25).

[42] For this point of view, see *British Quarterly Review* 9 (February 1849): 117–36.

[43] *Edinburgh Review* 89 (April 1849): 426.

respondent of not being able to go where she liked and ventured the wish that "poor Mary Barton could be annihilated" so that *she* could move about "naturally and simply" (*Letters*, p. 71). To Chapman she declared that she was not thinking of writing anything else because it simply wasn't worth it—"le jeu ne vaut pas la chandelle" (*Letters*, p. 72). Despite the praise *Mary Barton* received from many quarters, Gaskell felt exposed and stigmatized as its acknowledged author and was uncomfortable with the public identity that authorship had inevitably created for her.

Given the shock of publicity Gaskell experienced with her first novel and her apparent distaste for stirring up controversy, her decision to write a novel about a redeemed fallen woman—*Ruth* (1853)—suggests just how profound was her need to testify publicly about some of the most highly charged issues of her day. She courted the risk of exposure even as she claimed to detest it. Her letters surrounding the publication of *Ruth* are, predictably, even more anxious and agitated than the *Mary Barton* correspondence, and she anticipated disapproval even before the reviews appeared. To her friend Anne Robson she wrote that she had forbidden some people to speak to her about the new novel, and that she was already disturbed by the disapprobation of those around her (*Letters*, p. 220). Although she claims to have known in advance that many would find the book an "unfit subject," she compares her position as shunned author to "St. Sebastian tied to a tree to be shot at with arrows" (pp. 220–21). This image suggests how excessively vulnerable and wounded she felt, yet also how just and martyred. Like Mary Barton after her appearance in court, Gaskell became quite ill with what may have been influenza, and she connected the illness in her own mind with the response to her novel. She wrote to Eliza Fox:

> I *have* been so ill; I do believe it has been a "Ruth" fever. . . . [I] cd not get over the hard things people said of Ruth. I mean I was just in that feverish way when I could not get them out of my head by thinking of anything else but dreamt about them and all that. I think I must be an improper woman without knowing it, I do so manage to shock people. Now *should* you have burnt the 1st vol. of Ruth as so *very* bad? even if you had been a very anxious father of a family? Yet *two* men have; and a third has forbidden his wife to read it; they sit next to us in Chapel and you can't think how "improper" I feel under their eyes. (*Letters*, pp. 222–23).

Gaskell again reacts painfully to others' conflation of her private and public selves. But here, with *Ruth*, the aura of sinfulness and sexual impropriety that was only implicit in the controversy surrounding *Mary Barton* is made explicit by her choice of subject and her identification with its illicitness.[44] As in the case of women factory workers, condemned by contemporary cultural discourse as both unsexed and unchaste, the middle-class minister's wife felt herself accused of writing about subjects of which respectable women should have no knowledge, and in so doing sullying herself by association. Indeed, it seems to me that *Ruth*, a novel that is neither "industrial" nor "urban" (London is tellingly invoked only as the place where the wealthy Bellingham seduces Ruth), nevertheless sustains Gaskell's engagement with the debate about woman's public role and her meditation on the place women had been assigned in the culture of the city.

In *Ruth* Gaskell returned to the subject of work and female sexuality which she had initiated in *Mary Barton*. She rewrote the lives of both Mary and her aunt Esther in the character of Ruth Hilton, a seamstress who, unlike Mary, does fall and who, unlike Esther, is redeemed. Both Mary and Ruth are made vulnerable to the sexual interest of upperclass men through their employment as seamstresses, an occupation that, as both novels suggest, puts them on display through the calculated maneuvers of their employers. In *Ruth* Mrs. Mason cynically promises the girls who work in her shop that the "most diligent" will be asked to attend the annual hunt ball to take care of last-minute repairs, when in fact she plans to take only the most beautiful, those who will "do credit to the 'establishment.' "[45] Subtly making the connection between this kind of enterprise and the misguided and insidious appreciation of surface, the narrator records that Mrs. Mason's foibles were "natural to her calling" (p. 8). Ruth's occupation, as overseen by Mrs. Mason and her kind, exploits the conjunction of class inferiority and sexual desirability which the properly displayed working-class woman can project. The text literalizes the position in which Ruth's work places her in its representation of the moment when she is first admired at the ball by Bellingham, her eventual seducer: she kneels at the hem of Bellingham's partner, and he is struck by the "noble head

---

[44] It is Gaskell's own response to the publication of *Ruth* that I mean to emphasize rather than the response of others. In fact, reviews were substantially positive in nature, and negative critical reaction centered more on the awkwardness or tediousness of the narrative than on its scandalousness. This makes Gaskell's sense of her own impropriety all the more revealing. See A. B. Hopkins, *Elizabeth Gaskell: Her Life and Work* (London: John Lehmann, 1952), p. 125.

[45] Elizabeth Gaskell, *Ruth* (1853; rpt. London: Dent, 1967), pp. 7–8; subsequently cited in the text.

bent down to the occupation in which she was engaged" and by the contrast between this humbly dressed, (literally) subordinate figure and the "flippant, bright, artificial girl" by his side (p. 15).

The danger that Mary Barton eludes is here fulfilled. Bellingham seduces Ruth, and when the partly culpable Mrs. Mason discovers the relationship between them, she dismisses Ruth from her employ. Although the economic plot of the fallen woman story is underplayed in Gaskell's novel, it is nonetheless carefully worked out, as indeed it is in *Mary Barton*. Abandoned by her lover, facing poverty, illness, and death, Esther resorts to prostitution. By contrast, Ruth, whose essential innocence and unfortunate ignorance are insisted upon, never overtly contemplates this option, even in her deepest despair. Instead, the problem of how to support herself is resolved by the Bensons, who not only take her in but educate her and lend her enough respectability so that she can work as a governess. Later in the novel, however, the power of economic need and social ostracism to shape the choices of seduced and abandoned women such as Esther and Ruth is startlingly introduced by the observations of Bellingham himself and by the narrative of yet another dressmaker. When Bellingham, now reincarnated as the political candidate Mr. Donne, meets "Mrs. Denbigh" in Abermouth, he muses on her resemblance to "poor Ruth." We read: "For the first time in several years, he wondered what had become of her; though, of course, there was but one thing that could have happened, and perhaps it was as well he did not know her end" (p. 275). Still unspoken, though clearly signaled here, is the notion that a young woman in Ruth's position would surely have ended as a prostitute.

The unwritten counterplot of prostitution finds an author in Mrs. Pearson, the dressmaker whom Jemima Bradshaw visits and from whom she learns the story of Ruth's early life. Jemima, who acts as the reader's surrogate, hears the tale of a vicious young woman's entrapment of a man from a religious and respectable family. She asks what became of the woman. "Why, ma'am, what could become of her?" Mrs. Pearson replies. "Not that I know exactly—only one knows they can but go from bad to worse" (pp. 317–18). The reader, although aware of the falseness of much of this account, is struck by the possibility of that other trajectory which both Bellingham and Mrs. Pearson predict for Ruth with such certainty. The specter of Ruth as prostitute casts a different light on her story and also sheds new light on the meaning of prostitution itself: Ruth might have been a prostitute, but a prostitute might well be Ruth, or someone like her. Just as this narrative forces Jemima to rethink her relationship to Ruth and then to reexamine her assumptions about sexual sin, so must the reader reconsider his or her understanding of the prostitute on the street as well as of the unfortunate heroine of fiction.

Without addressing the issue directly, then, Gaskell nevertheless enters into the discussion of prostitution which by the 1850s had become a focus for social debate. In this decade, as Judith Walkowitz points out, prostitution became "the Great Social Evil," a subject of moral, economic, and medical concern.[46] Prostitution emerged as a public health issue in the works of physicians, sanitary reformers, and, as I have suggested in the case of Dickens, novelists. During the decade that followed, of course, this concern would be translated into the Contagious Diseases Acts, legislation designed to control the spread of venereal disease through the forced examination of prostitutes.[47] Woman as contaminant, capable of infecting "respectable" men and thereby invading and destroying the sanctity of middle-class life, became a powerful and often subtly deployed cultural image. In *Ruth*, I would argue, Gaskell incorporates this image and offers a critique of it, largely though not exclusively through the introduction of the themes of disease and nursing.[48] Although we cannot be certain that Gaskell was reading *Bleak House* (which began to appear in serialization in March 1852) while she was writing *Ruth*, it is certainly possible that she gave a particular inflection to the relationship between female sexuality and disease in response to Dickens's own construction of that relationship in his novel.[49]

Gaskell makes full use of the idea that those around Ruth who know of her past will regard her as a contaminant in their midst, and she shapes her plot in order to suggest that, on the contrary, both Ruth and her offspring possess the power to comfort and cure. The image

[46] Judith R. Walkowitz, *Prostitution and Victorian Society* (Cambridge: Cambridge University Press, 1980), p. 32.

[47] See ibid., chap. 4.

[48] See chapter 4 of Deirdre d'Albertis, "Elizabeth Gaskell and the Victorian Social Text: Politics, Gender, and Genre" (Ph.D. diss., Harvard University, 1991), for a similar but much fuller discussion of nursing and disease in *Ruth*.

[49] Gaskell first began to mention *Ruth* in the fall of 1852, and the novel was published early in 1853. *Bleak House* first began to appear in serialization in March 1852 and continued until the summer of 1853. It is likely, then, that Gaskell began to write *Ruth* in the early months of *Bleak House*'s publication. J. G. Sharps suggests that the typhus in *Ruth* may have been based on the cholera epidemic of 1831 (*Mrs. Gaskell's Observation and Invention*, p. 157); and readers have certainly seen cholera as a possible model for the smallpox in *Bleak House* (see my discussion in chapter 3 of this volume).

of Ruth as healer is established early in the novel, when she nurses Bellingham in Wales, and counteracts the vision of those such as Mrs. Bellingham and Mrs. Pearson who see her as a dangerous woman determined to entrap a series of young men and destroy their health and their fortune. When Mrs. Bellingham arrives in Wales to displace and dismiss Ruth, she virtually accuses her of making ill the man she has in fact been trying to nurse back to health.[50] Mr. Bradshaw shares this view of Ruth and focuses on the danger she poses to other women— specifically to his daughter Jemima—rather than to men. When he learns the secrets of Ruth's past, he articulates in a particularly wrathful manner common fears for the safety of the home: this woman has been accepted and embraced by his family, but now he finds that she has come "with [her] sickly, hypocritical face imposing upon us all" (p. 334). He rails against the "wantonness" that has crept into their midst unannounced. When Jemima, who has already absorbed Ruth's history, stands before her father to "bear witness to Ruth," he can only conclude that the contamination has already done its damage: "It only convinces me more and more," he says, "how deep is the corruption this wanton has spread in my family" (pp. 335–36). From Ruth's insidious influence on female purity, Bradshaw turns to the subject of her "bastard" child, using the language of stigmatization—the boy is "stained," "marked"—so common in contemporary discourses of sexual contamination.

In this context the typhus that spreads through Eccleston in the last chapters of the novel is yet another marker for sexual contagion. In describing the disease Gaskell employs the familiar tropes of invasion and invisible movement from class to class:

There came creeping, creeping, in hidden, slimy courses, the terrible fever— that fever which is never utterly banished from the sad haunts of vice and misery, but lives in such darkness, like a wild beast in the recesses of his den. It had begun in the low Irish lodging-houses; but there it was so common it excited little attention. . . . It had, like the blaze of a fire which had long smouldered, burst forth in many places at once—not merely among the loose-living and vicious, but among the decently poor—nay, even among the well-to-do and respectable. (p. 420)

[50] Deirdre d'Albertis suggests, quite convincingly, that Bellingham's "uncommon susceptibility to illness" is meant to suggest "moral laxity," and that the brain fever he suffers in Wales may hint at syphilis ("Elizabeth Gaskell and the Victorian Social Text," p. 91).

The metaphoric connection between the diseases of poverty and sexual taint which is established in the "vitiated air" passage of *Dombey and Son* or in the description of Tom-all-Alone's in *Bleak House* is played out in the plots of Dickens's novels, where the innocent are truly threatened with contamination. Edith Dombey shares the taint of the prostitute Alice Carker, and Mr. Dombey's family, especially Florence, is at risk; Esther Summerson is blighted at birth and must suffer the agony of smallpox before she can be purged of the sins of her parents. In *Ruth*, however, the danger of contamination from the sexually tainted woman is proved to be an illusion, a wrongheaded social myth. Jemima, like Mary Barton, represents the chaste woman whose innocence is never seriously jeopardized by contact with the fallen woman; indeed, Jemima is strengthened rather than diminished by knowing Ruth and her story.

Gaskell uses the idea of typhus, in fact, beyond this canceling out of the idea of Ruth's danger to the innocent, to *reverse* the standard paradigm of sexual and moral contamination—the paradigm offered by Mrs. Bellingham, Mrs. Pearson, and Mr. Bradshaw. It is Ruth who heals, and it is Bellingham who infects and kills. Ruth nurses many typhus victims before she catches the fatal disease from Bellingham, and her death reenacts his initial "infection" of her—the seduction and his insouciant destruction of her future. In addition, Gaskell extends the function of healing to Ruth's son, Leonard, who will be apprenticed to and adopted by the surgeon Mr. Davis, who is himself illegitimate. Here the sins of the mother are not visited on the child, as they inevitably are in the case of Lady Dedlock and Esther Summerson. In the context of powerful cultural assumptions about sexual taint, its indelibility, and its spread, the Reverend Benson's words about Ruth's absolute moral and physical integrity take on a radical, not simply a conventional Christian, cast: "In the eye of God she is exactly the same as if the life she has led had left no trace behind" (p. 118).

The origins of this novel in Gaskell's own experience make even clearer the purposeful nature of her subversion of popular cultural notions of sexual contamination. In January 1850 Gaskell wrote to Dickens about a young imprisoned woman she wished to help emigrate to the colonies. She hoped that Dickens might be of assistance because of his knowledge of Angela Burdett-Coutts's scheme for the rehabilitation through emigration of female prisoners. This particular young woman, the orphaned daughter of a clergyman, had been apprenticed to a dressmaker, a woman who "connived at the girl's seduction by a surgeon in the neighborhood" (*Letters*, pp. 99–100). Later, after the girl had entered the New Bailey Prison (for reasons Gaskell does not specify in her letter to Dickens), she fell ill and needed medical care. In a postscript Gaskell includes an account of the strange coincidence that brought the very same surgeon who had seduced the girl to examine and treat her for her illness in prison. The prison matron told Gaskell that when the two "came thus suddenly face to face, [the girl] just fainted dead away" (*Letters*, p. 100). Gaskell used this prisoner as a prototype for Ruth and incorporated the details of her occupation and the role of her employer as salient elements in her story; but she also took the incident of illness, exploited it as a metaphor for sexual sin, and reversed the roles of patient and doctor. In Gaskell's version the seduced but uncontaminated woman is called in to cure the diseased seducer, from whom she contracts a fatal illness. The sexually fallen woman, like the transgressing woman novelist, might be martyred like Saint Sebastian, but she retains the authority to bear witness to society's crimes and the power to cure its ills.

The saint whose spirit hovered over the writing of *North and South* (1854–55) was Florence Nightingale, whom Gaskell compared in her letters of that period to Saint Elizabeth of Hungary and Joan of Arc (*Letters*, p. 107). In the fall of 1854 Gaskell went for an extended visit to the Nightingale family home, Lea Hurst, at Matlock, where she would be able to write without the interruption of household duties and family demands. At times left completely alone in the house and at times in the company of her hosts, Gaskell was free to devote herself to her novel and to write long, meditative letters to friends on the subject of the woman whose life, like Charlotte Brontë's, she felt a "hunger to know." Gaskell seemed to be fascinated by Nightingale's heroism—especially by her recent stories of nursing cholera victims at Middlesex Hospital—and by her apparent "want of love for individuals," even as she risked her own health to care for the dying.[51] Particularly chilling to Gaskell was Nightingale's ministering to "the poor prostitutes" who were brought in from their Oxford Street "beats" filthy and gravely ill. Prostitutes, Nightingale told her, suffered from cholera more severely than anyone else, and Gaskell marveled at Nightingale's seeming immunity from contamination as she undressed the

[51] See especially Gaskell's letters to Catherine Winkworth, October 11–14, 1854, and to Emily Shaen, October 7, 1854 (*Letters*, pp. 305–10, 316–21).

diseased women (*Letters*, p. 305). The image of this saintly woman surrounded by contagious disease echoed in an uncanny way the heroine Gaskell had just created in *Ruth*; but the novelist's ruminations on Nightingale's unconventional femininity and subversion of traditional authority corresponded to the conflicts of the heroine she was then in the process of inventing—Margaret Hale.

Relieved temporarily of her own obligations to the people she loved, Gaskell judged Nightingale's freedom from responsibility to those close to her to be her chief fault and her reigning strength. So that Florence might be "at liberty to do her great work," her sister, Parthenope, had "annihilated herself, her own tastes, her own wishes in order to take up all the little duties of home, to parents, to poor, to society, to servants," writes Gaskell (*Letters*, p. 317). Her accounts of this and other aspects of Nightingale's single-mindedness and rejection of conventional feminine duties consistently mingle admiration and disapproval. For instance, she tells the story of a poor villager whose dying son Nightingale had once nursed. But when the woman's husband died, Parthe had to go to great lengths to persuade her sister to visit the widow just once. "She will not go among the villagers now," Gaskell writes, "because her heart and soul are absorbed by her hospital plans, and as she says she can only attend to one thing at once" (*Letters*, pp. 319–20). The novelist and the reformer had a "grand quarrel" one day about the rearing of children: Nightingale, who Gaskell thought believed too fervently in institutions, had proposed that all children, rich and poor alike, be raised not by their mothers but in crèches. "That exactly tells of what seems to be *the* want," Gaskell concludes, "but then this want of love for individuals becomes a gift and a very rare one, if one takes it in conjunction with her intense love for the *race*" (*Letters*, p. 320).

The minister's wife, herself a visitor of the parish poor and a dedicated mother, marvels at the scope and determination of Nightingale's will but finds her refusal of human attachments and family moorings disturbing.[52] She is obsessed with Nightingale for precisely this reason, and in *North and South* she makes central to the life of her new heroine "that most difficult problem for women," as Margaret herself understands it, of "how much was to be utterly merged in obedience to authority, and how much might be set apart for freedom in working"

---

[52] Gaskell seems to have been unaware of the anger Nightingale bore toward her mother and her sister, who for so long opposed her entry into the profession of nursing.

(p. 508). Will Margaret, as the hardly impartial suitor Henry Lennox phrases it, allow herself to "thaw" a bit and emerge as a Cleopatra, or will she adhere to her ambitious and commanding ways as a Zenobia (p. 505)?[53] Will she be renowned for her beauty and epic romances or for her power to challenge and conquer the established order? Or, to put Lennox's query in a less highly charged manner, will Margaret be able to salvage traditional ties to family, husband, and children and also find a way to claim authority for herself?

Issues of authority loom large in *North and South*, from Mr. Hale's questioning of the authority of his church, to Frederick's overt and aggressive challenge to his captain's authority aboard ship, to Mr. Thornton's initial desire for absolute authority over his workers, to the strikers' defiance of their employers' authority, to Margaret's own increasing authority—in her family, over Thornton, and in the public realm. The narrative ambivalence that colors all of these struggles and rebellions is suggested at the outset by the case of Mr. Hale, who abdicates responsibility within the family and causes suffering he does not have the courage to address as he acts out his crisis of conscience and leaves the clergy. Margaret defends her brother, Frederick's, mutinous acts as the justifiable defiance of "arbitrary power, unjustly and cruelly used," even as his forced exile from England, like his father's banishment to Milton-Northern, causes the family pain (p. 154). In order that these men might challenge authority and, as it were, take it into their own hands, Margaret herself (not unlike Parthenope Nightingale) must shoulder new burdens within the family: she arranges for the move to Milton, oversees the new household, sends for her brother when her mother is dying, and buries both her parents. The novel offers a critique of the egoism involved in the subversion of authority, and yet it endorses that subversion as a matter of conscience, both for individuals and for social classes. The masculine practice of rebellion places a heavy burden on women in the novel, but it also affords them the chance to seize what power the egoist overlooks. Gaskell uses the full range of masculine revolt to contemplate and comment on the moral implications of a female subversion of authority.

In Gaskell's novel it is two cities (Milton/Manchester and London) and two cultures (North and South) that set up the choice women have between obeying or dissenting from established authority. The contrast

[53] Zenobia was the queen of the Syrian city-state Palmyra who challenged the authority of Rome by invading Asia Minor and Egypt.

between London and Manchester remarked on by contemporary observers and subsequent historians is thematized in *North and South* in
terms of relations between the sexes and, in an analogous way, relations
between classes. In London, from the very first pages of the narrative,
middle-class women are represented as passive, narcoleptic creatures,
bred to be adorned, displayed, and married off. Margaret's cousin
Edith, likened at the outset to the fairy princesses Titania, Sleeping
Beauty, and Cinderella, never emerges from childhood into adulthood
in the course of the narrative, despite her experience of marriage and
motherhood. When Margaret returns to London after the death of her
parents in Milton, she sees that London will lull even the most active
woman into passivity, and she associates this threat to her northern-
bred independence with the invisibility of work and of the working
class:

> She was getting surfeited of the eventless ease in which no struggle or en-
> deavour was required. She was afraid lest she should even become sleepily
> deadened into forgetfulness of anything beyond the life which was lapping
> her round with luxury. There might be toilers and moilers there in London,
> but she never saw them; the very servants lived in an underground world of
> their own, of which she knew neither the hopes nor the fears; they only
> seemed to start into existence when some want or whim of their master and
> mistress needed them. (p. 458)

Margaret's residence in her aunt's home firmly allies her with an in-
sular, petted, professional middle class, a realm unconnected to production or producers of any kind. In Milton, by contrast, she is located
within the modest, genteel, and respected sphere of an ex-clergyman's
family and, by association, within the mixed-class world of manufacturing. In London, not only is she bereft of connection to those who toil,
but she is herself a dependent within a middle-class hierarchy.

The contrast between life for the middle-class woman in Milton and
in London is even more precisely defined in the novel by the experience of the street, the very site where Margaret first comes to know the
factory workers of the town. When first venturing out on Milton's
streets, Margaret remembers the sanctions her aunt had imposed on
her in London: "Mrs. Shaw's ideas of propriety and her own helpless
dependence on others, had always made her insist that a footman
should accompany Edith and Margaret, if they went beyond Harley
Street or the immediate neighborhood" (p. 109). Now, unaccompa-

nied but conscious of the need to adopt the "even and decorous pace necessary in streets" (p. 109), she learns to navigate the town on her own. This independence of movement matches the authority she now assumes in the Hale household, and it offers her the possibility of meeting workers, such as Nicholas and Bessy Higgins, with whom she strikes up an acquaintance on the street. Her friendship with the Higginses initiates her into a new way of understanding class relations. On their first meeting she assumes the father and daughter will be amenable to her visiting their home when she likes, just as her father's parishioners in Helstone had always welcomed the clergyman's daughter. When Higgins challenges this assumption, wondering why she has asked their name and where they live, and protests that he does not like to have strangers in his home, she is made to understand that what to her is a natural act of benevolence is to these factory workers a form of impertinence. Elbowing and being elbowed on the street, then, begins a movement for Margaret away from southern paternalism and deference and toward a more northern form of reciprocity and cooperation.

Margaret's education in reconstructed class relations leads to her learning a variety of new languages: the slang of the streets and the factory; new meanings for "man" and "gentleman" that reject old class hierarchies and depend on individualist values; the vocabulary of workers' anger and resistance in the strike; the discourse of ambitious and powerful manufacturers, which intoxicates her with its defiance of old limits. She gradually grows distant from the culture of what is called at various points in the novel the "aristocratic society" of the South. This aristocratic culture involves a particular mix of gender and class politics that in Margaret's experience ensures rigid class roles, prohibits certain kinds of autonomy for women, enforces idleness, and separates workers from employers and indeed from one another. For Mr. Thornton the South means sloth and complacency. "I would rather be a man toiling, suffering—nay, failing and successless—here," he tells Margaret, "than lead a dull prosperous life in the old worn grooves of what you call more aristocratic society down in the South, with their slow days of careless ease. One may be clogged with honey and unable to rise and fly" (p. 122).

Margaret, who initially insists that common people suffer less in the more conservative atmosphere of the South, later comes to believe that only in the North can working people find what is crucial to their survival—a spirit of community and self-conscious debate. When Nicholas Higgins, weary with grief, hard work, and struggle, announces to

Margaret his intention of trying out life in the South, the friendliness and comfort of which she herself had previously touted, Margaret warns him against it:

> You would not bear the dulness of the life; you don't know what it is; it would eat you away like rust. Those that have lived there all their lives, are used to soaking in the stagnant waters. They labour on, from day to day, in the great solitude of steaming fields—never speaking or lifting up their poor, bent, downcast heads. The hard spadework robs their brain of life; the sameness of their toil deadens their imagination; they don't care to meet to talk over thoughts and speculations, even of the weakest, wildest kind, after their work is done; they go home brutishly tired, poor creatures! caring for nothing but food and rest. You could not stir them up into any companionship, which you get in a town as plentiful as the air you breathe. (p. 382)

Implicit in this portrait of unreflecting workers is the notion, newly understood by Margaret, that struggle and contention are better for the worker than resignation and passivity. In this sense we see that she has accepted the spirit and necessity of the union and even of the strike, however much she objects to some of the workers' tactics and assumptions. She has not quite turned into the "democrat . . . red republican . . . member of the Peace Society . . . socialist" her father's friend Mr. Bell imagines her to have become, but the shift in her vision of class relations justifies his perception of a fundamental change (p. 409).[54]

In sexual politics as well, Margaret ultimately comes down on the side of struggle. The gender codes of the South are clear, as I have already suggested, from the early London chapters and from Margaret's retrospective musings on the constraints under which she lived in her aunt's home. But a subtler form of the sexual politics of the "aristocratic" South operates in Margaret's own household in the attitudes of her mother and Dixon, her mother's maid, who "remembered the day when she had been engaged by Lady Beresford as ladies' maid to Sir John's wards, the pretty Miss Beresfords, the belles of Rutlandshire," one of whom is now Mrs. Hale (p. 52). Dixon considered the former Miss Beresford's marriage to a poor clergyman her "affliction and

---

[54] In a letter to Eliza Fox in April 1850, Gaskell mused about the different aspects of herself—her "mes," as she called them—that coexisted within her: "One of my mes is, I do believe, a true Christian—(only people call her a socialist and communist)" (*Letters*, p. 108).

downfall" (p. 52), but stood by her mistress in her social descent, reminding everyone at regular intervals about the glory that was past.

What is particularly important in this context is not merely the nostalgia that Dixon and Mrs. Hale feel for an aristocratic past but the connection between this nostalgia and their attitudes toward the Hale children. Both older women favor Frederick Hale and depreciate Margaret, in part because Margaret, unlike Frederick, does not reproduce her mother's beauty, in part because in her seriousness and reserve Margaret resembles her father, and in part simply because a son has greater value and importance in the aristocratic world in which they once lived. Dixon keeps Frederick's room exactly as he had left it, consenting only to tidy this one room in the house. She tells Margaret that she will never be "like [her] mother for beauty . . . not if [she] lives to be a hundred," and threatens to "put [Margaret] in a passion" because, when in a rage, she physically resembles the adored Frederick (p. 179). The dying Mrs. Hale recalls the infant Frederick's beauty and laments that her daughter had been an "ugly little thing," and then insists that Margaret send for her exiled son (p. 262).

This family mythology, in which the son is valued over not only the daughter but also the father, persists even as Margaret holds the family together while Frederick, for reasons ostensibly beyond his control, deserts them in their time of most acute need. The novel remains silent on Margaret's response to this patriarchal dynamic. She expresses no bitterness toward Frederick or resentment of the insulting behavior of her mother and her mother's surrogate. We do know, however, that she rejects the kind of man her brother represents—her "preux chevalier" of a brother, as she calls him—in favor of the rough-hewn manufacturer who, in almost every way, offers a physical and temperamental contrast to Frederick. She also rejects the standards of femininity that her mother and Dixon value, the same standards that rule her cousin Edith's vapid life. Finally, in leaving her utterly bereft of her entire immediate family by the end of the narrative, the novel grants her a bittersweet but necessary independence from what is essentially a belittling and yet demanding daughterly role.

After Mrs. Hale's death, it remains for Margaret to come to terms with her mother's legacy in the form of her aunt, the other Miss Beresford, and with the London life this entails. It is on her return to London that Margaret realizes how passive the life there will make her, how foolish her cousin Edith seems, and how much she needs to assert herself and her need for "freedom in working" (p. 508). When Margaret confides to Edith her resolve to "take her life into her own hands," the latter begs her determined cousin not to be too "strong-minded" or too serious, or to visit working-class neighborhoods dressed in "brown and dust-colour [so as] not to show the dirt you'll pick up in all those places" (p. 508). Edith's response makes clear just what Margaret means by "freedom in working," and later, when Margaret is reported to be "pok[ing] herself into" all sorts of "wretched places," Edith laments the *"rambling habits"* her cousin had been allowed to develop in Milton (p. 520). Margaret tries to reproduce in London the kind of independent urban rambling in the neighborhoods of the poor to which she had become accustomed in Milton. It is striking, however, that the narrative only hints obliquely at this activity and never describes Margaret's experience of it. Her London rambling is simply reported secondhand, and then only in the vaguest way.

We know that at this stage of her writing Gaskell was rushing her work under pressure from Dickens, who was publishing the novel in *Household Words.* As a result, the narrative compresses a great deal into a small space.[55] Nonetheless, this segment of the story, which tells what happens to the "work" Margaret has begun in the North, seems central to the novel's engagement with the conflicts of femininity. I offer three possible reasons other than haste for the novel's failure to imagine Margaret's work in London or to see it through her eyes. First, the narrative suggests through this elision that what Margaret did in Milton she cannot in fact continue in London: the London rambling simply, literally, cannot be imagined, and no appropriate context for it, analogous to that of the industrial city, can be reproduced in the metropolis. Gaskell herself cannot conjure it, and the urban culture of the South cannot sustain it. In this sense the incomplete representation of this part of her London experience points in the direction of a return to Milton, to a place that makes possible a fuller representation. Second, and to some degree in tension with the first explanation, the obscuring of Margaret's labors in the metropolis also points toward a suppression of vocation in the novel's conclusion and toward the ascendancy of marriage as the resolution of Margaret's conflicts. Third, by evading the representation of a public identity for Margaret in the final chapters, the narrative also escapes the vexing problem of sexual

[55] For the publishing history of *North and South* and Gaskell's editorial relationship with Dickens at the time, see Dorothy W. Collins, "The Composition of Mrs. Gaskell's *North and South*," *Bulletin of the John Rylands Library* 54 (1971–72): 67–93.

exposure which had complicated each of her major ventures into the public arena in Milton.

Beginning with Margaret's experience of being jostled, inspected, and appraised by working people on Milton's streets, her entry into public life, her independent navigation of the city, and her assumption of authority at points and places of conflict result in the sexualization of her image. Milton offers the possibility of public engagement, autonomy, and authority, but it also ensures that, by taking advantage of these possibilities, Margaret will find her chaste reputation sullied almost beyond redemption. Her experiences act as a mirror of Gaskell's own: the novelist's forays into public debate on controversial subjects left her with the sense that she had overstepped the bounds of propriety and announced her complicity in sin.

Much has been written about the extraordinary confluence of politics and sexuality in the riot scene of *North and South*.[56] Here Margaret tries to act as mediator by inserting herself between Mr. Thornton and the crowd of striking workers, who are enraged that he, like other employers, has hired Irish scabs to do their work. After encouraging Thornton to confront the angry mob at his door, Margaret realizes that he will surely be attacked and rushes to his side, throwing her arms around his neck to shield him from the crowd with her body. A sharp pebble meant for Thornton grazes her forehead, and dark red blood trickles down her face in an image suggestive of both defloration and the wounds of martyrdom.[57] Thornton catches her as she faints and carries her into the house, where he declares his love over her unconscious form (pp. 231–41). A number of onlookers, including Thornton's mother and a servant, interpret Margaret's gesture as an embrace, a sign of her love for Thornton, and Thornton himself is emboldened by the incident—and by his mother's interpretation of it—to tell Margaret of his love for her.

There are a number of points to be made about this climactic episode in the context of a discussion of the risks of public exposure for a woman in the city. The account of the riot emphasizes how others

[56] See especially Deirdre David, *Fictions of Resolution in Three Victorian Novels* (New York: Columbia University Press, 1981), chap. 3; and Barbara Leah Harman, "In Promiscuous Company: Female Public Appearance in Elizabeth Gaskell's *North and South*," *Victorian Studies* 31 (Spring 1988): 351–74.

[57] Deirdre David emphasizes the fear of working-class passions expressed in the image of the hurled stone and the wound it inflicts on Margaret (ibid., p. 43).

perceive Margaret once she steps out into public view, once she engages in political conflict and allows herself *to be seen*, her gestures read and misread. She becomes part of a spectacle, the meaning of which is constructed by others. Once she crosses Thornton's threshold, she can no longer control the meaning or even the appearance of her actions. Furthermore, the spectators involved tend to read these actions according to a sexual script, as if it were the only script available to them. No discourse of Margaret's heroism, class sympathies, or physical courage emerges in the wake of these events. Margaret, the only one who understands the public meaning of what others merely construe as private, seems ultimately powerless to resist the notion of her own disgrace. "Oh how I am fallen that they should say that of me!" she laments as she absorbs insults to what she calls her "maiden pride" (p. 247). Unable to shake off the image of herself as a fallen creature, Margaret feels "a deep sense of shame that she should thus be the object of universal regard—a sense of shame so acute that it seemed as if she would fain have burrowed into the earth to hide herself, and yet she could not escape out of that unwinking glare of many eyes" (p. 249). Margaret cannot hide from the watchful public nor, ultimately, from the truth of their vision. Gaskell loads the dice here in a way that confirms the private meaning of public action. Margaret must gradually come to the realization that she does love Thornton, and the reader is left with the possibility that her shielding him owed as much to passion as to civic concern. The sense that Margaret cannot escape the absolute commingling of personal desire and political involvement suggests that Gaskell cannot write or imagine her way out of her own feeling that her work casts her as a transgressor, a woman who sinned against her own class and who wrote "firebrand" novels because she was "an improper woman."[58]

The narrative goes on to confirm rather than resist the idea of Margaret's fall by framing the episode at the railway station with her brother Frederick as a replication of the riot scene with Thornton. Once again Margaret chooses to act courageously to protect someone

[58] Although I agree with much of the analysis in Barbara Harman's "In Promiscuous Company," I think she is far too sanguine about the mixing of public and private in the novel. She suggests that Gaskell *celebrates* the erosion of the distinction between the two realms as "oddly beneficial, . . . positive and educative," and that the novel "transforms private sexual shame into an opportunity for sexual self-recognition" (p. 374). I would say rather that Gaskell does not—cannot—resist the interpretation of public gestures as private ones, even though she does demonstrate the unfairness and painfulness of the community's, and especially Thornton's, sexualization of Margaret's public actions.

in need, first to help her brother escape without notice from the country in which he is now an outlaw and then to cover up for him by lying about what had transpired at the station. This time it is Thornton who takes the role of the misinterpreting spectator. He sees Margaret walking arm in arm with another man, gazing at him with love, once again in a place where she is not expected to be. We read: "He was haunted by the remembrance of the handsome young man with whom she stood in an attitude of such familiar confidence. . . . At that late hour, so far from home! It took a great moral effort to galvanize his trust . . . in Margaret's pure and exquisite maidenliness" (p. 339). When he later finds out that Margaret has lied about the events at the station (which include a man's fall from the platform and his subsequent death), he is further confirmed in his suspicions that she must love this young man "blindly" to tell a falsehood that so "stains" her. This revelation causes him to reflect on the riot and to realize that the way she looked at *him* at that time could mean nothing compared with the "tender glances" she directed toward this other man (p. 387). Interestingly, Thornton never considers the possibility that if he and others had misread her before, he may be misreading her again.

Mrs. Thornton, who acts here as the "world's wife," avers that Margaret has lost her "character," and Margaret herself feels a deep sense of shame for having lied, a shame the text makes inseparable from the sexual shame others impose on her. When she realizes that Thornton not only knows she has lied but also has mistaken Frederick for her lover, she accepts this loss of "character" in the public eye as an indelible judgment and, accordingly, feels herself to have become ineligible for marriage. "I have passed out of childhood into old age," she laments. "I have had no youth—no womanhood; the hopes of womanhood have closed for me—for I shall never marry" (p. 401). Because she loves Thornton and doubts now that he would ever have her, she imagines herself a spinster; and she also senses that she has squandered the chaste reputation she would need to become the wife of a respectable man.

Just as the novel joins Margaret's lie to the suspicion of sexual impropriety, so too does it seem to sustain that image of defloration which is the result not so much of working-class passions as of the middle-class woman's trespass into a forbidden public arena. To return to the saintly spirit of Nightingale which haunts this novel, Margaret has now (temporarily, as it turns out) removed herself from the possibility of a conventional feminine role by making *the many*—what Gaskell called "the race"—her concern. She has been tainted by exposing herself to public scrutiny and unwittingly inviting suspicions of sexual impropriety. Even Nightingale, whose reputation eventually took on an angelic cast, ran the risk of sullying herself in body and in image by nursing outcasts such as the cholera-ridden prostitutes of Oxford Street.[59] Authority, claimed and made possible for Margaret in the northern culture of Milton, carries with it the liability of public disgrace.

I end my discussion of *North and South* here, rather than with Margaret's recovery of respectability through marriage and authority through the inheritance of property, in order to suggest how powerful, how unavoidable, was the sexualization of woman's entry into urban space and into the social conflicts that circulate within that space. As the example of Margaret's wound suggests, the sexual imagery in the novel, and indeed the general evocation of her sexuality, is determined by the shaping vision of the male observer. Recall that in *Mary Barton* the narrator shifts responsibility for the comparison between Mary and Beatrice Cenci onto another observer, as if disowning the troubling association with sexual scandal called up by this image. In *North and South* the narrator repeatedly inhabits the position of the male gaze—usually Thornton's—to describe Margaret's physical presence and to establish the erotic tension between the two. When they first meet in chapter 7, the narrative moves jarringly from within Margaret, describing her feelings of fatigue and impatience, to a position outside her, implicitly if not explicitly entering Thornton's perspective:

> She wished that he would go, as he had once spoken of doing, instead of sitting there, answering with curt sentences all the remarks she made. She had taken off her shawl, and hung it over the back of her chair. She sat facing him and facing the light; her full beauty met his eye; her round white flexile throat rising out of the full, yet lithe figure; her lips moving so slightly as she spoke, not breaking the cold serene look of her face with any variation from the one lovely haughty curve; her eyes, with their soft gloom, meeting his with quiet maiden freedom. (p. 100)

A few chapters later Thornton watches mesmerized as Margaret's bracelet falls down around her wrist and she repeatedly pushes it up "until it tightened her soft flesh" (p. 120). Still later, at a dinner party at

---

[59] Before the professionalization of nursing, tending the sick was considered an occupation for women of low birth or ill repute. Sairey Gamp, Dickens's drunken midwife and nurse in *Martin Chuzzlewit*, exemplifies this particular cultural stereotype.

Thornton's home, he watches her as she talks to Fanny, his sister, and the narrator records "the curving lines of [her] red lips . . . the smooth ivory tip of the shoulder; the round white arms" (p. 215).

It is Thornton's erotic vision of Margaret that establishes the evolving nature of the feelings between them, just as, in a parallel way, the erotic interpretation of her gestures during the riot foretells the story of their eventual union. The construction of her sexuality by those who observe her ultimately *becomes* her sexuality. In the final scene of the novel, when Margaret offers Thornton her wealth and he offers her marriage, he arranges her arms around his neck in an intended reenactment of her posture during the riot. "Do you remember, love?" Thornton asks her, referring to this ambiguous embrace, "And how I requited you with my insolence the next day?" She replies, "I remember how wrongly I spoke to you,—that is all" (p. 530). This concluding moment, then, essentially affirms the sexual meaning of Margaret's gesture and seriously mitigates, without completely canceling out, the possibility of its civic meaning. As the novel closes, the future of Margaret's public identity is left in question, even as she chooses to throw in her lot with the manufacturer and the life of the North.

When Elizabeth Gaskell entered the battleground of competing middle-class ideologies that was Manchester in the 1840s and 1850s, she made a bid for public authority that unsettled and perplexed her. The contradictory nature of her position—her wanting to have a voice but dreading the private response to it—had its analogy in woman's place on the streets of the industrial city. As author and as urban spectator Gaskell wanted to take her place as an observer and reformer of the social scene, to fix her urban vision and offer it to her middle-class peers. The impossibility of remaining invisible, however, of claiming the uninhibited status of urban rambler and walking the streets with complete impunity, made exposure a necessary and unavoidable concomitant of spectatorship. Inevitably it was this experience of being jostled or scrutinized by those she wished to observe that gave form to her particular vision of urban life. The moment on the street that appears and reappears in her fiction is a moment of exposure, of engagement with the crowd, of awakened consciousness.

Manchester did, however, provide her with the possibility of immersing herself in the crowd and confronting the world of work in a way that the more diffuse class configuration of London could not. The public exposure of working-class women, both on the street and in the factory, offered Gaskell a social and rhetorical context into which she could insert herself and her fiction. Her own sense of transgression, fueled as much by private anxieties as by the shocked responses of certain readers, became linked for her with the ostensible transgressions of the woman laborer and the woman of the streets. She began, after all, with the working-class heroines of *Mary Barton*—the dressmaker's apprentice and her prostitute aunt—before moving on to the fallen seamstress in *Ruth* and, finally, to her own alter ego, the middle-class heroine of *North and South*. The continuity of concerns in the three novels should by now be clear: Gaskell returned repeatedly to woman's need to bear witness and to the public disgrace that inevitably follows. The heroic images of Mary Barton's testimony in the Liverpool courtroom, Jemima Bradshaw's public defense of Ruth, Margaret Hale's intervention in class strife, Gaskell's championing of the starved worker and the fallen woman are simultaneously images of danger and shame.

Gaskell resisted and wrote against prevailing discourses of contagion in *Mary Barton* and in *Ruth*, but she did not avoid the connection between civic participation and sexual stain that her culture had so forcefully constructed. Mary Barton's illness and rebirth, Ruth's martyrdom, and Margaret Hale's retreat from vocation all attest to the trauma of exposure and the trespassing woman's need for radical cleansing. Emigration, death, and marriage complete the respective processes of rehabilitation in these three novels. Gaskell did not, of course, withdraw from the literary marketplace, but her subsequent novels avoided the overt and controversial topicality of this early phase of her career.[60]

[60] It is important to remember, of course, that *Cranford*, a novel that created no controversy, appeared between *Mary Barton* and *Ruth*, and that not all of Gaskell's early novels were "firebrands." By the same token, *The Life of Charlotte Brontë* (1857) also provoked some outraged response that unsettled its author. See Hopkins, *Elizabeth Gaskell*, chap. 10. The controversy in this case, however, revolved around personal issues, matters affecting Brontë's private life, rather than around issues of public debate.

PART THREE

New Women

SIX

"Neither Pairs Nor Odd": Women, Urban Community, and Writing in the 1880s

Remarkable for the "revival" of British socialism, the birth of New Unionism, and the creation of empirical sociology, the decade of the 1880s also produced a generation of women who imagined, and for a time lived out, the possibility of social and economic independence. London was the site of these efforts, and the metropolis served as the very material for their work, whether literary, philanthropic, or activist. Born in the late 1850s and early 1860s, these middle-class women represented a moment of transition in the history of women's communities. They attempted to live outside the sphere of family, but chose not to enter into the alternative domestic structures created by like-minded women.[1] Although they did not form residential communities as some teachers, nurses, and settlement house workers did, they nevertheless depended on a loosely organized community or network of other unmarried women in whom they saw their own ambitions reflected and affirmed. Whether thought of as "new women" or "glorified spinsters," they were united by no single vocation or ideology but rather by their revolt against the constraints of bourgeois family life and by their attraction to London as the place where those constraints might be escaped and where a field for intellectual, political, and professional engagement might be found.[2]

---

[1] Martha Vicinus has richly described this group in *Independent Women: Work and Community for Single Women, 1850–1920* (Chicago: University of Chicago Press, 1985).

[2] Judith Walkowitz, in *The City of Dreadful Delight* (Chicago: University of Chicago Press, 1992), devotes an entire chapter to what she calls the "contested terrain" of London in the 1880s. She chronicles the entry of middle- and working-class men and women into

The opportunities afforded by London attracted aspiring female novelists, social investigators, and political activists; but the city also represented the antithesis of those private and protected spaces that
middle-class women had traditionally occupied.[3] The metropolis offered anonymity, community, and distance from provincial and familial
expectations, but it also proved a difficult and threatening place to be
a woman alone. Martha Vicinus reminds us that even in the 1880s a
"lady was simply not supposed to be seen aimlessly wandering the
streets in the evening or eating alone," and that it was to some extent
the difficulty of commuting from their homes in middle-class neighborhoods to work in the East End that first brought women into residential settlement houses.[4] In *The Pargiters*, which later became *The
Years*, Virginia Woolf characterizes the year 1880 dramatically as a time
when what she calls "street love" made it impossible for the unmarried
Pargiter daughters to walk unescorted beyond their immediate neighborhood.[5] Woolf's seemingly hyperbolic assertion suggests that the
young woman observed alone without parent, male escort, or spouse,
was sexually vulnerable, her singleness interpretable as sexual availa-
bility. Just as there was no wholly adequate social or economic structure
for the independent existence of the genteel single woman, so there
was no wholly respectable context for her appearance in the city landscape.

As Woolf understood, the decade of the eighties was a pivotal time
in the public lives of women, and the work they produced reflects a
certain precariousness or tentativeness in their social positions and, as
a consequence, in their own notions of themselves. London was a place
of opportunity for women: mixed-sex political and social clubs welcomed them; women's clubs cropped up, where they could take refuge
and take tea; the tops of double-decker buses were now open to them;

urban spaces previously cordoned off from their purview. Shopping ladies, glorified spinsters, charity workers, matchgirls on strike, and Salvation Army lasses all contributed to
and transformed a new urban scene (pp. 41–80).

[3] See Susan Squier's introduction to *Women Writers and the City: Essays in Feminist Literary
Criticism*, ed. Susan Merrill Squier (Knoxville: University of Tennessee Press, 1984), pp.
3–10. Squier observes that women have "traditionally been relegated to pastoral or interior settings, both in life and in literature," but that cities "hold out the possibility of
sisterhood, as women who have escaped from the private home gather in public spaces
to work, to play, and to discover that . . . they like each other" (pp. 4–5).

[4] Vicinus, *Independent Women*, pp. 297, 218.

[5] Virginia Woolf, *The Pargiters*, ed. Mitchell A. Leaska (New York: Harcourt Brace Jov-
anovich, 1977), p. 37. For an interesting discussion of "street love," see Susan Merrill
Squier, *Virginia Woolf and London: The Sexual Politics of the City* (Chapel Hill: University of
North Carolina Press, 1985), chap. 7.

and dwellings for women were built. But it was also a place of danger, the city of Jack the Ripper, in which women like the Pargiter sisters felt threatened and exposed.[6] Being single was to be celebrated for the freedom it brought and female community for the support and companionship it provided. Most of the women I describe here, however, thought of themselves as "neither pairs nor odd," neither coupled nor committed to celibacy. These women occupied a middle ground between the earlier Victorian women whose female communities and homosocial worlds existed within the context of married domestic life and the early twentieth-century women who chose spinsterhood, celibacy, and female companionship outside patriarchal domesticity as a self-conscious political gesture.[7]

Beatrice Potter Webb, Margaret Harkness, and Amy Levy, among other women with whom they were linked in a wide circle of London acquaintances, resisted rigid notions of separate spheres on the one hand and the necessity of a feminist or suffragist politics on the other. They rejected the idea of "women's work," the notion that women's public engagement must be an extension of domestic virtues and talents.[8] But though they accepted celibacy as an aspect of their lives, they did not cling to it as a permanent and necessary condition; for the most part they sought personal emancipation outside an aesthetic or political sensibility based on gender. They understood their own marginality not only—perhaps not even primarily—as a condition of their

[6] For mixed-sex clubs, see Judith R. Walkowitz, "Science, Feminism, and Romance: The Men and Women's Club, 1885–1889," *History Workshop* 21 (Spring 1986): 37–59. This world of sexually integrated organizations would also include the Fabian Society, the Fellowship of the New Life, the Progressive Association, the Society for Psychical Research, the Zetetical Society, the Dialectical Society, the Land Reform Union, and the Shelley and Browning societies. In an essay published in *Woman's World* in 1888 titled "Women and Club Life," Amy Levy mentions the Albemarle Club (established in 1881), the Alexandra Club, the University Club for Ladies, and the Somerville Club. See *The Complete Novels and Selected Writings of Amy Levy, 1861–1889*, ed. Melvyn New (Gainesville: University Press of Florida), pp. 532–38.

[7] For the earlier group, see Carroll Smith-Rosenberg, "The Female World of Love and Ritual: Relations between Women in Nineteenth-Century America," *Signs: Journal of Women in Culture and Society* 1 (Autumn 1975): 1–30; reprinted in Carroll Smith-Rosenberg, *Disorderly Conduct: Visions of Gender in Victorian America* (New York: Oxford University Press, 1985), pp. 53–76; for the later group, see Sheila Jeffreys, *The Spinster and Her Enemies: Feminism and Sexuality, 1880–1930* (London: Pandora's Press, 1985), chap. 5. Jeffreys cites a number of women between 1909 and 1912 who chose celibacy as a "silent strike" against the unequal relations between men and women (pp. 90–91).

[8] The single women Vicinus describes celebrated, or at least took advantage of, notions of sexual difference imposed on them by social convention. She writes, "If the larger society exaggerated the difference between men and women, so too did they, redefining these differences as a source of strength" (pp. 288–89).

sex but also as a product of their socialist politics, of their aspirations to enter male-dominated areas of work, or of their religion or class. Despite their reluctance to commit themselves wholeheartedly to organized or de facto single-sex communities, their membership in a more amorphous community of women, demarcated spiritually rather than by specifics of geography or address, sustained them and gave them identity and purpose. They exhibited the kind of ambivalence about the idea of female community that Nina Auerbach identifies in fiction of the period as a "contradictory vision of a unit that is simultaneously defective and transcendent."[9]

When these women came to write about the city, their poems, novels, and social investigations represented or expressed in a variety of ways the marginality they experienced. Out of their revolt against family and domesticity they saw arising new social and class relations, new spaces for life and work. Out of their spinsterhood they delineated the tensions between men and women that made marriage what Webb once called a "felo-de-se."[10] Out of their experience of vulnerability in the city they forged a new urban vision, in which they struggled to become subject and observer rather than object and observed. As Amy Levy remarks in her 1888 essay on female club life, the "female club-lounger, the *flâneuse* of St. James's Street, latch-key in pocket and eye-glasses on nose, remains a creature of the imagination."[11] If the *flâneuse*, the leisurely stroller and street spectator, did not yet exist in reality, how did these women conceive of themselves when they took on the role of urban observer? Webb tried hard to assume the professional, "scientific" stance of the male social investigator, suppressing her gender and sense of vulnerability, except when, in an act reminiscent of Flora Tristan, she donned the protection of a disguise. Margaret Harkness adopted the techniques and tone of social realism or naturalism, marking her difference from other (male) novelists in her overtly political perspective. Amy Levy chronicled the life of the single intellectual woman in London more overtly than either Webb or Harkness, but she too deployed strategies of displacement and disguise. We do not find in these women's writings the inescapable sense of exposure and trespassing that we saw in Tristan's and Gaskell's urban nar-

[9] Nina Auerbach, *Communities of Women: An Idea in Fiction* (Cambridge: Harvard University Press, 1978), p. 5.

[10] Deborah Epstein Nord, *The Apprenticeship of Beatrice Webb* (Ithaca: Cornell University Press, 1989), p. 100.

[11] Levy, "Women and Club Life," p. 536.

ratives; we find instead a proliferation of ambiguous identifications and personae as the *possibility* if not the reality of female spectatorship begins to emerge.

Beatrice Potter Webb, her cousin Margaret Harkness, and the poet and novelist Amy Levy were all part of a scattered London network that also included Eleanor Marx and Olive Schreiner, author of *The Story of an African Farm* (1883) and *Woman and Labour* (1911).[12] Harkness, her cousin's confidante since adolescence and the person who introduced Beatrice Potter to the young Fabian Sidney Webb, was a moderately successful novelist and sometime associate of leading labor militants in the 1880s. She acted as Eleanor Marx's guide around the slums of the East End and befriended Schreiner during the South African novelist's early years in England.[13] Webb met Marx, Schreiner, and Levy through her cousin, and although female friendships did not come easily to her, she was fond of Schreiner, admired Levy, and was fascinated by, if somewhat disapproving of, Marx.[14] Eleanor Marx, a talented linguist as well as an active socialist and labor organizer, translated Levy's most successful novel, *Reuben Sachs*, into German. Levy published two novels, a novella, three volumes of poetry, and numerous essays and short stories before she took her life in 1889 at the age of twenty-seven.[15] Her

[12] For other women associated with this group, see Nord, *Apprenticeship of Beatrice Webb*, pp. 129–36. On Harkness, see John Goode, "Margaret Harkness and the Socialist Novel," in *The Socialist Novel in Great Britain: Towards the Recovery of a Tradition*, ed. H. Gustav Klaus (New York: St. Martin's Press, 1982), pp. 45–66; and Eileen Sypher, "The Novels of Margaret Harkness," *Turn-of-the-Century Woman* 1 (Winter 1984): 12–26.

[13] For Harkness's friendship with Eleanor Marx, see Yvonne Kapp, *Eleanor Marx* (New York: Pantheon, 1976), 2:261; and for her relationship with Schreiner, see *The Letters of Olive Schreiner, 1876–1920*, ed. S. C. Cronwright-Schreiner (London: T. Fisher Unwin, 1924), pp. 76, 101–2, 112, 135.

[14] Beatrice Webb, *My Apprenticeship* (London: Longmans, n.d.), pp. 147, 341, 258.

[15] Amy Levy was the author of *Reuben Sachs* (1888); *The Romance of a Shop* (1888); "Miss Meredith" (1889); *Xantippe and Other Verse* (1881); *A Minor Poet and Other Verse* (1884); and *A London Plane Tree* (1889). For a discussion of her career, see Melvyn New's introduction to his valuable edition of Levy's writings. The reasons for Levy's suicide are not absolutely clear. We know from the letters of her contemporaries that she was depressed. Olive Schreiner wrote to Havelock Ellis: "In her last note to me she said, 'You care for science and art and helping your fellow-men, therefore life is worth living to you; to me it is worth nothing'" (*Letters*, p. 207). In his *Dictionary of National Biography* entry on Levy, Richard Garnett writes of the suicide: "No cause can or need be assigned for this lamentable event except constitutional melancholy, intensified by painful losses in her own family, increasing deafness, and probably the apprehension of insanity, combined with a total inability to derive pleasure or consolation from the extraneous circumstances which would have brightened the lives of most others." He refers to her "habitual melancholy" and to the "sadness [which] grew upon her steadily, in spite of flattering success."

suicide, and later Eleanor Marx's, remind us of the tenuousness of the late Victorian independent woman's life. Beatrice Webb fastened onto Levy's story as somehow emblematic of what she called "these terrible days of mental pressure": "It is the supreme courage of fighting a battle for an unknown leader, for an unknown cause," she wrote, "that fails us now and again."[16]

The world these young women inhabited was in part the one Virginia Woolf sought to evoke in the "1880" section of *The Years*: the world of rent collecting and visiting the poor Jews of the East End which so attracts Eleanor Pargiter in the first pages of the novel. To conjure up the year and the decade, Woolf underscores the social marginality that the middle-class Pargiters share with groups more explicitly on the margins, the people who make up what Jane Marcus has called the "diaspora" of "women, Jews, workers, [and] homosexuals."[17] Webb, Levy, Harkness, and others like them—all middle-class women and all in some profound sense socially marginal—were linked not just by their aspirations toward vocation and achievement but also by a critical political stance and by a social position peripheral to the traditional configurations of their class. Each was at odds with family or with some aspect of social convention: Harkness because of her socialist politics, Webb because of her choice of the vocation of social science, and Levy because of her Jewishness on the one hand and her vexed relationship to middle-class Jewry on the other. But they were also anomalous because each woman, already close to the age of thirty by the mid-1880s, regarded marriage as an unlikely or undesirable fate, and each chose London as the locus and subject of her work.

A rector's daughter, Margaret Harkness left her home in Salisbury at the age of twenty-three to make her living in London. She had apparently resisted her family's injunction to bolster their fortune by marrying a wealthy man. Like her cousin she had no formal education, but her family, unlike the wealthier Potters, could not afford to support her bid for independence. "So few women have enough character to live an unmarried life," she wrote to her cousin from Earl's Court in 1878, "or not sink into a nobody, or still worse into a general nuisance. I think an unmarried woman living a true life is far nobler than a married woman. . . . For myself, I know I should have made my people

---

[16] Webb, *My Apprenticeship*, p. 341.

[17] For an extremely suggestive discussion of *The Years*, see Jane Marcus, "*The Years* as Greek Drama, Domestic Novel, and Götterdämmerung," *Bulletin of the New York Public Library* 80 (Winter 1977): 276–301; the quotation is from p. 285.

happier if I had married. I could have made the lives of all easier. . . .
Have I been very selfish?"[18] Complaining in another letter that in London "the life is hard and the work heavy," she nevertheless concluded
that "one has more liberty and freedom here than in other places."[19]
Harkness trained as a nurse, worked as a dispenser, and, with financial
help from the Potters, tried her hand at journalism and then novel
writing.

When Beatrice Webb came to London for a more serious and more
extended stay than her family's yearly visit for the season usually allowed, she roomed with Harkness in a number of different—and contrasting—urban locations. They shuttled between rooms at Katherine
Buildings, a tenement built for casual laborers near St. Katherine's
Dock, where Webb worked as a rent collector, and a comfortable flat
that belonged to her sister Kate Courtney on Cheyne Walk (she would
take a river steamer between Chelsea and the Tower Pier). During the
mid-eighties she struggled with a troubling and ultimately futile relationship with the Radical politician Joseph Chamberlain, a man who
attracted her but disapproved of her ambitions. As the possibility of
marrying Chamberlain seemed more and more remote, she began to
conceive of herself as a spinster—a "glorified spinster," she liked to
say—who had a mission to other unmarried women, particularly those
of her own class, and who would work at the career that Chamberlain
had scorned.[20] In her diary she described her life in London in a pen-
sive but uncharacteristically contented tone:

> Journeys down the Thames in the ferry steamers, especially back by the eve-
> ning light; the picturesque side of London lower-class life, the background
> of grand public buildings with their national historic associations. And then
> once back in that perfect house, Maggie Harkness fresh from her novel-
> writing to greet me to chat on all subjects, human and divine, and to play
> snatches of good music on the parliamentary piano [Webb's brother-in-law,
> Leonard Courtney, was an M.P.]; I, lying the while on the sofa, watching the
> river and the barges on it creeping by. Happy fellowship in work, rest, and

[18] Margaret Harkness to Beatrice Potter, 1878, Passfield Papers, sec. II–1–ii, London
School of Economics and Political Science.

[19] Margaret Harkness to Beatrice Potter, February 22, 1878, Passfield Papers, sec. II–
1–ii. Despite her sense of "liberty and freedom," Harkness told her cousin in this same
letter, her parents had insisted she leave a boarding house in Westminster because "they
think a place where all classes are mixed and no difference made, unfit for a lady to be
in."

[20] See Nord, *Apprenticeship of Beatrice Webb*, pp. 129–36. See Walkowitz, *City of Dreadful
Delight*, pp. 61–68 on the idea of the "glorified spinster."

also in memories. "Who would have thought it," we said constantly to one another, "when we two as schoolgirls stood on the moorland near Bournemouth, . . . discussed our religious difficulties and gave vent to all our world-sorrow, and ended by prophesying we should in ten years be talking of cooks and baby linen, . . . who would have thought of our real future?"[21]

Both women had "passed through the misery of strong and useless feeling" and were at work making lives for themselves beyond domesticity. Would their lives change again, or had they settled into "the groove [they were] destined to run in"?[22]

Amy Levy's vision of her social and familial role can be guessed at from her novel *Reuben Sachs*, in which the marriage market of the upper-middle-class London Jewish community is imagined as crass, hypocritical, and cruel. Love does not provide a strong enough motive to marry in the face of economic considerations, and women without a dowry, regardless of their talents and intelligence, must await promotion by marriage. In a whimsical poem called "A Ballad of Religion and Marriage," Levy imagines that adherence to the great duality of married and unmarried would ultimately go the way of belief in God:

> Monogamous, still at our post,
> Reluctantly we undergo
> Domestic round of boiled and roast,
> Yet deem the whole proceeding slow.
> Daily the secret murmurs grow;
> We are no more content to plod
> Along the beaten paths—and so
> Marriage must go the way of God.
> . . . .
> Grant, in a million years at most,
> Folk shall be neither pairs nor odd—
> Alas! we sha'n't be there to boast
> "Marriage has gone the way of God!"[23]

[21] *The Diary of Beatrice Webb*, ed. Norman MacKenzie and Jeanne MacKenzie (Cambridge: Harvard University Press, 1982), 1:139.

[22] Ibid.

[23] Amy Levy, "A Ballad of Religion and Marriage," n.d., Houghton Library, Harvard University, published privately.

Levy was distinctly one of the "odd women," like the heroines of George Gissing's 1893 novel of that title, and like the four sisters in her own first novel, *The Romance of a Shop*. She regarded herself as singular in a world of the paired and, because she was a Jew and an unmarried woman, as an outsider and virtual foreigner in English society.

Beatrice Webb took advantage of the acceptable middle-class avocation of slumming to enter into the world of the East End, first as a Charity Organization Society worker and then as a rent collector in Katherine Buildings. For the self-taught but highly intellectual Webb, the question of vocation was a particularly problematic one: How could she serve humanity, as both gender and zeitgeist would dictate, and yet exercise the talents of a "brain-worker" and aspiring social scientist? She discovered her vocation—that of social investigator—in the process of keeping track of the tenants of Katherine Buildings. Following the example of Octavia Hill, Webb and her co-collector Ella Pycroft carefully screened tenants, collected rents, tried to help with family crises, and evicted disruptive tenants and delinquent rent payers.[24] They kept a large ledger, now in the archives of the London School of Economics, in which Webb wrote case histories of the tenants and recorded the details of their origins, employment, illnesses, marriages, and offspring. It is clear from the ledger and from Webb's diaries that her authentic activity at Katherine Buildings was not policing the tenants or bringing moral enlightenment to their lives but rather observing and analyzing their positions in society in relation to the objective circumstances that had determined them. Patterns of unemployment and the insidious effects of casual labor began to emerge in her records, and they formed a basis for the investigation of dock labor and the tailoring trade that she was soon to undertake with Charles Booth. This interest in the analysis of poverty separated her from women such as Octavia Hill or Emma Cons, then managing a similar working-class dwelling in South London. In her discussions with both of these women, Webb discovered that neither kept accurate records of tenants' lives and movements, and neither considered it necessary. What was wanted was *action*, Hill told

[24] Pycroft, a Devonshire physician's daughter, came to London in 1883 to look for work. She spent five years at Katherine Buildings, turned to teaching, and in the 1890s became adviser to the Technical Education Board of the London County Council. She was engaged briefly to Maurice Paul, son of the publisher Kegan Paul, who ran a boys' club in the tenement.

her, not more "windy talk."[25] "Did not attempt to theorise about her work," Webb noted of Emma Cons in her diary, "no desire to solve the general questions of the hour."[26]

It seemed clear to Webb that in choosing to take an analytic rather than an active posture toward poverty and the poor, she was embarking on a masculine rather than a feminine form of vocation. To be an investigator and to use the information derived thereby in order to speculate on social structures and policies was the province of male social scientists and theorists; women might investigate as a help to managing or serving, or as a way of gleaning information for others. Pondering the "questions of the hour" and theoretical analyses of social problems would only deflect women from their proper sphere of influence. It was as if, for Webb, the act of analyzing what investigators observed amounted to a presumptuous and unseemly extension of masculine spectatorship. "If I were a man, and had an intellect," Webb wrote in her diary in a fit of insecurity, "I would leave political action and political theorising to those with faith, and examine and try to describe correctly and proportionately *what actually happened* in the different strata of society."[27] Not only were service and activism seen as appropriately feminine gestures, but the particular ethic of female service promoted by Octavia Hill valued, above all, the contributions of married women—or at least women who were committed first and foremost to their own homes. Hill did not want professionals or even full-time volunteers, nor did she favor women workers who gave up their own domestic happiness and went to live among the poor.[28] As Martha Vicinus points out, unmarried settlement house workers operated under the paradox of enforcing middle-class domestic values while they themselves were "walking evidence of the opposite."[29]

Eventually, for reasons both personal and cultural, Webb abandoned an activism that embodied private and traditional feminine virtues and adopted for herself a masculine intellectual stance. When she turned to the work of social investigation, she assumed the "scientific" tone she found appropriate to her descriptions of dock laborers, workers in the tailoring trades, and the Jewish community of the East End. I have

---

[25] Webb, *My Apprenticeship*, p. 239.

[26] Ibid., p. 229.

[27] Ibid., p. 166 (July 1884).

[28] See Octavia Hill, *Homes of the London Poor* (London: Macmillan, 1883), pp. 66–67.

[29] Vicinus, *Independent Women*, p. 239.

talked elsewhere about the distance, presumed objectivity, and unconscious censoriousness that characterized her contributions to Charles
Booth's *East London* (1889).[30] It is clear that in these essays she is striving to suppress feelings of sympathy and identification, as well as any
hint of consciousness of gender, taking as her model the practice of
scientific analysis, a mode of inquiry and discourse associated with masculine intellectual enterprise. By suppressing gender, she suppressed
sympathetic identification as well. In two other striking instances of
observation, however, she departs from efforts to reproduce the "objective" stance of the social scientist, expresses feelings of identification
with her working-class subjects, and betrays an awareness of gender as
an important part of that identification. Neither piece of writing—the
first a series of letters she wrote to her father about the workers of
Bacup in Lancashire, and the second an account of her experiences as
a "trouser-hand," or seamstress, in an East End tailor's shop—was published as a work of investigation, and the latter was taken by many of
its readers as a work of fiction.[31]

What emerges from these two less conventional texts of investigation
is that when Webb could allow herself to write as a woman (a stance
she generally avoided in order to assume the authority of science), she
also allowed herself to express feelings about her subjects other than
disapproval and detachment. In her evocation of Bacup she stresses the
camaraderie between male and female workers. She writes: "They are
a happy lot of people . . . men and women mixing together in a free
and easy manner—but without any coarseness that I can see, the masculine sentiment about marriage being 'that a man's got no *friend* until
he's a woman of his own.' Parties of young men and women go off
together for a week to Blackpool, sometimes on cheap trips to London—and as the women earn as much or nearly as much as the men
. . . there is no assumption of masculine superiority!" In her piece on
the East End tailor's shop she conjures up a congenial community of
Jewish women workers, an ostensible matriarchy in which she is encouraged by her boss, Mrs. Moses, despite her obvious ineptness at
sewing and is comforted by her co-workers when she feels humiliated.
Her feelings of class superiority and professional distance fade in the

[30] See Nord, *Apprenticeship of Beatrice Webb*, chap. 6.
[31] Webb's letters on Bacup can be found in *My Apprenticeship*, pp. 132–48; and her
account of the tailor's shop, "Pages from a Work-Girl's Diary," appeared in *The Nineteenth
Century* 25 (September 1888): 301–14.

face of possible disgrace as a working girl, and she finds herself moved to the point of tears by the surreptitious gift of a slice of bread and butter from a co-worker who sees that she has no food for tea.[32]

In the context of this discussion what seems most significant about Webb's shifting voice and consciousness is her ability to express feelings of solidarity with other women, specifically working-class women, when she is *disguised*—when she is *not herself* in the minds of her public, and when she is, therefore, able to *be herself* on the most private level. On her trip to Bacup she passed herself off as a Welsh farmer's daughter, and in the East End she was taken for a Jewish worker.[33] After rejecting the traditional feminine stance of service and adopting the masculine posture of "brain-worker" or scientist, Webb could expose her personal sense of marginality only in the guise of someone else.

Susan Squier has written suggestively of Virginia Woolf's ambivalent identification with urban "outsiders" on the one hand and "insiders" on the other. In the 1927 essay "Street Haunting" Woolf projects herself imaginatively into the roles of washerwoman, publican, dwarf, and street singer, but without fully relinquishing her middle-class, male-identified stance.[34] In Woolf's case it is not a visible disguise that allows for this projection but an invisible and tentative gesture of mind: "Into each of these lives one could penetrate a little way, far enough to give oneself the illusion that one is not tethered to a single mind, but can put on briefly for a few minutes the bodies and minds of others."[35] As her title suggests, Woolf's is a ghostly presence on the city streets rather than an actively engaged one, and her identification with urban outsiders—women as well as male workers and street people—is, like Webb's, incomplete.

Female identification had indeed become problematic for Webb. The bond she felt with women such as Maggie Harkness emerges in her work only covertly, as in her evocation of Mrs. Moses's tailoring shop, and socialist politics took her even further from overt female identification. By 1889 she had given up the chance to undertake a

[32] Webb, *My Apprenticeship*, p. 144; and Nord, *Apprenticeship of Beatrice Webb*, pp. 165–70, 174–77.

[33] Webb's maternal relatives, the Akeds, came from Bacup, and some of Webb's cousins were among the people she "observed." Her paternal grandmother, Mary Seddon, was believed by some—including Webb—to have been Jewish. Her disguises were, therefore, also attempts to recover identity.

[34] See Squier, *Virginia Woolf and London*, pp. 48–49.

[35] Virginia Woolf, "Street Haunting, A London Adventure" (1930), in *Collected Essays* (London: Hogarth Press, 1967), 4:165.

study for Booth of women's work in the East End and had embarked instead on her history of the cooperative movement. Neither the investigation of women per se nor the adoption of a supposedly genderless investigative stance appeared to Webb to solve the problem of who and what she was when she scrutinized and assessed the urban poor.

The now nearly forgotten novelistic career of Webb's cousin Margaret Harkness began with *A City Girl* (1887), a novel that grew out of her observations of the tenants of Katherine Buildings—called Charlotte Buildings in the novel—where the cousins lodged together for a time, Harkness because the rooms there were cheap and Webb because she was working as the rent collector.[36] If Harkness is remembered at all, it is as the recipient of a letter from Friedrich Engels about this first novel, which she had sent to him for comment. In what is now a classic statement of socialist aesthetics, Engels praised the truthfulness with which Harkness had represented the circumstances of poverty but regretted that she had not shown the "convulsive attempts" of the working class to subvert those circumstances. Proletarian rebellions, he wrote, "belong to history and may therefore lay claim to a place in the domain of realism."[37] Whether because she chose to follow Engels's advice or because her own political and aesthetic evolution took her in that direction, Harkness set her next novel, *Out of Work* (1888), against the background of the Hyde Park riots and a later one, *George Eastmont, Wanderer* (1905), during the period of the 1889 dock strike. In these later novels she focuses on both the demoralization and the will to resistance that typify the urban poor.

Just as Webb departed from traditions and patterns of middle-class women's relations with the poor in her work, so Harkness introduced in her novels elements alien to the conventions of late nineteenth-century social realism. The social realist or naturalist fictions of Arthur Morrison, George Moore, Rudyard Kipling, and George Gissing depicting working-class life are almost without exception apolitical. Many focus on the demoralization of the urban poor by representing them

[36] In an essay in the *Fortnightly Review* 52 (August 1892): 191, Evelyn March Phillipps comments that, in light of the difficulty of finding appropriate and affordable lodgings in London, genteel working women "have utilised to a considerable extent the huge blocks of artisans' dwellings which have sprung up in all parts of London." Harkness was one such woman, and Honnor Morten, nurse, graduate of Bedford College, and founder of a settlement house in Hoxton, was another (Vicinus, *Independent Women*, p. 223).

[37] See George J. Becker, ed., *Documents of Modern Literary Realism* (Princeton: Princeton University Press, 1963), p. 484.

in isolation, separated from any interchange with the middle class, insulated within the slums. Arthur Morrison's novel *A Child of the Jago* (1896), which tells of a criminal enclave within the East End, and Kipling's "Record of Badalia Herodsfoot," which relates the story of a single East End street, are both successful examples of what Peter Keating has described as a "horizontal" cutting into society.[38] While brilliantly evoking the horrors of slum life, these novels and stories tend to ignore both the class rebellion that the Hyde Park riots and the dock strike represented and the class relations that provide an analysis or interpretation of poverty and degradation.[39] Not only is there no way out of the "nether world," as Gissing named it, but in these works, there is also no real explanation for its existence.

In *Out of Work*, set in the year of Queen Victoria's first Jubilee, Harkness records the rage of the unemployed as well as the gradual disintegration of the casual laborer, forced into idleness by irregular work and into the workhouse by scant wages. As in most of her novels after *A City Girl*, however, she also hints at the certainty of political change and attempts to put the condition of the working class into historical perspective. The narrator of *Out of Work*, speaking of casual dock labor in the 1880s, notes:

> Years hence, when children read in lesson-books about the Age of Competition, the docks will be given as an illustration of the competitive system after it reached a climax. Boys and girls will read that thousands of Englishmen fought daily at the dock gates for tickets; that starving men behind pressed so hard on starving men in front, that the latter were nearly cut in two by the iron railings which kept them from work; that contractors were mauled by hungry men; that brick-bats and stones were hurled at labour-masters by men whose families were starving.[40]

In her third novel, *Captain Lobe* (1889), a tale of the Salvation Army later renamed *In Darkest London* after William Booth's *In Darkest England*

[38] Peter Keating, *The Working Classes in Victorian Fiction* (New York: Barnes and Noble, 1971), p. 130. Keating credits the influence of Zola in discussing this aspect of English naturalism and points out that giving a horizontal portrait of working-class life enabled the novelist to refrain from passing moral judgment. Although this is clearly the case, isolating the working class in fiction also depoliticized its identity.

[39] Keating has commented that Harkness "attempted to reverse the class bias of industrial fiction and correct the blindness of late-Victorian novelists to the urban workers' revolutionary potential" (ibid., p. 245).

[40] John Law [Margaret Harkness], *Out of Work* (London: Swan Sonnenschein, 1888), p. 162. Here, as in Harkness's use of the setting of Katherine Buildings, her experience and evocation of East End life are very close to Webb's.

(which was, in turn, named after Henry M. Stanley's account of Africa), a brutal tour of the degradation and domestic violence of Seven Dials is followed by a warning—if not a threat—that the "enforced idleness" of the unemployed is dangerous: "Remember that a million men throughout the United Kingdom are out of work; and then think what your fate will be if the police take the part of the unemployed."[41] Later, in *George Eastmont* (1905), this anticipation of social revolution becomes more complex and ambivalent, as Harkness gives vent to her disillusionment with the leadership of the dock strike and with armchair socialists. Yet even in this novel it is the relations between classes and, above all, the importance of politics and the dynamics of history that are underscored. Even in *A City Girl*, her first novel, she rewrites the traditional story of the working-class girl ruined by the upper-class gent as the East End seamstress seduced by a married West End radical in order to expose both the ideological hypocrisies and the personal callousness of the politically committed bourgeois.

In addition to introducing an agenda of socialist politics into fin-de-siècle realism, Harkness added the perspective of the socially engaged, independent middle-class woman whose relationship to her own class is marginal and strained. Although writers such as Morrison, Kipling, and Moore used working-class women—Lizerunt, Badalia Herodsfoot, and Esther Waters—as the centerpiece of urban description, none of them took as his subject the consciousness of the middle-class woman who discovers the life of the city and its slums. (Gissing is exceptional here only in a limited sense, in that his novel about independent middle-class women, *The Odd Women*, is an urban novel but not, like *The Nether World* or *Demos*, a story of working-class life.)

In Harkness's novels, as Eileen Sypher has pointed out, the "strong, individual woman, whether she be poor and struggling, a slum savior, an upper class political woman, or a socialist 'labor mistress,' " plays a prominent role.[42] Although Harkness's working-class heroines seem familiar literary types, her middle-class slum workers, Salvation Army officers, and Fabians reflect a contemporary reality that had as yet no literary existence. Here Harkness consciously creates new types, the most interesting of which is Mary Cameron, the woman who has a platonic bond with George Eastmont and who helps to care for his

---

[41] John Law [Margaret Harkness], *In Darkest London: A Story of the Salvation Army* (London: William Reeves, 1891), p. 58.

[42] Sypher, "Novels of Margaret Harkness," p. 21.

laudanum-addicted working-class wife. Cameron is a portrait of Harkness, with aspects of Olive Schreiner, Beatrice Webb, and others mixed in. She lives in Ladies' Chambers, "a funny place, full of medical students—she-boys she called them—lady-journalists, artists, and widows." Cameron has left her parents' rectory in the country at an early age and makes her living in London correcting publishers' proofs and teaching typing and shorthand. She tries to do good works in the slums and quickly joins the socialists in protest against the social misery she observes. It is the physical reality of Cameron's life—her room "furnished with Japanese ware, art muslin, and the various nick-nacks that lady-students and their consoeurie gather," her short, stout frame, and her exhausting but precious work—that makes her a compelling and original character, a new urban type in the novel of city life.[43]

But as Eileen Sypher has also suggested in writing about Harkness, the novelist cannot sustain the initial attention and importance she gives her independent women. Mary Cameron remains a secondary figure, playing a supporting role to Eastmont, the male hero of the people, and she virtually disappears from the novel before the novelist, as if in an afterthought, marries her off to a fellow Fabian.[44] Like Olive Schreiner, who used the pseudonym Ralph Iron, Harkness chose a pen name—John Law—which suggests a kind of masculine authority and forcefulness; and, like Webb in her official works of social investigation, Harkness did not wish to declare her female identity in her work or to write from an openly feminist or even avowedly female point of view. As terms such as "she-boys" and "lady-journalists" imply, Harkness partly disowns her own identity through irony, even as she betrays it, and she repeatedly uses only male characters to represent the public world of working-class or middle-class politics. Socialism and labor organizing are imagined primarily as male spheres of action and thought, even though Harkness herself played a role in the dock strike and was active in the Social Democratic Federation.[45] Her allegiance to socialist politics and to the idea of class rebellion, like Webb's adherence to the principles of scientific inquiry, took precedence over her tie to the

[43] John Law [Margaret Harkness], *George Eastmont: Wanderer* (London: Burns and Oates, 1905), pp. 49, 88. Olive Schreiner lived in Ladies' Chambers on Chenies Street near the British Museum (see *Letters*, p. 164); and Martha Vicinus discusses such dwellings for single women in an appendix to *Independent Women* (pp. 296–97).

[44] Sypher, "Novels of Margaret Harkness," pp. 23–25.

[45] See Keating, *Working Classes in Victorian Fiction*, p. 242, on Harkness's role in the dock strike; and Goode, "Margaret Harkness and the Socialist Novel," p. 51, on the Social Democratic Federation.

community of marginal, independent women. As in her novels, the consciousness and representation of female experience and conflict were displaced into a genderless politics and an identification with the distress and the heroism of the workers.

Amy Levy, the least well known of the three women under consideration here, addressed most directly the question of singleness and urban existence, and was also the most overtly ambivalent about the sexual identification of her public persona. Her Jewishness made her more thoroughly and permanently an outsider in English society than either Webb or Harkness: theirs was at least in part a willed marginality; Levy's was inherited and indelible. Still, in her poetry she writes only obliquely of her alien status, and her novel *Reuben Sachs* signals a marked ambivalence about her ties to her own people. She was the only one of the three who had been to university—she was educated at Newnham—and her experiences at Cambridge may well have heightened her feminist sensibilities while, at the same time, binding her to certain male traditions of learning and literature, especially in the realm of poetry.

Her second volume of poems, *A London Plane Tree*, published posthumously in 1889, contains two illustrations: the first is a frontispiece drawing of a plane tree next to a church, and the second shows a young woman seated, hand on brow, at a desk, surrounded by papers that cover the desk and spill off onto the floor. Placed in front of an open window through which the spires and rooftops of city buildings can be glimpsed, she is the quintessential woman writer alone with her work in a London garret (see figure 15).[46] She is a descendant of Elizabeth Barrett Browning's Aurora Leigh, who sits in her room above the streets of London, "serene and unafraid of solitude," writing her poetry and watching the sun "startle the slant roofs and chimney-pots / With splashes of fierce colour."[47] A quotation from Austin Dobson opposite the frontispiece reads, "Mine is an urban Muse, and bound / By some strange law to paven ground." The first poems in the collection celebrate urban life, chronicling the omnibus ride and the newspaper seller's cry, and summon up the poet's view from behind "garret-pane."

[46] Amy Levy, *A London Plane Tree and Other Verse* (New York: Frederick A. Stokes, 1890). The two illustrations are by J. Bernard Partridge, who appears in Levy's novel *The Romance of a Shop* (Boston: Cupples and Hurd, 1889) as the artist Frank Jermyn.

[47] Elizabeth Barrett Browning, *Aurora Leigh and Other Poems* (London: Women's Press, 1978), p. 120.

Figure 15 J. Bernard Partridge, "Odds and Ends." Amy Levy, *A London Plane-Tree and Other Verse* (1890).

Levy's own experience of the city is here, in her untiring enjoyment of seeing the human pageant unfold from the top of a bus, and in her sense that for burdened souls like hers the city is preferable to village garden calm: "For me, the roar and hurry of the town, / Wherein more lightly seems to press the burden / Of individual life that weighs me down."

In more cases than not, however, personal experience is noticeably camouflaged by the use of a male persona. In "London in July" the poet, speaking in the voice of a lovesick man, wonders "that all the people in the street / Should wear one woman's face," and in numerous other lyrics in the collection the beloved, usually an unresponsive one, is imagined as a woman. In these poems Levy uses conventional forms, among them the ballade, as if practicing as an apprentice the traditional modes of her poet's trade.[48] Somewhat paradoxically, the lyric enabled her to achieve impersonality, to use another's voice, a man's voice, while other, more impersonal forms—dramatic monologues and verse plays—allowed her to speak as a woman, to express private feeling in a veiled or disguised way. There are, however, a couple of interesting exceptions. In the poems "Philosophy" and "To E." the poet speaks more personally of relations with men that are tensely, and perhaps misguidedly, platonic. In the former she writes: "Proudly we sat, we two, on high, / Throned in our Objectivity; / Scarce friends, not lovers (each avers), / But sexless, safe Philosophers." But her most powerful expressions of female passion, resentment, and longing are to be found not among her lyric verses but in her first volume of poems, *A Minor Poet,* in the dramatic modes she learned from Tennyson and the Brownings.

"Xantippe" and "Medea," in which she inhabits the personae of two classical antiheroines, are Levy's most memorable and original poems, and they are also, not coincidentally, her most feminist poems.[49] In form they resemble the works of her Victorian forefathers, but in perspective they look forward to "Helen" and "Eurydice" of H.D. In "Xantippe" the rejected and ridiculed wife of Socrates, famous for her legendary shrewishness and slow wit, reveals what it was like to be married to the "high philosopher" who "deigned not to stoop to touch so slight a thing / As the fine fabric of a woman's brain." Socrates saved his love and learning for "this Athenian city and her sons" and failed to teach Xantippe what as a bride she yearned to have, a "tongue / That should proclaim the stately mysteries." Her "tender language wholly misconceived," she becomes to all the world a "household vessel," untutored and ill-tempered, ignorant and bitter. In "Medea," written as a fragment of a play rather than as a dramatic monologue, we have the plaint of another ill-used, apparently monstrous woman. Medea rails against her husband's treachery and betrayal, accuses him of duplicity and ungratefulness; but it is, above all, her sense of foreignness, of being a lusty Colchian in the midst of cold Corinthians, which dominates the poem. A citizen of Corinth declares to Medea

[48] It is possible that Levy addressed such poems to women because she was a lesbian, but her conventional love lyrics do not at all give that impression. These poems seem rather like exercises, often spirited ones, in which she carries convention to the point of taking a male poet's voice. Rather than revealing intimate feeling, they seem instead to be burying it almost completely.

[49] Amy Levy, *A Minor Poet and Other Verse* (London: T. Fisher Unwin, 1884), pp. 15–30, 31–58. "Xantippe" was originally published in *Dublin University Magazine* in 1880.

that he likes not "your swart skins and purple hair; / Your black fierce eyes where the brows meet across"; he prefers instead "gold hair, lithe limbs and gracious smiles." Levy, the anomalous Jewish woman, surely stands behind the alien and enraged Medea, the stranger in a strange land who is marked as much in physical type as in temperament.

In her two novels, *The Romance of a Shop* and *Reuben Sachs*, both published in 1889, as well as in other prose writings, Levy found it possible to express more directly her personal experience of marginality. Her essays and short stories, published in a variety of jounals—among them Oscar Wilde's *Woman's World*—give a fictional account of the world of intellectual London women in the 1880s which historians have recently begun to reconstruct.[50] And they evoke the social world of the British Museum Reading Room, where "dusty people . . . bustled and dawdled, whispered and flirted"; the difficulty of reentering metropolitan society after the rarefied atmosphere of Newnham; the humiliations of working as a governess and being a genteel but poor single woman (Jane Eyre is a frequent point of reference for her); and the paradoxes of life in a liberating but still frustrating decade. Says the narrator of "Wise in Her Generation": "My room is full of blue-books, pamphlets, and philosophical treatises. *Sesame and Lilies* and Clifford's *Essays* are hobnobbing on the table; the *Bitter Cry of Outcast London* and a report of the Democratic Federation stand together on the shelf. This is an age of independence and side-saddle; but how often is woman doomed to ride pillion on a man's hobby-horse!"[51]

The chronicle of independent urban women—or urban women striving to be independent—continues in Levy's first novel, which anticipates Gissing's novel *The Odd Women* in a number of interesting ways. It tells the story of the four unmarried orphaned Lorimer sisters, who are left virtually penniless by a brilliant but reckless father, and who determine to make their living as something other than governesses or

---

[50] See Melvyn New's introduction to *The Complete Novels and Selected Writings of Amy Levy* for Wilde's estimate of Levy.

[51] See, in New's edition of *The Complete Novels and Selected Writings of Amy Levy*, "The Recent Telepathic Occurrence at the British Museum" (1888), p. 432; "Between Two Stools" (1883); "Griselda" (1888); and "Wise in Her Generation" (1890), p. 494. In *The City of Dreadful Delight* Judith Walkowitz describes the British Museum Reading Room in the 1880s as "the stomping ground of the 'bohemian set,' a place where trysts were made between heterodox men and women" (p. 69). Beatrice Potter first laid eyes on Eleanor Marx in the refreshment room of the British Museum, and she was first introduced to Sidney Webb by Margaret Harkness in rooms across from the British Museum. See Nord, *Apprenticeship of Beatrice Webb*, pp. 53, 134.

teachers.[52] Unlike Gissing's Madden sisters, however, they have a skill, photography, which they have learned from their father, and they undertake to set up a photographer's shop in Baker Street. Gertrude Lorimer, the sister who seems closest to Levy herself, finds the idea of business appealing: it is "progressive" and "a creature capable of growth," the "very qualities in which women's work is dreadfully lacking."[53] In their zeal for the world of business and in their belief that it is a means to independence, the sisters look forward to Gissing's Rhoda Nunn and Mary Barfoot rather than to his Alice, Gertrude, and Monica Madden.

The Romance of a Shop succeeds at conveying how difficult and yet how exhilarating it was to be a woman alone in London in the 1880s. Like the unprotected women imagined by Woolf in *The Pargiters*, another work that Levy's novel anticipates, the Lorimer sisters are made so convincingly vulnerable that the eldest sister, Fanny, prudish and old-fashioned in her instincts, feels them to be as "removed from the advantages and disadvantages of gallantry as the withered hag who swept the crossing near Baker Street Station."[54] The shop, quite realistically, is always on the verge of failure, and even the sisters' friends expect female photographers to produce cheap photographs. But, as Lucy Lorimer says when she sees the studio and rooms in Baker Street that Gertrude has rented, "This is work, this is life." Gertrude, referred to as the most "inveterate cockney" of the lot, regrets not at all that she has been "transported from the comparative tameness of Campden Hill to the regions where the pulses of the great city could be felt distinctly as they beat and throbbed," and she harbors a "secret, childish love for the gas-lit street, for the sight of the hurrying people, the lamps, the hansom cabs, flickering in and out of the yellow haze, like so many fire-flies."[55]

Levy's first novel shares the urban sensibility of her "London Plane Tree" poems but combines it with a self-consciously female urbanism. As she reminds us in another piece, the *flâneuse* remains a thing of the

---

[52] I can find no evidence that Gissing read *The Romance of a Shop*, but in his diary he does mention taking *Reuben Sachs* out of the library in April 1892, a very few months before he started to write *The Odd Women*. See *London and the Life of Literature in Late Victorian England: The Diary of George Gissing*, ed. Pierre Coustillas (Hassocks, Sussex: Harvester Press, 1978), p. 276.

[53] Levy, *The Romance of a Shop*, p. 10.

[54] Ibid., p. 100.

[55] Ibid., pp. 61, 113.

imagination; the gaslight must be enjoyed by women in private. Like Aurora Leigh and the *London Plane Tree* poet pictured in her garret, Gertrude finds that her favored vantage point for observing the city is from within her flat. We most often see her gazing longingly and lovingly at the street from her window, able to relish the "London pageant" only in the safe position of hidden spectator, of voyeur, seeing but not being seen. (The sisters first get to "know" their neighbor Frank Jermyn by watching him from the window, so that when he finally appears at their flat, they justifiably feel a certain familiarity with him.) Gertrude cannot occupy the city street as men do; she must enjoy its public life from a largely private vantage point. She identifies with the kinds of scorned and tortured heroines Levy used for her dramatic poems: when the novel begins she has been writing a play about Charlotte Corday, and she refers to herself repeatedly as "Cassandra."

But Levy's failure in the novel is precisely that she does not know what to do with her independent, idiosyncratic heroines—particularly Gertrude—and resorts to killing off the beautiful, "fallen" sister and marrying off the remaining ones. Lucy's fiancé, Frank, has gone off to cover the Boer War as an illustrator and is reported dead; but he makes a miraculous reappearance and saves Lucy from spinsterhood. Even Gertrude, who in the closing pages of the novel still believes that she will continue to pay "the penalty, which her sex always pays one way or another, for her struggles for strength and independence," is reunited at the very last minute with the older, distinguished Lord Watergate, a man she has earlier rejected.[56] More disappointing than these marital dei ex machina is the thrust of the entire final third of the novel. It begins to resemble a shoddy *Pride and Prejudice*, with all four sisters searching for an appropriate mate, and ceases to foreshadow the far more sobering and clear-eyed *Odd Women* (although that too owes something to Austen's novel, more as a subversion, perhaps, than as a recapitulation). After the struggle for independence is essentially won in the novel, Levy cannot sustain it, at least in part because she understands that independence as painful, precarious, and exhausting, and because as a fledgling novelist she shies away from writing a book that might tell an uncomfortable truth.

Levy's second novel, *Reuben Sachs*, confronts directly that aspect of herself that she so obliquely expresses in her Medea poem—her Jewishness. But her story of middle-class London Jewry is told initially from

---

[56] Ibid., p. 294.

the point of view of a man. The novel's eponymous hero, who suffers from a nervous condition and unlimited ambition, turns his back on the poor Jewish woman he loves so as not to thwart a budding political career. The novel exposes the crassness of the Sachs family in terms that understandably earned Levy the disapproval of some of her coreligionists. As one cynical member of the family says about a Gentile friend in the novel: "I think that he was shocked at finding us so little like the people in *Daniel Deronda*. . . . Ours [is] the religion of materialism. The corn and the wine and the oil; the multiplication of the seed; the conquest of the hostile tribes—these have always had more attraction for us than the harp and crown of a spiritualized existence."[57] If Margaret Harkness tried to capture the nature of interactions between classes, in *Reuben Sachs* Levy sought to pillory the upper-middle class through her portrait of London Jewry. That Eleanor Marx translated the novel into German is not surprising, for its indictment of upper-bourgeois life—in this case Jewish life—is scathing.[58] *Reuben Sachs* can indeed be seen as a latter-day *Daniel Deronda*, a revision from inside the Jewish community and ultimately, as we shall see, from a woman's point of view.

Something interesting happens about two thirds of the way through the novel: it ceases to be written from the perspective of Reuben Sachs and shifts its focus onto Judith Quixano, the woman Reuben loves but rejects, and becomes a novel about the choices a poor but genteel woman must make rather than one about the vexed ambitions of a young man. The novel emerges as a *Daniel Deronda* that puts Mirah rather than Daniel at its center and imagines a fate for her quite different from that of Eliot's eclipsed Jewish heroine. From the moment of Reuben's rejection of Judith, it is her consciousness that dominates the narrative. It is as if Levy ceases to throw her voice, as she had done in so many of her poems, and allows herself to imagine without disguise the chilling position of the unmarried woman trapped in lifelong celibacy or loveless marriage. As a result of her sorrow and disappointment, Judith is awakened from a kind of willed ignorance about the ways of the world, but her fate is to be a soul grown "frozen and ap-

---

[57] Amy Levy, *Reuben Sachs* (London: Macmillan, 1888), pp. 115–17. For the response to the novel, see Richard Garnett's entry on Levy in the *Dictionary of National Biography*, 11: 1041.

[58] Yvonne Kapp notes that Marx must have translated *Reuben Sachs* immediately after its publication (the German edition also appeared in 1889), and that it is the only work she is known to have translated out of, rather than into, her native tongue. See Kapp, *Eleanor Marx*, p. 258.

palled.''[59] She marries a man she does not love (he is rich and Gentile, and finds her exotic), and as the novel closes we leave her absorbing the news of Reuben's premature death and anticipating the birth of a child. The chilling sense of limited possibilities that Levy avoided in the conclusion of her first novel here dominates the ending. The aspirations of middle-class manhood and womanhood alike have been utterly thwarted.

The particular community of independent women I have been describing dissolved by the end of the 1880s. Amy Levy committed suicide in September 1889, and Olive Schreiner sailed for South Africa the next month; in the fall of 1890 Margaret Harkness left England, having broken with her cousin as well as with her labor allies Tom Mann and John Burns; and Beatrice Potter turned to the Fabians by the end of the decade and became engaged to Sidney Webb in 1891. The strains that had always existed in these women's friendships finally overwhelmed them. Both Webb and Schreiner complained of Harkness's constant requests to borrow money, and when Harkness announced her departure from England, Webb mourned the end of a "fifteen years' friendship" with the cousin who had been "as tender to one in one's trouble as she has been traitorous to me in success."[60]

The creation of an autonomous existence outside family or residential community remained elusive for single women in the 1880s. There was as yet no adequately comfortable social or economic niche for the single woman who did not exist, or did not want to exist, within an institutional framework; and the kind of loosely defined network of women of which Webb, Harkness, and Levy were a part was of necessity a fragile one. The physical and psychological difficulties of a self-sufficient urban life overcame, indeed defeated, many women who wanted to live neither as daughters nor as wives nor as members of a sisterhood that would act as surrogate family. The familial roles invented for them by society held no appeal, but neither did the role of spinster, at least as it was defined by those groups of women who found strength in celibacy and continued to make use of the power of sexual difference.

At the end of the decade, as if to declare her independence from the community of emancipated women, Beatrice Webb signed the in-

[59] Levy, *Reuben Sachs*, p. 266.
[60] See Schreiner, *Letters*, p. 112; and Webb, *Diary*, 1:341.

famous antisuffrage petition drafted by Mary Ward and published in the *Nineteenth Century*, a gesture she later referred to in *My Apprenticeship* as a "false step." Buried in a footnote to this episode in the autobiography is its revealing sequel. Frederic Harrison implored her to write a rebuttal to Millicent Fawcett's suffragist response to the petition, but Webb declined on the grounds that she had "as yet accomplished no work which gives me the right to speak as a representative of the class Mrs. Fawcett would enfranchise: *celibate women.*"[61] About to embark on a career as social investigator, eager to be regarded first as a professional and only second as a woman, Webb did not want a label— whether antisuffragist, spinster, or celibate woman—that put gender at the core of her identity. For each of the women I have considered here, other aspects of identity—religion, politics, vocation—seems to have taken precedence over gender, but contemporary constructions of spinsterhood, whether they embraced or opposed conventional notions of femininity, made gender the unavoidable and central issue with which women were forced to contend.

Webb, Harkness, and Levy, like other women who found it difficult to reconcile the goals of their work with the dictates of femininity, all had a highly ambivalent relationship to female culture, and all vacillated between an identification with masculine forms and postures and a need to adopt or reinterpret feminine modes and traditions. Although this was also true of many women of earlier generations (think, for example, of George Eliot), what distinguishes this group in the 1880s is their dependence on one another, on an unstructured but for them powerfully real urban female community, and on the *possibility* of being single without being odd. The temporary social dislocation of these women and their tenuous coming together in London made it possible for them to do a kind of work they never managed to reproduce. This was obviously and sadly the case for Levy, but it was true, too, for Harkness and even for Webb, whose subsequent work, whatever its merits, never recaptured the empirical immediacy and methodological inventiveness of her social-investigative contributions of the 1880s.

In a real sense both Webb and Harkness lost their subject—London—when they abandoned the independent if marginal urban community to which they attached themselves in the 1880s. Webb's earliest writings were tied to a rhetorical mode of social investigation and to the urban observation that shaped it. She left these behind for a variety

[61] Webb, *My Apprenticeship*, pp. 302–3; emphasis added.

of complex reasons, but among them was the difficulty of finding her place—and her voice—as a female spectator within the social scientific mode. Those aspects of urban working-class life that animated her imagination—religious community, for example, and the gender relations of working men and women—found no clear place in the dispassionate and analytical discourses of an emerging social science. She could allow her closest identifications to come into play only when she felt assured that disguise gave her license. For Harkness the real drama of urban life lay in the streets and courts of the slums, in the politics of working-class resistance, and in the intrigue of cross-class relations. Her distinctly political voice and her desire to capture the immediacy of topical events placed her outside the feminine realm of domestic fiction and on the margins of an apolitical naturalist literary movement. Amy Levy, whose future as a writer can only be imagined and mourned, drew sustenance as a poet and prose writer from the euphoria of urban life and from the tensions inherent in a young, single, female intellectual's encounter with independence. In the works of all three, a woman's vision of the city begins to emerge, but it is a vision defined by tentativeness, hesitation, ambivalence. Observing London from the top of a bus, gazing through a sitting room window, disguised as a "trouser-hand" or a Welsh farmer's daughter, appearing as a "she-boy" or "glorified spinster," these London women invented tangible and rhetorical defenses against vulnerability, exposure, and accusations of trespass.

❧ SEVEN ❧

The Female Social Investigator: Maternalism, Feminism, and Women's Work

In the final two decades of the nineteenth century and the first decade of the twentieth, the enterprise of British social investigation was joined by women. Although women writers had contributed extensively and incisively to the ongoing Victorian project of social analysis, they had done so largely in the form of fiction and not in a social scientific mode. The statistical and journalistic studies of slums, poverty, labor, disease, and sanitation that appeared throughout the middle decades of the nineteenth century were the direct results of government commissions, newspaper investigations, and medical surveys, and their authors were journalists, physicians, clergymen, and royal commissioners—men with professional authority and access to the principally urban objects of their investigations. Now, at the end of the century, women began to publish investigations in what was for them a new mode, scientific and empirical, focused on individual towns or urban neighborhoods, based on personal observation, and often directed at specific social reforms.

These women adopted the role of urban investigator, but their province of scrutiny was not the street or the workplace but the home. They took as their point of entry or analytic center the domestic sphere of working-class life and, to a striking degree, directed their critical energies toward bolstering woman's domestic role. This choice of subject was a strategic one: home was the realm in which they had license to observe and authority to judge. In working-class homes, in the company of women and children, they avoided—or so they felt—the scrutiny of men of their own or another class, the sense of trespass they experienced on city streets. Indeed, the social historian Ellen Ross makes the point that while male ramblers and observers took in urban life through the eyes, the female investigators' mode of observation was aural. They listened to the talk of working-class women, and, as Ross remarks, they eavesdropped, enjoying at times a nearly complete invisibility.[1]

Entering the homes of the poor had become, as we shall see, an accepted duty of middle-class women, but entering the sweatshop or interviewing dock laborers was, as Beatrice Webb had discovered, a questionable undertaking. The problems of identity and identification Webb experienced in her investigations of the 1880s did not impede the project of the domestic observers. They positioned themselves as female investigators and middle-class experts, using a language borrowed not necessarily from male social scientific discourse but in part from the commonsense business of housekeeping and care. What did disturb their work, however, was the need to suppress their own distance from conventional domesticity, their feminist politics, or their critique of patriarchal marriage in order to present themselves as reliable observers of the home. Their own sense of grievance as women, kept convincingly in check for a time, surfaces in these texts under the pressure of identification with the struggles of working-class women. It is as if their legitimacy as social investigators depended on their creating a conventionally feminine persona even though the actual unconventionality of being a female investigator—a writer, a professional, an authority—was at odds with their obligatory support of traditional gender roles.

In this chapter I focus on four sustained works of social investigation written by women just before or after the turn of the century: Helen Bosanquet's *Rich and Poor* (1896), a proposal for constructive philanthropic intervention in the East End of London; Mary Higgs's *Glimpses into the Abyss* (1906), a proto-Orwellian account of going "on the tramp" through the towns and doss houses of England; Florence Bell's *At the Works* (1907), a portrait of labor and survival in the iron manufacturing town of Middlesbrough; and Maud Pember Reeves's *Round*

---

[1] Ellen Ross, *Love and Toil: Motherhood in Outcast London, 1870–1918* (New York: Oxford University Press, 1993), p. 18. Ross's first chapter, "'Miss, I Wish I Had Your Life': The Poor of London and Their Chronicles," includes invaluable material and insights for an understanding of the historical moment of these female social investigators and their work.

About a Pound a Week (1913), a study of domestic economy in Lambeth conducted by the Fabian Women's Group.[2] I will suggest how and why each of these works of social investigation, although different from one another in subject and ideological bias, endorses a traditional link between woman and the home and yet ultimately mounts a critique of domestic life and of the economic and social position of women. Each text works within and argues against conventional notions of womanhood, translating the late-century dislocations of middle-class women's lives into analyses of the domestic plight of working-class women. But before looking closely at these investigative texts, I offer some general observations about women's entry into social service in the Victorian period, about turn-of-the-century obsessions with the home and maternity, about the enormous changes in middle-class women's circumstances at the end of the century, and, finally, about what were perceived by middle-class women to be points of convergence between working-class women's lives and their own.

The first and most obvious reason for the domestic emphasis in works of social investigation by female authors lies in the history of women's entry into the public sphere of social service—an entry effected not through the factory or workshop door but through the kitchen, the sickroom, and the nursery. As many historians have observed, women in the middle decades of the nineteenth century justified their public work by casting it as an extension of their domestic duties, a fulfillment of private responsibilities in the public realm.[3] If women had the maternal skills to tend their own families, then they were the logical choice to nurse and mother the poor, the sick, and the orphaned. A few women, almost all of them unmarried, expanded these opportunities into full-fledged careers or lifetime crusades; but whole armies of middle-class Victorian women with families of their own engaged in occasional philanthropic work and in virtually obligatory "visiting" (see figure 16 for an illustration of a charitable visit).

Protected by class privilege and emboldened by the ethic of charity,

[2] Mrs. Bernard Bosanquet, *Rich and Poor* (London: Macmillan, 1896); Mary Higgs, *Glimpses into the Abyss* (London: P. S. King and Son, 1906); Lady Bell, *At the Works: A Study of a Manufacturing Town (Middlesbrough)* (London: Edward Arnold, 1907); and Mrs. Pember Reeves, *Round About a Pound a Week* (1913), intro. Sally Alexander (London: Virago, 1979). All subsequent citations will be given in the text.

[3] For a summary of this argument, see Martha Vicinus, *Independent Women: Work and Community for Single Women, 1850–1920* (Chicago: University of Chicago Press, 1985), p. 15.

Figure 16 Gustave Doré, "London Charities." Gustave Doré and Blanchard Jerrold, *London, A Pilgrimage* (1872). Department of Rare Books and Special Collections, Princeton University Libraries.

women entered the neighborhoods and dwellings of the poor, bringing nourishment, clothing, and advice on housekeeping and child rearing. However paternalistic—or maternalistic—an element of bourgeois life this visiting was, and however presumptuous and invasive was the bourgeois woman's counsel, the visitor herself could benefit from this practice in two ways: first, it offered her a means of participating in civic life without apparently transgressing the appropriate bounds of gender, and second, she could glean a great deal of knowledge about the domestic side of poverty, which was visible only to that relatively small

Figure 17 Hablot K. Browne, "The Visit at the Brickmaker's." Charles Dickens, *Bleak House* (1853). Department of Rare Books and Special Collections, Princeton University Libraries.

group of professional middle-class men—principally doctors and clergymen—who routinely entered working-class homes. Victorian fiction offers as an unremarkable phenomenon many instances of the "visiting" heroine, and in some notable cases—*Bleak House* (see figure 17) and *North and South* among them—visiting marks the heroine's initiation into wider experience, the beginning of social and personal revelation.

By the last two decades of the century, home visiting by middle-class women had become an integral part of the distribution of charity as organized by the Charity Organization Society and of the system of rent collecting pioneered by Octavia Hill.[4] This more systematic and regular exposure to working-class homes gave visitors the chance to record their observations, note changes, register a decline or an improvement of circumstances, and in so doing learn something of the economic rhythms of families dependent on casual labor and intermittent wages. By the time a small number of these women made the transition from

[4] See Deborah Epstein Nord, *The Apprenticeship of Beatrice Webb* (Ithaca: Cornell University Press, 1989), pp. 119–28.

visitor to investigator, their methods of observation and inquiry were already well established and remained fundamentally unchanged. Helen Bosanquet was herself a Charity Organization Society worker and author of its history; Florence Bell asserts that *At the Works* was the result of thirty years of "intercourse" with the ironworkers of Middlesbrough and of visits by several women to more than a thousand homes (p. vii); Maud Pember Reeves and the Fabian Women's Group distributed funds to Lambeth families between 1909 and 1913 and recorded their daily patterns of life and expenditure with a particular eye to the effect of proper nourishment on newborn infants.[5] For middle-class women the techniques of visiting became the techniques of their own particular mode of social investigation.

Two phenomena of the late century—one methodological and one ideological—helped to pave the way for a female-authored social investigation. First, Charles Booth's inquiry into urban poverty, which began in the mid-1880s, established the importance of the "scientific" study of social life and emphasized statistical analysis based on just the kind of personal observation in which lady visitors had been engaged.[6] In fact, Booth's first sources of data were the written reports, notebooks, and personal accounts of school board visitors, whose method of inquiry was home visiting and whose object of study was domestic arrangements. Booth employed other female investigators—Beatrice Potter Webb and Clara Collet foremost among them—and also included in *Life and Labour of the People in London* essays by Octavia Hill and one other anonymous woman on the working-class tenements, or "model dwellings," they visited and supervised (one such dwelling is illustrated in figure 18).[7] Although Booth's emphasis on the nature, and particularly the extent, of urban poverty and on the connection between labor and poverty differed from the focus on domestic life of much social investigation by women, his methods and his acknowledgment of the essential information gleaned from home study gave women a sense of the intellectual value of their practical work. Finally, Booth's importance as a model for women investigators, suggested by Florence Bell's decision to dedicate *At the Works* to him, also derived

[5] Helen Bosanquet, *Social Work in London, 1869 to 1912: A History of the Charity Organisation Society* (London: John Murray, 1914).

[6] See Nord, *Apprenticeship of Beatrice Webb*, pp. 153–59; and Harold W. Pfautz, ed., *Charles Booth on the City* (Chicago: University of Chicago Press, 1967), pp. 15–26.

[7] Charles Booth, ed., *Life and Labour of the People in London*, vol. 3 (London: Macmillan, 1892). This volume contains chapters by Hill on the "influence on character" of model dwellings (pp. 29–37) and by "A Lady Resident" on "life in buildings" (pp. 27–58).

Figure 18 "Jersey Dwellings, Ancoats, 1897." Manchester Central Library: Local Studies Unit.

from his status as amateur; that is, he was not a physician, scientist, clergyman, politician, or academician but a well-to-do man of business with an interest in the question of poverty and the methodology of statistical analysis. His authority rested on professional credentials not very different from women's own.[8]

The end of the nineteenth century also produced an ideological climate receptive to women's efforts at investigation—a climate of anxiety about the health of the family, the role of motherhood, and the successful breeding and care of children. A falling birthrate, high rates of infant mortality, insecurities about Empire brought on in part by the Boer War, worries about international economic power, and new knowledge about the extent of poverty combined with eugenicist ideas about the "degeneration" of the race to create a vision of a national crisis

[8] When Booth first presented his research to the Royal Statistical Society in 1887, his use of the findings of school board visitors and the absence of data based on actual budgets were greeted with suspicion. See Pfautz, *Charles Booth on the City,* p. 27; also Judith R. Walkowitz, *City of Dreadful Delight* (Chicago: University of Chicago Press, 1992), chap. 1.

with roots in the domestic sphere.[9] News about family life became news about the nation, indeed about Empire. If economic and political weakness really resulted from physical and moral degeneracy, then information about how mothers raised children would be crucial to understanding and bolstering not just private but public life. Organizations for promoting domestic hygiene proliferated at the turn of the century, and politicians of various stripes offered plans for supporting, improving, and "endowing" motherhood.[10] This ideology of maternalism had conservative, liberal, and socialist variants, and women of the working as well as the middle class joined their male counterparts in variations of the cause. In short, domestic life headed the national agenda, making valuable the information that women visitors and investigators had to offer and giving these women a context of national debate into which to insert themselves and their writings. The ideology of maternalism lent validity to their knowledge and expertise, both as investigators of domestic life and as women. They entered the fray, then, from within a tradition of nonprofessional "women's" work and yet with a keen understanding of how this tradition might serve national concerns.

Of course, this fervor for solving national problems through the scrutiny of motherhood also masked a conservative response to the extraordinary changes that some women's lives had undergone since the middle of the century. It became common for women at the turn of the century who wanted to define these changes in their social and economic positions to look back thirty or forty years to the way women lived then. In an address in 1890 delivered to the South Place Ethical Society, titled "The Economic Position of Educated Working Women," Clara Collet began by quoting a passage from *Aurora Leigh* (1856) and then proceeded to compare Elizabeth Barrett Browning's time to her own:

---

[9] See Sally Alexander's superb introduction to the Virago edition of Reeves, *Round About a Pound a Week;* and Anna Davin, "Imperialism and Motherhood," *History Workshop* 5 (Spring 1978): 9–65. Ellen Ross remarks that by the 1870s and 1880s the figure of the mother entered the lexicon of middle-class representations of working-class types, and that by the 1890s mothers had become the "figures around whom this working-class culture had coalesced" (*Love and Toil,* pp. 21–23).

[10] Davin, "Imperialism and Motherhood," p. 12. For a renegade Fabian socialist's version of the endowment of motherhood, see H. G. Wells, *The New Machiavelli* (Harmondsworth: Penguin, 1970). In this 1911 novel Wells declares himself "altogether feminist" after proposing that "a conscious and deliberate motherhood and mothering" is woman's "special function in the State" (p. 308–9).

At that time it would not have been possible for a woman "to prove herself a leech and cure the plague" [here she paraphrases *Aurora Leigh*]; for on the one hand she was debarred from obtaining the necessary qualifications, and on the other she was prohibited from practising without them. The hospitals and lecture rooms were closed to her by prejudice, and practice was therefore forbidden her by Act of Parliament. . . . Women were prohibited from doing what they could, on the ground that they could not if they would.[11]

Now, in the 1890s, women went to university, studied to be doctors, worked as journalists, typists, high school teachers, nurses, decorators, engravers, and electricians. By the 1890s, even in comparison to the 1880s of Harkness, Webb, and Levy, more professionally trained and educated women had come of age, were finding employment, and managed to support themselves.

In 1911 Lucy Moor, historian of the YWCA, recalled that in the period when the organization was founded, in the 1850s and 1860s, young women in London had "no idea of independence, and very little of self-support"; that they could feel comfortable and complete walking in the City only if they strolled on the arm of a male relation; that nurses' uniforms could not be seen on the streets and that offices were for women an "unknown sphere."[12] In the *Fortnightly Review* in 1892 one writer estimated that at least several thousand "working ladies" could be found in London and that a new kind of woman was on the rise. As Evelyn March Phillipps wrote, "Fewer girls sit down with folded hands nowadays, waiting for a possible husband to solve the problem of the future, or resign themselves to the monotony of making one of several gradually aging spinsters in a not always harmonious family interior."[13] For the first time, then, middle-class women could manage to survive—both economically and psychologically—outside the family.[14]

[11] Clara Collet, "The Economic Position of Educated Working Women, A Discourse delivered in South Place Chapel, Finsbury, February 2, 1890" (London: E. W. Allen), p. 205.

[12] Lucy M. Moor, *Girls of Yesterday and To-Day: the Romance of the YWCA* (London: S. W. Partridge, 1911), p. 31. The YWCA had its roots in the organized training and lodging of women who were preparing to go off to the Crimea in the 1850s to work as nurses. Often unwilling or unable to return to their families, these middle-class women also needed a place to live after their service in the war (p. 34).

[13] Evelyn March Phillipps, "The Working Lady in London," *Fortnightly Review* 52 (August 1892): 191.

[14] See Vicinus, *Independent Women*, pp. 5–6.

The "new woman" of Gissing, Wells, and Shaw was but the literary incarnation of scores of middle-class women who found it possible to define themselves neither as daughters nor as wives and mothers. The "new woman" and the cult of maternalism shared the same historical moment, for the woman outside the family contributed unwittingly to a reactionary sanctification and distrustful inspection of motherhood by virtue of her own rebelliousness.

Women who participated in the movement away from traditional domesticity struggled to maintain their economic independence and to negotiate their marginal social status. Some pondered the problematic nature of marriage and of relations between the sexes in general; some campaigned for political rights, divorce law reform, suffrage, and higher wages; some occupied themselves with creating alternative domestic arrangements for women; and some understood their own sexual vulnerability as a link with those whose sexuality was bought and sold in the marketplace.[15] They were engaged in a multitude of political and social issues that touched on the lives of women who worked, went to university, left their husbands, never married, or simply imagined autonomous lives for themselves. These concerns about economic, legal, and sexual independence emerge as strong undercurrents even in their work on behalf of women's traditional roles.

A feature of much social-investigative writing by women during this period was the middle-class woman's conviction that her concerns converged with those of working-class women. At the crux of this convergence lay the issue of economic precariousness, a condition that middle-class women now confronted and acknowledged perhaps for the first time. A secondary issue—and one understood in relation to economic anxieties—was the general question of self-sufficiency, even within marriage. Some unmarried middle-class women also faced and feared the likelihood of downward mobility: Evelyn March Phillipps began her article on the "working lady" by defining a lady precisely as a woman "who cannot sink to the level of the daughter of the artisan, or even of the small tradesman, without undergoing real hardship and suffering of mind and body."[16] As Phillips's language suggests, this perceived convergence of concerns involved a measure of dread as well as a sense of sympathetic identification.

Female social observers developed the occasional but striking habit

---

[15] Ibid., p. 290.
[16] Phillipps, "The Working Lady in London," p. 193.

of comparing the situation of working-class girls and women to that of the "new woman" of the upper classes. May Craske wrote an article titled "Girl Life in a Slum" for the *Economic Review* in 1908, describing her experiences living and working in the East End over a period of nine years. She delineates the different types of slum girls she had observed: the reserved, genteel club members in whose future it is easy to have faith; the boisterous, flamboyant "flash girls" who work at unskilled labor in factories and flaunt their feathered hats and fringed coiffures; and the very young "drudges" whose families harness them prematurely to a life of toil. It is the "flash girl," Craske realizes, who makes the worst impression on her middle-class readers, perhaps because of her independent and insouciant air, and she ends her essay with a plea for understanding these girls in more familiar terms. West or East, she insists, girls' natures are the same: "When you see her coming out of her factory, laughing loudly and romping roughly in the street, remember how young she is, and for how many hours her spirits have chafed in silence. Think of the cultured girl who throws her energies into hockey, fencing, and gymnastics; who skips and runs gracefully; whose energies are never cramped. Forgive the working girl her noisiness and all her faults, and try to see beneath the rough exterior the same charm of the natural girl."[17] Without a new breed of privileged or "cultured" girls, a breed of hockey-playing, physically active, and institutionally educated upper-class girls, Craske could not have drawn this comparison or made her pitch for understanding the high-spirited "flash girl" as a "natural girl."

We see the same kinds of comparisons at work in the writings of Clara Collet, one of Charles Booth's researchers and contributors. Collet wrote about the labor of both middle- and working-class women, and her concerns are consistently economic ones. In her 1890 lecture on the economic position of educated working women, she examines the progress women have made in entering new occupations and forging independent lives, and concludes that the central, ongoing problem faced by women is that of outrageously low pay, especially for jobs such as teaching, to which many had flocked.[18] Women could no longer assume that they would be supported by a father or husband, and therefore needed to become economically self-sufficient. She encour-

---

[17] May Craske, "Girl Life in a Slum," *Economic Review* 18 (1908): 185–87, 189. The "flash girl" is a familiar type in the slum fiction of Arthur Morrison and in Rudyard Kipling's "Record of Badalia Herodsfoot," whose heroine is prominently "fringed."
[18] Collet, "Economic Position," p. 207.

aged women to enter business, farming, and industry, and she urged employers to welcome them in these fields. Here women might actually earn a living wage and, in the process, provide a new perspective, perhaps a spirit of cooperation, to the commercial world.[19]

Because Collet saw the need for middle-class women to venture beyond the more traditionally female, genteel occupations to a broader spectrum of jobs, she was able to see women's labor as a continuum not always easily divisible by class. When she wrote extensively on "women's work" in Charles Booth's volume *The Trades of East London*, she began with a discussion of skilled and unskilled manual labor (the manufacture of boxes, umbrellas, ties, corsets, shirts, and furniture; book folding and sewing; ostrich feather curling; laundry), continued with a comparison between home work and factory work, and then moved on to an analysis of the labor and wages of what she calls "middle-class" women. Here her vision of the continuum of women's work becomes evident. She criticizes the low pay offered to the clerk's daughter, whose family contributes to the problem by supplementing her income. These women, she writes, must be able to support themselves, for in later life their fathers will not be there to do so; starvation, unhappy marriage, or the "sacrifice [of] maidenhood itself" may otherwise be the result. At this point Collet brings into the continuum the university-educated woman also engaged in supporting herself and living on the edge of genteel poverty:

> The workgirl in the lower middle class, when she begins to reflect on the future, does dread it. There is hardly one thing which the Girton or Newnham girl requires in the way of food, clothing or lodging, which is not equally desired by the City workwoman in this rank. Of the two the Girton girl can resign herself the more easily to shabby dresses and hats, has no fear of losing caste on account of poverty, and can offer her friends weak tea and a biscuit without any dread of being considered mean and inhospitable.[20]

Collet brings together in the same discussion working women of a variety of nuanced class differences, suggesting how wages, marriage, education, social status, and birth affect them in interconnected ways. The university woman is protected by the aura of her class and her educa-

[19] Ibid., p. 213.
[20] Clara E. Collet, "Women's Work," in *Life and Labour of the People in London*, ed. Charles Booth (London: Macmillan, 1893), 4:320.

tion; the lower-middle-class woman cannot withstand the damage done to her precarious status by poverty and so is forced to marry; but the factory worker of the "lowest class" in the East End has a better chance of marrying than the woman of the "poorer middle class." Shifts in middle-class women's lives at the end of the century made possible this perception of an unbroken continuum of women's work and experience. In the four works of social investigation I am about to describe, this affiliation of gender complicates the class barriers between investigator and investigated and makes especially problematic the middle-class investigator's professed conviction that the working-class woman's place was in the home.

Helen Bosanquet, supporter and historian of the Charity Organization Society (COS), wrote *Rich and Poor* as a tract criticizing indiscriminate and ignorant philanthropy and arguing the need for "intercourse" between those who give and those who receive. But rather than offering the COS philosophy in undiluted form, she sought to give her readers and would-be almsgivers a true, indeed a "scientific," picture of life in the poorest districts of London. She gently mocks the middle-class traveler into the "unknown region" of the East End as a "modern knight-errant [who] looks to win his spurs, to challenge all oppressors and wrong-doers, to defy the dragons of poverty and disease" (p. 7). These knights-errant, well-meaning though they may be, are sadly ignorant of what she repeatedly calls the "nature of the *organic* life" in the parishes of the East (pp. 6, 8; emphasis added). This stress on the "organic whole" of slum life and her heavy reliance on the work of Henry Mayhew and Charles Booth signal her alliance with empirical investigation (see e.g., pp. 51, 65). Without this kind of knowledge, she insists, no charity can be beneficial, and all aid will destroy rather than improve the lives of the poor. Voicing one of the dominant attitudes toward philanthropy of the period, she tries to reconstruct the workings of local institutions and communities and unveil something of the every-day life of the poor.

For the most part Bosanquet represents the "organic whole" of East End life by drawing on the research and statistics of other investigators and institutions rather than by offering firsthand accounts of individual cases. Her work—in this particular text, at least—is in fact much less empirical than that of Florence Bell, Mary Higgs, or Maud Pember Reeves, even though visits by COS workers would have yielded just such case-by-case information.[21] Bosanquet herself, as narrator and investigator, remains rather a remote figure, at least until we read the affective and contradictory center of *Rich and Poor*, chapters 3 and 4, "The Family Income and Its Expenditure" and "The Women of the East." Here Bosanquet talks about the condition of women in the East End without ultimately being able to separate their predicament from that of the middle-class woman. She begins her discussion in a wholly conventional "maternalist" mode but cannot sustain it, both because her own observations of East End families finally come into play and because controversies about the position of women in her own class impinge on her expression of the received wisdom about motherhood in the lower classes.

"The Family Income and Its Expenditure" is devoted to the idea that mothers working outside the home are doing irreparable harm to their children. She begins: "One of the most hopeful signs of social improvement is the extent to which married women are withdrawing from the labour market; that the working classes should recognise the importance of the woman's home duties is a sign of their higher intellectual standard, and . . . proof of their improved material conditions" (p. 80). When mothers work, homes are neglected, children become ill, and earnings are wasted. Children must either be locked in or locked out of the home when mothers are absent and, as a consequence, are never properly fed. Even childless wives, she claims, ought to be able to find the activities of homemaking fulfilling and sufficient, and need not be "driven" to work by the "vacancy and *ennui*" of their lives (p. 81). So eager is she to discredit all employment for women that she criticizes even piecework done in the home as an insidious distraction from their real duties (p. 90). She grants the possibility that in some circumstances—when husbands are ill or dead—women need to work, but she very quickly recovers her theme, asserting, "We will all agree that for the woman to have to work is an *unmitigated evil* where there are children" (p. 81; emphasis added). This chapter is written neither to assess the economic needs of poor families nor to promote broad social reforms in labor or education, but rather out of an un-

---

[21] Bosanquet, as paid COS district secretary for Shoreditch, did in fact live for a time among the poor in the East End. Between 1890 and 1894 she stayed at the Women's University Settlement and then lived alone in Hoxton. See Jane Lewis, *Women and Social Action in Victorian and Edwardian England* (Stanford: Stanford University Press, 1991), p. 150. Lewis's chapter on Bosanquet in her extraordinarily helpful study places her in the context of other women activists, among them Beatrice Webb.

questioned belief that a nonworking wife and mother is the one thing needful to set the working-class home aright.

When Bosanquet turns her attention to working-class women themselves, however, not as linchpins of the family but as individuals in their own right, she automatically sees their struggles in terms that are similar to those of women of her own class. And she is immediately defensive about it: "In devoting a short chapter especially to the position of women of East London," she begins, "it is not with any desire to raise the question of women's rights and wrongs" (p. 100). A proponent of women's suffrage, Bosanquet did not naively employ the language of Wollstonecraft and the fight for women's emancipation.[22] But she did deny her intention to write about women's rights even as she declared it, for she believed that the "interests of men and women are in the long run the same" (p. 100). The chapter that follows undercuts this disclaimer at a number of points. She paints a portrait of the working-class wife who, with "patient endurance," shoulders all the "unwelcome burdens" of unreliable husbands and sons, writing:

> And as the children grow older the chances are that the burden of maintaining the family falls entirely upon the mother. It is so easy now for the father to disappear and take up life free of responsibility in some of the many shelters or lodging-houses in London; to change his name if necessary, but in any case to elude the necessity of feeding more than himself. Or if he carries his ideas of irresponsibility still further, he may—as many indeed do—dispense with the trouble of seeking new quarters [and] remain at home an idle loafer, living upon oddments of charity and his wife's poor earnings. (p. 105)

Contemplating what she calls "this terrible devotion of the woman," she concludes that many poor mothers might have done better had they chosen "the burden of a solitary life" (pp. 108, 112).

As if carrying on a debate with herself in the pages of her text, Bosanquet wonders if, given the habitually low wages women are able to garner, spinsterhood could ever be preferable to an oppressive marriage. In answer to her own query she proposes better training and a greater diversity of jobs for potentially self-sustaining women, proposals that echo discussions about middle-class women and their labor. She acknowledges, too, the belief of many that training is wasted on girls and young women, who may then marry and ultimately give up work-

[22] Ibid., p. 149.

ing. Confirming the intimate connection between her discussion of the women of the East End and debates about the "woman question" among the upper classes, she concedes that "the whole question of women's work is of course complicated, both here and in the professional classes, by the prospect of marriage and all that it involves" (p. 114). Prompted, perhaps, by this vision of convergence between middle- and working-class women's needs and concerns, she ends her chapter with a firm and ringing endorsement of training and education for women as the "remedy for all" (p. 116). Women, she concludes, need better skills to manage their homes and to improve their economic position, whether they are married or single. Only as a result of education can they be raised out of what she calls "bondage," a term that by this point in the text refers not only to the slavery of poverty but to that of marriage as well (p. 117). It is difficult to reconcile this view of the "rights of woman" with Bosanquet's celebration of women's motherly role and exclusive devotion to home.

In 1909 another working-class district of London, Lambeth, drew the attention of the Fabian Women's Group (FWG) when its members decided to study the household economy of working families and to find out exactly how women managed domestic life on "about a pound a week." The fundamental assumption underlying their research was the need for state support of women and children, or what they ultimately called the "state endowment of motherhood." If the Charity Organization Society philosophy of privately distributed and carefully rationed charity represented one dominant strain of late nineteenth-century philanthropic thought, the Fabian philosophy of collectivism and state responsibility exemplified the most powerful competing approach to the problem of poverty. Despite the fact that its ideological stance toward individualism and collectivism differed radically from that of women such as Helen Bosanquet and Octavia Hill, the Fabian Women's Group shared their conviction that the mother was the key to the reform of working-class life and their assumption that they, as women, could be the agents of this reform. In her wonderful introduction to the Virago edition of Maud Pember Reeves's *Round About a Pound a Week*, Sally Alexander discusses the Fabian women's relationship to the "national pastime" of "thinking of ways to improve the nation through 'improving' motherhood" (p. ix). She points out that, although their research allowed for "equating the national interest with motherhood and children," their emphasis on mothers had an important feminist, as well as socialist, dimension (p. xix). Let us now look more closely at the way this "feminism" operated within a framework that appears to have made traditional assumptions not about the state but about relations between the sexes.[23]

To investigate the effects of proper nourishment and care on newborns in working-class families, the FWG distributed subsidies to mothers with infants in Walworth Road, Lambeth, and visited them regularly over the course of the child's first year of life.[24] They wanted to see if a supplement to weekly income would make a difference in the health and well-being of children, to discover if direct aid to mothers had beneficial results, and to determine in a general way how "a working man's wife bring[s] up a family on 20s. a week" (p. 21). Babies were weighed every two weeks, mothers were asked to keep weekly accounts of expenditures, and the Fabian women themselves took notes on what they observed and what they read—or deciphered—in the Lambeth women's accounts.

The practical part of the investigation drew on the traditional skills of "visiting"—doling out charity and advice and closely observing and recording working-class habits. Reeves's narrative contains transcripts of the Fabian women's reports. Their descriptions of the Lambeth women recall the notes of other "lady visitors": "Mrs. L. is older and larger and more gaunt. . . . Mrs. S. could tell you a little about Mr. S. if you pressed her. . . . Mrs. K. liked being read to" (pp. 90–92). In *Round About a Pound a Week* what had constituted the private notes of rent collectors and COS visitors became a text for public perusal. The methodological familiarity of the volume is matched by an extremely conventional, even middle-class vision of the family: mothers do not work outside the home; husbands have permanent work and bring in a steady if inadequate wage; families have their own cottages; domestic violence does not exist.[25] Men occupy the public sphere and women the private; laborers are male, parents female. These particular Lambeth women, Reeves tells us, live so exclusively in the domestic realm that they have no need for new or presentable clothing: men must have clothes for work and children to attend school, but women, who have

---

[23] For the Fabian Women's Group, see Polly Beals, "Fabian Feminism: Gender, Politics and Culture in London, 1880–1930" (Ph.D. diss., Rutgers University, 1989).

[24] Reeves, *Round About a Pound a Week*, chap. 2, pp. 8–10.

[25] See Ross, *Love and Toil*, chap. 3 ("Marriage"), for a discussion of the prevalence of domestic violence among working-class husbands and wives. She writes: "The threat of male violence was one of the daily fixtures of married life for women" (p. 84).

"no need to appear in the light of day," seldom spend money on their own apparel and often go even without boots (p. 64).

That these families deviate so little in their sexual division of labor from traditional norms can be attributed in part to the relatively stable economic circumstances in which they lived. The inhabitants of Walworth Road were not "slum people," Reeves informs us, nor could the FWG have conducted its study in households where wages were so low that any subsidies would have been devoted to bare necessities for the entire family rather than to improved nutrition for newborns (pp. 8–9). These women were apparently not forced to go to work in factories or sweatshops, and given the focus of the Fabian women's project, the families chosen for study had to be relatively young and intact. But Reeves's text also displays a desire to impress her readers with the reliability, respectability, and indeed resemblance to themselves of these Lambeth families and, in particular, these Lambeth mothers. Her purpose was, after all, to establish that with the proper resources these women could be exemplary mothers and that nothing stood between their children and ideal care but money. Anything that might detract from this image of competent and devoted maternality—such as a mother's need to work or to place her child in a crèche while she did so—was kept out of the representational frame constructed around these families' lives.

If Maud Pember Reeves and the FWG took such great pains in *Round About a Pound a Week* to represent working-class mothers in the most traditional of roles, how then did this tract reflect their feminist principles, their commitment to "equality in citizenship and women's economic independence"?[26] Although Reeves emphasizes throughout the heavy and unrealistic burden placed on these Lambeth women in the management of their families, not until the ninth chapter, "Menus," does she begin to introduce the concept of women's economic independence, and she does so almost as a red herring. Describing the skimpy, unhealthy meals prepared by these women, Reeves acknowledges that many readers will be deeply critical of the inadequate materials from which they are made. "It is quite likely," she concedes, "that someone who had strength, wisdom, and vitality, . . . who was not bowed down with worry, but was herself *economically independent* of the

---

[26] I am quoting Sally Alexander's introduction to Reeves, *Round About a Pound a Week*, p. xiv.

man who earned the money, could lay out his few shillings with a better eye to scientific food value" (p. 131; emphasis added). It is, however, quite as likely, she continues, that her husband would turn up his nose at "scientific" food and request his "old tasty kippers and meat."[27] The idea of economic independence, which here might refer to separate women's wages but more likely alludes to state subsidies for mothers, drops out of the discussion so that Reeves can make the point that women are not necessarily to blame for the poor diet of their children. She does, however, begin to sound a feminist theme which takes the place of and subsumes the idea of economic independence: the theme of separate interests.

Continuing with the topic of food and money in the next chapter, Reeves argues that in the best of circumstances families are able to afford both an "adult's" diet and a "children's" diet, but that in poor families "only one kind of diet is possible, and that is the man's" (p. 144). (Notice how "man" takes the place of "adult.") Her defense of mothers' good intentions is sustained: it is not the wife's ignorance or indifference that is to blame but rather the sheer impossibility of both "maintain[ing] a working man in physical efficiency and rear[ing] healthy children" on an income of twenty shillings a week (p. 145). No longer is it adults and children whose interests diverge but *fathers* and children; and mothers thus need outside support in order to accommodate both sets of requirements. Without it, Reeves makes clear, fathers' interests will always take precedence, so at some basic level men and women exist in the family in opposition to each other's needs and purposes.

This is precisely the point that Reeves goes on to make explicitly in the next chapter, "The Poor and Marriage." By contrasting women's lives before and after marriage, she reintroduces the issue of economic independence and continues to build on her critique of marriage. Young women's lives change far more radically than do men's when they marry, she asserts, because women give up public existence for a wholly private one even before they have children. They then miss the companionship of a working life and the money of their own that it brings (p. 151). Without addressing directly the issue of *married* women's work, Reeves makes clear the loss of independence that nonwork-

---

[27] In *Love and Toil* Ellen Ross's chapter "Feeding a Family" provides an illuminating context for Reeves's "Menus." Reeves's evocation of the culinary divisions within the family is borne out at every point in Ross's wider study.

ing women experience. With the birth of children and increased
economic strain, "the separation of interests soon begins to show itself." She writes:

> The husband goes to the same work—hard, long, and monotonous—but at
> least a change from the growing discomfort of the home. He gets accustomed
> to seeing his wife slave, and she gets accustomed to seeing him appear and
> disappear on his daily round of work, which gradually appeals less and less
> to her imagination, till, at thirty, she hardly knows what his duties are—so
> overwhelmed is she in the flood of her own most absorbing duties and econ-
> omies. Her economies interfere with his comfort, and are irksome to him;
> so he gets out of touch with her point of view. . . . The unvarying amount
> paid for the bread-winner's necessary daily food becomes a greater portion
> of the food bill, and leaves all the increasing deficit to be met out of the
> food of the mother and children. It is unavoidable that it should be so;
> nobody wastes time thinking about it; but the fact that it is so forces the
> mother to take a different point of view from that of the father. So each of
> them gradually grows to understand the other less. (pp. 155–57)

Reeves carefully establishes a portrait of the working-class household
in which wives—and their children—need additional funds to meet
their own needs, and in this way she makes the case for state support
of motherhood which is the Fabian Women's Group's cause. But she
also describes a family in which the sexes are marked by mutual lack
of understanding, and in which the utter and rigid separation of their
spheres is directly to blame. Men's absence from the home blinds them
to their children's needs; women's confinement to the home makes
the husband's world invisible and incomprehensible. Unwilling to record domestic violence or to evoke the abdicating and disappearing
fathers Helen Bosanquet describes, Reeves nevertheless sees the working-class family through a feminist lens. The economic remedy she offers—the state's assumption of responsibility for the material well-being
of all children—seems, by the end of the text, an insufficient answer
to the problems she has raised. She underscores the extent of the difficulty, whether unwittingly or not, when she berates for its maltreat-
ment of poor families "this masculine State, representing only male
voters" (p. 215). A political agenda, one that would profoundly change
women's relation to the state, and by implication all gender relations,
must accompany the economic reforms Reeves recommends. The
middle-class Fabian women's push for suffrage, kept scrupulously out
of the text of *Round About a Pound a Week*, surfaces in the recognition

that, without the vote, women's "separate interests" will never be fully understood.

With Florence Bell's *At the Works* we leave London for the industrial North and the iron manufacturing community of Middlesbrough. On a much smaller scale Middlesbrough presented the same simplified class configuration that inspired Elizabeth Gaskell's imagination in Manchester. A Yorkshire town virtually created by the discovery of iron ore nearby and by developments in the technology of ironmaking, Middlesbrough seemed to Bell to be made up of workers and industrialists, or, as she phrases it, the "cottage people" and the "well-to-do."[28] The wife of an ironmaster, Bell had spent thirty years visiting the homes of his workers and had detailed knowledge of their lives as well as of the processes of iron manufacture, which she describes so brilliantly in her book. She assiduously avoids the language of class and, like Gaskell in her preface to *Mary Barton*, pleads innocent of dealing with issues of economic theory or class relations in the abstract, with what Bell calls the "great questions involved in the relations between capital and labour, employer and employed" (p. vii).

Like the ideal working-class wives imagined by Helen Bosanquet and Maud Pember Reeves's Lambeth housewives, the women of Middlesbrough do not work outside the home. This manufacturing town differs from others, and from textile manufacturing towns in particular, in offering no possibilities for women's labor in its principal industry. Middlesbrough employs no women in the iron trade, has no large factories or "organized women's labour," and in short offers women "no independent existence of their own" (p. 178). Like the wives of Lambeth, these women have no public life. They must satisfy their need for community and sociability by chatting in the doorways of their homes, and by making the streets they observe their place of entertainment and education (p. 228). Bell regrets that there are so few public places where a workingman's wife can go for relaxation and pleasure, even when accompanied by her husband. She argues gently: "It would make a difference to many an overworked wife and mother if she could go out with her husband ... and have a cup of tea, perhaps, which she had not made herself, in some warm and pleasant surrounding" (p. 133).

[28] The population of Middlesbrough went from 35 in 1811 to 18,892 in 1861 after the building of the railroads and the discovery of ironstone in the area. See Bell, *At The Works*, pp. 10–11.

Her protest against the domestic confinement these women endure remains muted, however, and is overshadowed by a more conventional response to the role of working-class wives. In the first of two chapters devoted to the wives and daughters of the ironworkers, Bell begins: "The key to the condition of the workman and his family, the clue, the reason for the possibilities and impossibilities of his existence, is the capacity, the temperament, and, above all, the health of the woman who manages his house; into her hands, sometimes strong and capable, often weak and uncertain, the future of her husband is committed, the burden of the family life is thrust" (p. 171). It is not, however, only the individual working-class family for whose fate the woman is responsible. Her task is nothing less than the prevention of the "much-discussed deterioration of the race" (p. 171). In a nod to the popular rhetoric of maternalism and to widespread anxiety about the decline of the nation, Bell acknowledges the truth that women are the "pivot of the whole situation" (p. 171). They marry too young, while still ignorant of the skills required to manage a home. After children arrive, the home often takes a downward slide as the woman becomes "more of a slattern day by day from sheer incapacity to keep up with her work" (p. 184). An untidy and disorganized home might ultimately lead the husband to retreat to the public house, the wife to take refuge in bed, and the family to suffer total disintegration, both physical and moral (pp. 188–89). Despite intermittent flashes of sympathy for the women who must cope with such inordinate burdens, Bell nonetheless paints a portrait of working-class families as undermined almost exclusively by the incompetence and progressive deterioration of wives and mothers.

At some point in her discussion of these delinquent women, however, she loses confidence in the rhetoric of maternal responsibility and blame and is no longer able to make a satisfactory connection between talk of national decline and these women's reproductive lives. She breaks off her discussion of working-class mothers' frequently heroic efforts to sustain unwanted children to remark: "It is bewildering and paralyzing in these days when we are lamenting at once the declining birth-rate and the deterioration of the children who are brought into the world, to look at some of the houses which keep up that birth-rate and see what is the result on the health of the average woman and, therefore, on the health of her children" (p. 195). If, she suggests, we all understood what it meant to these women to give birth to ten or fifteen or seventeen children, many of whom would die in infancy or childhood, to have their health worn away by childbirth, we would no longer be able to offer glib prescriptions about keeping up the birthrate and improving the nation through improving motherhood.[29] Bell is aware that her own observation of working-class mothers' experience of childbirth *paralyzes* her, makes it impossible for her to pass judgment or offer help. Moreover, she realizes that although words do not fail her completely, her imagination does. After describing one woman who gave birth to ten stillborn children, she comments: "It is easy to write these words; it is wellnigh impossible for the ordinary reader to call up the true picture of what they really mean" (p. 199). Contrast becomes the only mechanism she can use to "call up" the meaning of this reality. The experience of the well-to-do woman is so remote from that of the "cottage woman" that the gap itself may prove instructive. "A woman among the well-to-do who should have had seventeen children and lost twelve," she continues, "would be one marked out as she went about the world for the wonder and compassion of her fellows; but such a destiny is accepted as possible by the working people, and is cruelly frequent among them" (p. 200). Only by describing what is unimaginable to the middle-class woman can Bell begin to make imaginable what the working-class woman endures.

Bell maintains her resolve and avoids discussion of class relations through most of her text. She offers no analysis of the differences between the prosperous lives of the ironmasters and the meager lives of some of the workers—until she reaches the section on childbirth. But here her contemplation of what it would mean to give birth to seventeen babies and lose twelve leads her into an extended meditation on the radical differences between childbirth in her own class and in the cottages. The pregnant well-to-do woman rests, relinquishes household duties to others, makes her health her first consideration; the delivery of her baby will involve sanitary precautions, well-qualified doctors, and the possibility of chloroform. The pregnant working-class woman, by contrast, must continue her "daily round of toil" until the moment of delivery, and when she gives birth it will be in a small, unventilated room next to the kitchen or in the kitchen itself; she will have no privacy, no insulation from the noises, smells, and activities of the household, no anesthetic, and no trained physician. The maternalist rhetoric of woman as "pivot" in preventing the "deterioration of the

[29] Ross notes that the contrast in birthrates between poor and middle-class women increased as the nineteenth century progressed, as more well-to-do families began to limit the number of their children (pp. 92–93).

race" collapses in the face of this identification with female experience that is both familiar and utterly, alarmingly different. In a striking passage close to the end of her text, Bell's sense of the incompleteness and one-sidedness of her enterprise surfaces: "A fierce light beats in these days upon the working classes [a term Bell scrupulously avoids for most of her text], revealing much that in more prosperous quarters is not seen; but it is probably there all the same. From the fact that so far, unfortunately, it has not been the custom to investigate, tabulate, report upon the private and individual lives of the well-to-do, it has come to pass that the working class is used, so to speak, as the unit of the moral investigation" (pp. 270–71).

Bell arrives here at an understanding of the project of social investigation rare among investigators, whether male or female. Who examines the family lives and reproductive practices of the middle class? And how has a moral assessment of the working classes become a legitimate enterprise for the nation? In contemplating childbirth and child rearing among the working-class women of Middlesbrough, Bell is moved to turn in on herself and her class, to understand it as the other necessary part of the picture. The gulf between classes and the investigator's distorting objectification of the working class have become apparent to her through the affiliation of gender.

Mary Higgs's *Glimpses into the Abyss*, an investigation of lodging houses, tramp wards, and shelters up and down the length of England, differs radically from the other three texts I have looked at, for it is not about home but homelessness. This extraordinary work follows in the tradition that was established by James Greenwood's *Night in a Workhouse* (1866) and extended to Orwell's *Down and Out in Paris and London* (1933) and *The Road to Wigan Pier* (1937): the literary record of the middle-class journalist or reformer who goes "on the tramp" disguised as a down-and-outer to discover how the vagrants of England live. Higgs's text also differs from Bosanquet's, Reeves's, and Bell's because Higgs herself appears as the central figure in her narrative and because it puts her back on the street, as it were, exposed to public view. Like Tristan's and Gaskell's heroines, Higgs walks the streets; and, like Tristan and Beatrice Webb, she employs disguise both to enter forbidden spaces and to protect herself and her identity. What she discovers, however, is that class disguise exposes her as a woman and increases her personal and sexual vulnerability.

Mary Higgs, like Elizabeth Gaskell the wife of a minister in the North

of England, was educated at Cambridge. She first glimpsed the world
of the homeless as secretary to the Ladies Committee of the Oldham
Workhouse.[30] She set up a lodging for destitute women in Oldham and
oversaw it for six years, studying, classifying, and examining its residents, as she reports in *Glimpses into the Abyss*, "as [through] a social
microscope" (p. v). Searching still for national solutions to the problem of vagrancy, she tells us in the preface, she decided to take to the
road to investigate "the depths" and explore "Darkest England" (p.
vi). With this last reference to Salvation Army founder General William
Booth's study of poverty, *In Darkest England and the Way Out* (1890),
Higgs allies herself with a particular turn-of-the-century strain of
"tramp" writing: the plunge into the "abyss" of destitution. From the
chapter of Booth's study titled "On the Verge of the Abyss" to H. G.
Wells's short story "In the Abyss" (1895) to C. F. G. Masterman's *From
the Abyss* (1902) to Jack London's *People of the Abyss* (1903), middle-class
observers recorded the descent into the netherworld of poverty not as
a journey into unknown territory, as Peter Keating notes, but as a fall
into a gaping hole at the edge of society.[31] During this period of increased unemployment, migration of workers from the provinces to the
cities, and immigration from abroad, a host of transients who seemed
to linger permanently on the periphery of society captured the public
imagination and caused anxiety by their very rootlessness.[32] They occupied not another world but, according to the rhetoric of the abyss,
a void out of which they would never emerge.

The abyss of homelessness, however remote it might seem from the
working-class domesticity described by Bosanquet, Reeves, and Bell, was
nevertheless rhetorically and ideologically linked to the national glorification of home and family which influenced their work. This link
becomes clear in the concluding chapter of *Glimpses into the Abyss*, in
which Higgs offers her analysis of the problem of vagrancy. A mobile
population, migratory workers, scattered families, and the "disintegra-

[30] For Mary Higgs, see Peter Keating's headnote to a selection from *Glimpses into the
Abyss* in his *Into Unknown England, 1866–1913* (Manchester: Manchester University Press,
1976), p. 273, and the author's preface to *Glimpses*.
[31] London claimed that he got his title initially from Wells's "In the Abyss." But as
Keating points out, the Wells work of greatest relevance here is *The Time Machine* (1895),
where the concept and class meaning of the abyss—if not the word itself—exist in Wells's
creation of the subterranean Morlocks. Peter Keating, *The Working Classes in Victorian Fiction* (New York: Barnes and Noble, 1971), p. 21. The world of poverty described by
midcentury social investigators such as Henry Mayhew was evoked as a terra incognita.
[32] The ancient problem of the tramp, Higgs writes, is now the modern problem of the
"fluidity of labour" (*Glimpses*, p. 288).

tion of the home" are at fault, for "by the preservation or extinction of the home a nation stands or falls" (p. 288). The "citadel of national life" is home, and only by making it "the centre of all our thought, the focus of national consciousness," can we solve the problem of vagrancy or homelessness (pp. 288, 296). She argues the need to cherish the child; and, not unlike the Fabian Women's Group, she believes that the community and the nation must take on a parental role (p. 297). The state has an obligation to shore up the family by reconstructing civic life and by ensuring people's right to work, for the state will not survive the disintegration of the home. Combining progressive political ideas about the state's responsibility in matters of employment with a (perhaps defensive) conservative rhetoric, she makes the obligatory connection between the well-being of the family and the strength of the nation.

The familiar ring of Higgs's cultural conservatism in this final chapter does not, however, reflect the central story she tells in *Glimpses*, a story that grows out of her experience as a disguised vagrant and marks a growing sense of the utter and insurmountable vulnerability of the female tramp. Almost from the very first Higgs's disguise transforms her relationship to the world and, more specifically, to men. As she and her female tramping companion walk from town to town, they are subjected to shouts and taunts. She writes: "We walked away and took no notice, but repeatedly on our journey we were spoken to, and I could not help contrasting the way in which men looked at us with the usual bearing of a man toward a *well-dressed* female. I had never realised before that a lady's dress, or even that of a respectable working woman, was a *protection*. The bold, free look of a man at a destitute woman must be felt to be realised" (p. 94). Were she to be on the tramp alone, without a female companion, Higgs concludes, her task would be impossible. She concurs with the advice of a destitute woman who tells her that if you tramped, "you had to take up with a fellow" (p. 94).

The altered responses of others to what is no more than a layer of clothing sets off in the narrator of *Glimpses* a steady, growing realization that, for the female tramp especially, the circumstances of poverty and homelessness are virtually inescapable. A male pauper who admits her to a workhouse issues an invitation for "a bit of funning" and tries to kiss her companion while interviewing her (p. 109). She is relieved and delighted finally to reach a women's shelter, where she is free from taunts and looks and propositions. She comes to realize that the appearance of indigence itself makes women susceptible to an endless

and wholly involuntary descent into the abyss. Once a respectable ve-
neer is shed, any chance of economic independence is lost, and then
follows inevitably a loss of self-respect and "decency." "The last article
gone, cleanliness lost, clothing dilapidated or dirty—what then?" she
wonders (p. 135).

The power of circumstance to make the homeless into permanent
vagrants and, ultimately, into an amoral and corrupt class overwhelms
Higgs when she decides she can take no more filth, sleeplessness, and
hunger and yet knows that she can escape because of the money and
clean clothes she keeps hidden in her bag. The urgency of her desire
to take refuge in the home of friends awaiting her at various meeting
points impresses upon her the horror of the life she does not have to
continue to lead. What would become of her, she muses, if she did not
have the ability to change herself from "tramp to tourist"? (p. 135).
She wonders if a "better class of friends . . . placed in like circumstances" would bear the test of destitution as well as the strong, patient
women she encounters in the shelters (p. 152). Like Florence Bell, who
falters when she tries to imagine middle-class women undergoing the
trials of childbirth routinely suffered by working-class women, Higgs
finds her most powerful moment of identification in the apprehension
of class difference.

As her observation of female vulnerability continues from town to
town and from shelter to shelter, her assessment of the inevitable connection between vagrancy and prostitution becomes more assured and
more vehement. She abandons the euphemistic language of "sinking"
and "temptation" and asserts that "the harlot is the *female tramp*, driven
by hard social conditions to primitive freedom of sex relationship" (p.
215). The male "wanderer" merely becomes a tramp, but the female
tramp inevitably becomes a prostitute. "When all else is sold," she concludes, "she sells herself" (p. 230). Finally, Higgs warns, warming to
the theme of home as the citadel of national life, if a woman has neither home nor work, she will almost certainly "get her living on the
streets" (p. 292). The overblown rhetoric of family glorification con-
verges with and is reinforced by the specter of moral disintegration and
sexual chaos. Behind this rhetoric—and obscured to some degree by
its polemical quality—is the sense of personal identification with sexual
and economic vulnerability which Higgs had so powerfully experienced. The female social investigator's connection to the woman of the
streets is a harder, more unsettling link to sustain than her affiliation
with her working-class housewife double, and Higgs allows that sense

of connection to dissipate in the prose of her final chapter. But her paean to home as the antithesis and answer to vagrancy appeals not to the mother as "pivot" of domestic health but rather to the *state* to care for children and provide work for parents. Her apprehension of un- avoidable decline in the face of circumstance grows immediately out of her experience as a *female* on the tramp and leads her to make the structure of law and labor, rather than woman, the object of her re- proach.

Female social investigators who made the family their intellectual pro- ject, their entrée into professional life, wrote out of a contradictory relationship to the ideology of maternalism. They adopted the very same cultural stance that was in part a reactionary response to their own personal emancipation. Their writing betrays their sense of pre- cariousness, their opposition to strictures of traditional femininity, and their discomfort with women's economic dependence. Although they chose the sphere of home as their object of investigation in part as a cover for their own professionalism and ideological commitments, they also revealed their investment in gender equality in writing about the families and marriages of the poor. They produced what Ellen Ross calls "mixed texts," in which their own voices mingle with the voices of working-class women. At times, says Ross, the poorer women seem to be "speaking on behalf of their better-off sisters who were prohibited from vulgar language, talk of sex, or open man hating."[33] The osten- sible object of study for these female investigators was the working-class family, and they felt obliged to offer suggestions for improving the conditions of the whole household. But their own identification with their sources of information—working-class women—made it difficult to see the interests of the household and interests of the woman as in all cases identical. A maternalist perspective, which addressed the needs of the family as a whole and with the woman's role *as mother*, competed with the feminist perception that the rights of woman, whether middle- class or working-class, were not always answered in a rhetoric of mater- nalism and an assessment of her duties toward home.

The maternalism that served both to inspire and to stifle women transcended class boundaries. Middle- and upper-class women were found wanting for pursuing careers and education, for not marrying readily enough, or for marrying without producing enough children,

[33] Ross, *Love and Toil*, p. 20.

just as working-class women were censured for "maternal ignorance" and irresponsibility toward the children they bore but appeared to neglect.[34] But if women of all classes were found wanting in "mothercraft," they also managed to react to maternalist ideology by taking advantage of the support society offered them in this arena of their lives. Working women sought recognition as political and economic beings through their maternity. Writing the history of the Women's Cooperative Guild, started in 1883, Catherine Webb explains the creation of the guild as "the emergence of the married working-woman from national obscurity into a position of national importance."[35] And just as the women of the cooperative derived collective strength from their identities as wives and mothers, their success must also have depended on the national willingness to see mothers as important consumers. In the first decade of the twentieth century, the guild made maternity the centerpiece of its campaign to ensure health care for children and mothers, and in 1915 it published a book, *Maternity: Letters from Working Women*, to argue for state-supported medical care for mothers.

As I have noted, social investigators and reformers took advantage of maternalist rhetoric to carve out areas of work and expertise for themselves, to contribute to a national debate, to claim professional authority, and to find an arena for uninhibited spectatorship and observation. Although Mary Higgs bravely pursued investigation of the extradomestic world, she also discovered that, like Tristan and Gaskell before her, her sex made it impossible to ramble with impunity or to lose herself in the crowd, to lose consciousness of herself as a woman exposed. In the first chapter of *The People of the Abyss*, Jack London describes with a kind of elation the transformation he undergoes as he trades his "soft, gray travelling suit" for worn trousers, a frayed jacket, and coal dust–encrusted brogans: "Presto! in the twinkling of an eye . . . I had become one of them. My frayed and out-at-elbows jacket was the badge and advertisement of my class, which was their class. . . . The fear of the crowd no longer haunted me. I had become a part of it."[36] This latter-day flaneur, achieving anonymity in the crowd through class disguise, bears little resemblance to Mary Higgs, whose ragged dress invites

[34] Davin, "Imperialism and Motherhood," p. 14.
[35] Catherine Webb, *The Woman with the Basket: A History of the Women's Co-operative Guild, 1883–1927* (Manchester: Cooperative Wholesale Society's Printing Works, 1927), pp. 10–11.
[36] Jack London, *The People of the Abyss* (n.p.: Joseph Simon, 1980), pp. 9–11.

rather than inhibits the stares and taunts of men on the road. Only in the sex-segregated women's shelters does she find a refuge from scrutiny and anxiety. Like the working-class homes that Bosanquet, Reeves, and Bell explored, the women's shelter enables the female social investigator to transcend the status of spectacle.

Conclusion:
Esther Summerson's Veil

The traditions of urban rambling and investigation I have touched on in this book involve a variety of kinds and degrees of disguise. From the flaneur's incognito to the investigator's masquerade of poverty to the female walker's veils and masculine garb, the urban observer obscures his or her identity in order to consume and explore the city. The flaneur's privileged position depends on the reserve and the chaos of the crowd; it protects him and lends him anonymity. He can see and be seen without himself becoming the object of anyone else's scrutiny, for *his* is the consuming and "botanizing" glance. His class, his masculinity, his posture of leisure shield him from the curiosity of the crowd. In this brief summing up I draw together the patterns of disguise I have sketched throughout the book, suggest how they operate in the navigation and representation of the city, and extend the discussion speculatively into the twentieth century.

In the George Cruikshank illustration to "The Streets—Morning" (figure 6), Boz, dressed in the uniform of the all-night stroller, leans against a post in top hat and evening coat and regards from a distance the street sellers of the earliest morning hours. There is no mistaking who is observer and who observed, who is spectator and who spectacle. In *Life in London* Pierce Egan promises to make his readers wholly invisible companions to his rambling gents, Tom and Jerry. By giving his audience a "*Camera Obscura* View of London," he can offer them the advantages of "SEEING and not being *seen*." Safe and obscured in a darkened chamber, peeking through the opening the author provides onto the colorful metropolitan stage, the reader enjoys vicariously the urban sprees of Egan's swells and, like the flaneur, takes pleasure in the stance of the voyeur. The incognito of the flaneur and the invisibility of the consuming spectator give way ultimately to the disembodied narrator of urban fiction who sees all but is never seen.

Paired with Esther Summerson in *Bleak House* is a narrator whose powerful voice and all-seeing eye achieve the status of what Michel de Certeau calls "a viewpoint and nothing more." Certeau meditates on the urban observer's desire to see the whole, to be lifted "out of the city's grasp," to become a voyeur-god who disentangles himself from the level of practice.[1] The *representation* of the city, according to this analysis, requires the obscuring or erasure of the observer's self, or the distillation of that self into an all-perceiving Eye. The practitioners of everyday life, by contrast, wear no camouflage, and because they are immersed in the comings and goings of the city, they are blind, unable to read the urban texts they produce by their movements and intersections.[2] The urban novelist, offspring of the flaneur, creates the "panorama-city" out of his ability to see everywhere and all at once. His invisibility gives him a kind of immunity and frees him from becoming the subject of the urban plot. In *Bleak House* it is Esther Summerson's body that draws our attention and carries the marks of urban contagion.

The disguise of the flaneur, spectator, or narrator may be only invisibility, anonymity, or the urban incognito of a privileged gaze. For the urban investigator, however, something more elaborate is required. Like the detective, he—or she—must be accepted as someone else in order to obtain a particular kind of knowledge. Thus in *Bleak House* Inspector Bucket dresses as a doctor to gain entrance to the Shooting Gallery and find Gridley. We read: "The physician stopped, and taking off his hat, appeared to vanish by magic, and to leave another and quite a different man in his place."[3] Bucket, like the omniscient narrator of the novel, navigates the city with complete mastery but, unlike the narrator or the flaneur, must protect and transform himself to achieve his ends unimpeded. More often than not, the social investigator must use class disguise in order to shed the appearance of privilege and thereby coax the "lower orders" to reveal themselves. Like the detective, the

[1] Michel de Certeau, *The Practice of Everyday Life*, trans. Steven F. Rendall (Berkeley: University of California Press, 1984), pp. 92–93.
[2] Ibid., p. 93.
[3] Charles Dickens, *Bleak House* (1853; rpt. Harmondsworth: Penguin, 1985), p. 404; subsequently cited in the text.

investigator has a mission and must obscure his or her identity in order to succeed.

Charles Egremont, the aristocratic, restless younger son in Disraeli's *Sybil* (1845), passes himself off as a journalist in order to find out about the other of the "Two Nations." He declares: "I resolved to live . . . among my fellow-subjects who were estranged from me; even void of celebrity as I am, I could not have done that without suspicion, had I been known; they would have recoiled from my class and my name."[4] Egremont is one of the first social investigators of nineteenth-century literature. His motives and method were replicated repeatedly in life as the century progressed and into the twentieth century as well. James Greenwood, George Sims, Charles Booth, Jack London, C. F. G. Masterman, Stephen Reynolds, and George Orwell all frequented the haunts of the poor disguised as down-and-out workingmen or classless men who had fallen on hard times, and each wrote about the experience or used it to unmask conditions of poverty. For Jack London in *The People of the Abyss*, the suit acquired at a secondhand clothes shop in Stepney puts him on an equal footing with the people of the streets. "It made me of like kind," he declares, "and in the place of the fawning and too-respectful attention I had hitherto received, I now shared with them a comradeship."[5] Not only does the disguise invite others to approach him as a confidant, but it also relieves London's fear of the crowd and gives him the secure sense that he can become safely lost within it. The investigator seeks not invisibility per se but rather the ability to move around in certain class-segregated spaces without raising suspicion, without being an object of curiosity or scrutiny. To see and hear without becoming a spectacle oneself was the investigator's purpose in adopting disguise.

George Orwell understood some of the deeper psychological motives of class masquerade, and he also understood its limits and delusions. In some instances, Orwell wrote in *The Road to Wigan Pier*, he needed no visible masquerade, not even a change of accent. With only the invention of a fictitious history he could convince a tramping partner or fellow occupant of a casual ward that he was a comrade. But to work as a coalminer or navvy turned out to be impossible—he simply could not do the work—and to be accepted fully as a lodger in a working-class family also proved elusive. "I was not one of them, and they knew

---

[4] Benjamin Disraeli, *Sybil, or the Two Nations* (Harmondsworth: Penguin, 1980), p. 299.
[5] Jack London, *The People of the Abyss* (n.p.: Joseph Simon, 1980), p. 10.

it better than I did," Orwell writes, concluding "That accursed itch of class-difference [was] enough to make real intimacy impossible."[6] In Piccadilly, Covent Garden, or Seven Dials, the middle-class onlooker's incognito of flanerie or rambling could suffice; in the doss house a tattered suit and a hard luck story would do; but for taking up a daily presence in the lives of what Orwell calls the "normal working class," even full class masquerade fails to convince. The "itch of class-difference" makes the investigator too conspicuous, as much a curiosity as the subjects of his inquiry.

For women observers of the urban scene, as I have suggested in a number of ways, femaleness itself constitutes an object of curiosity and subverts their ability to act as either the all-seeing eye or the investigator of public life. To see without being seen, or to be seen without becoming spectacle, is rendered impossible. No reserve or incognito protects the female rambler, and class disguise makes the likes of Mary Higgs more, rather than less, sexually vulnerable. When Beatrice Webb disguised herself as a "trouser-hand" to investigate the sweating system, she found herself among a protected group of working women. Yet her ineptitude with a needle caused her acute anxiety. Fearing she would be exposed as a fake, she learned something of what Orwell later discovered about the impossibility of passing as a fully functioning member of the working class. Rent collectors, visitors, charity workers, and social investigators of the domestic sphere—Helen Bosanquet, Maud Pember Reeves, Florence Bell—relied on their respectability, femininity, and class privilege to enter the homes of the poor and even, to a certain extent, to navigate the streets of the slums. But investigation of public life, city streets, workplaces, and commercial districts threatened middle-class women's respectability and challenged their authority.

If a female spectator wanted to trespass onto forbidden ground or to turn the tables so as to be consumer, not consumed, she could attempt to disguise her identity in some fundamental way other than class. Lady Mary Wortley Montagu and other European travelers abroad adopted foreign garb, especially if it obscured identity altogether, if it hid the form of the body and covered the face and seemed to offer liberty through what Lady Mary called "perpetual masquerade." The

[6] George Orwell, *The Road to Wigan Pier* (1937; rpt. New York: Berkley Publishing, 1961), p. 133.

Muslim or Catholic injunction to veil (and, from a certain perspective, stigmatize) femininity—as in Lady Mary's Turkey or Flora Tristan's Peru—struck the European woman as a means to escape stigma. When Flora Tristan entered Parliament in the robes of a Turkish gentleman, she employed a variety of disguises at once: she obscured her nationality, her bodily form, her religion, and her sex, achieving not precisely anonymity—and certainly not invisibility—but visual ambiguity. She might become a spectacle in Parliament, but not exactly as herself. Intermittent cross-dressing enabled women to enter places ordinarily prohibited to them, and it also offered the possibility of obscurity and sheer freedom of movement. George Sand could attend the theater alone without being recognized ("No one paid attention to me"), and Vita Sackville-West could walk down Piccadilly secure in the knowledge that even her own mother could not identify her. Gender disguise might provide an exhilarating sense of invisibility, interrupt the circuit of objectification, and deflect the attention habitually attracted by a lone female in a public place.

Instances of female disguise in nineteenth-century fictional texts are far less sensational than the escapades Flora Tristan describes in the *Promenades* or those alluded to in Lady Mary's letters and George Sand's memoirs. Margaret Hale favors "brown and dust-colour" dresses for the London visiting mentioned only briefly at the end of *North and South*; and Aunt Esther, in a kind of parody of class descent through costume, ascends with ease in respectability of rank simply by dressing as a mechanic's wife in *Mary Barton*. But by far the most complex and telling use of urban disguise in the novels I have discussed is to be found in Dickens's *Bleak House*, in which the veils worn by three female characters suggest a number of paradigms associated with women's navigation of city streets. The novel employs a convention of Victorian women's dress—the covering of the head and occasionally the face with bonnet and veil to go into the street—to enhance the mystery of the plot, to suggest the interchangeability of women within the context of the city streets, and to dramatize the female street walker's need for disguise. What I hope to show in the discussion that follows, however, is that *Bleak House* ultimately exposes the veiling of women as a sign rather than a concealment of stigma.

The veils worn by Lady Dedlock, her maid Hortense, and her daughter, Esther, function on a dramatic level to confuse the reader's apprehension of the novel's mystery and to disorient and terrify the streetsweeper Jo, who sees all three women veiled and thus apparently indistinguishable. Lady Dedlock comes to him veiled and in plain dress to question him about her lover, Nemo, and to be shown his grave in the paupers' burial ground. She seeks to conceal her identity, her class, and indeed her passion and to separate herself from the taint of her past; but though she manages to carry out her mission, her efforts at concealment and camouflage are only partially successful. Like Flora Tristan, who cannot really fool the gentlemen in Parliament, Lady Dedlock "sufficiently betrays herself" by the discrepancy between her "refined manner" and her upper-servant's attire that she causes many who pass her to "look round sharply" (p. 276). The disguise also works metonymically to suggest her inability to escape the stigma of her past, as she cowers in the entrance to the paupers' graveyard, "into a corner of that hideous archway, with its deadly stains contaminating her dress" (p. 278).

The interchangeability of women's bodies, suggested almost comically by Jo's bewilderment, is further emphasized by the ambiguous origins of Lady Dedlock's "plain dress." When we see her disguised as a servant, we assume she has borrowed an outfit belonging to Hortense; but later, after the lawyer Tulkinghorn has displayed a veiled Hortense to Jo in order to glean information about Lady Dedlock, we discover that it is Hortense who has borrowed her mistress's clothes for the ruse. Similarly confounding is the fact that Bucket and Tulkinghorn have dressed Hortense as they think Lady Dedlock must have appeared to Jo in order to establish both the resemblance of one to the other and the telling differences between them. When Jo responds to seeing the veiled Hortense with "that there's the wale, the bonnet, and the gownd. It is her and it an't her. It an't her hand, nor yet her rings, nor yet her voice," he is answering exactly as Bucket had hoped (p. 369).

The third woman in this proliferating pattern of doubles is, of course, Esther, whose physical resemblance to Lady Dedlock does not end with clothing. When Jo, feverish and semidelirious, sees a veiled Esther in the brickmaker's cottage, his initial terror gives way to the realization that there might be "*three* of 'em," but he also asserts that, although Esther's bonnet and gown are different from the first woman's, "she looks to me the t'other one" (p. 486). Jo recognizes a physical resemblance between Esther and her mother which signifies inheritance on a number of levels. Like Mary Barton, whose figure resembles her Aunt Esther's, Esther Summerson is marked and threatened by her biological link to a disgraced woman. In the novel's economy of female fallenness,

Hortense embodies Lady Dedlock's debased passions and Esther the legacy, and possible transcendence, of a tainted past.

Indeed, the veils Esther Summerson wears tell the story of her evolving relationship to the city and to the inherited taint she bears. When she dons a veil on the night she is exposed to the fever, she does so neither to disguise her identity, as her mother does, nor at anyone else's request, as Hortense does, but rather as an expression of her sense that she needs protection in negotiating the city. When Esther had walked in the city for the very first time, early one morning on her way to Bleak House in St. Albans, she had seen it through wholly innocent, uninitiated eyes—it was to her "the wonderful city," "delightful to see"—and she had no need of a veil. But when she goes out to the brickmaker's on that fateful night, she sees London overhung with a "lurid glare," an "unearthly fire" that gleams on people and buildings alike (p. 484). Her vision of the city has now come to match that of the omniscient narrator, and it seems fitting that she should now have need of a veil through which to view the corrupt and fallen city. Not only has she been exposed to the dire circumstances of the brickmaker's family and the agony of a chancery suit, but she has by this point in the narrative seen Lady Dedlock's face, which, "like a broken glass," reflects back to her a version of her own (p. 304). Veiling now becomes linked to the question of Esther's facial resemblance to her mother.

Although the veil *hides* Esther's face in the brickmaker's cottage, it also transforms her identity, causing her to be mistaken for her mother. After Esther falls ill, she continues to wear a veil at all times to hide her disfigurement. But at this point too, mother and daughter replicate each other, as Lady Dedlock comes around—veiled—to inquire after Esther's health. The veil had both hidden the daughter's resemblance to her mother and accentuated it, and it is paradoxically the effects of the smallpox that render the veil unnecessary. When Esther draws first the muslin veil and then the cascade of hair from in front of her scarred face, she recognizes that she has, in some important sense, become someone else. As I have discussed earlier in this book, Esther now wears the stigma of her past on her face: it has been extracted from her being and externalized, making her shame more manifest but also easier to endure. This loosening of ties to her guilty origins is articulated explicitly when Lady Dedlock reveals herself as Esther's mother, and Esther's first reaction is relief that "any trace of likeness" to her mother has been obliterated by her illness (p. 565). She claims to be relieved for her mother's sake, but the erasure of her physical resemblance to her mother emancipates Esther as well. Her final link to shame, to her mother, and to her own psychological demons is severed at the moment when she unveils her dead mother—the woman she thinks to be Jenny, the brickmaker's wife—who lies outside the paupers' burial ground. In a gesture that repeats the unveiling of her own disfigured face, Esther draws aside the dead woman's hair and sees her mother. Lady Dedlock's last true double is Jenny, and the death of "the mother of the dead child" also marks the exorcism of Esther's stillborn self. No longer in need of veiling her association with shame, Esther can even ultimately regain her looks—the beauty that may or may not be like her mother's.

The veils in *Bleak House*, and particularly Esther's, suggest that although the superficial motive for female disguise is the desire to obscure identity, the deeper impulse involves a need to hide sexuality and the suspect forms of it that the street imposes on the lone female walker. And just as Esther's veil both hides and reveals her link to her mother, so does the iconography of woman's urban disguise both obscure and signify transgression. The veiled women in *Bleak House*—Lady Dedlock, Hortense, and Esther—announce their suspiciousness, their trespass, their secretiveness by endeavoring so visibly to conceal their identity. Each is associated with sexual taint: Lady Dedlock through her history of nonmarital liaison and illegitimate motherhood; Hortense through her caricatured Gallic, unlicensed, and ultimately murderous passions; and Esther through her birth "in sin" and her nearly indelible connection to her mother. They carry this taint as they move about on the streets of London, and in their particular cases they also venture forth as pursuers, stalkers, detectives of sorts. They trespass not simply by virtue of their femaleness but because they are determined to read and uncover the city's mysteries.

Can the female walker, rambler, investigator, or detective move about the city undisguised and unmarked by her sex? I conclude with some speculations derived from the work of a female urbanist of the twentieth century, Virginia Woolf, who creates a number of different textual possibilities for navigating the streets of London. Indeed, these possibilities can be understood as strategies imagined in response to the barriers to unimpeded female strolling she describes in *The Pargiters*. If Bond Street seemed "as impassable . . . as any swamp alive with croco-

diles" and Burlington Arcade a "fever-stricken den," even granting
that these images are used to evoke the London of the 1880s, how did
she invent herself and her female characters as citizens of the city?
Androgyny, growing old, mental travel, reduction to the organ of sight,
utopian aspiration: these are some of the methods her texts offer as
means of mitigating the experienced obstacle of femaleness.

When the narrator of *A Room of One's Own* (1929) speculates on the
kind of writer the hypothetical Mary Carmichael, the woman writer of
the near future, will be, she imagines her walking and describing the
city streets. Mary Carmichael will be able—or, rather, compelled—to
do what the narrator can enact only in her mind's eye: "[I] went on
in thought through the streets of London. . . . For *in imagination* I had
gone into a shop." She conjures up a cast of female types: plump
women gesticulating in doorways, violet sellers and match sellers, old
crones, aimless girls, and, in the shop, the "girl behind the counter."
The London she imagines for Mary Carmichael's exploration is a woman's London, in which female rambler and female street folk coexist
without encroaching on one another's psychic territory and in which
the history of the shopgirl is found to be more interesting than "the
hundred and fiftieth life of Napoleon or seventieth study of Keats."[7] A
few pages later, continuing her meditation on the city but now *describing*
rather than *imagining* a London walk, she is propelled into speculations
on androgyny. A woman on the street, she says, "is often surprised by
a sudden splitting off of consciousness . . . when from being the natural
inheritor of that civilisation, she becomes, on the contrary, outside of
it, alien and critical."[8] This split consciousness, the result of a woman's
identification with yet alienation from the dominant culture, coupled
with the narrator's glimpse of a man and a woman getting into a taxi,
causes her to muse on a desired mental synthesis of male and female.
One androgynous consciousness might unite the two perspectives of
identification and alienation, of possessing the city and being possessed
by it.

These two modes of street travel—the imaginary and the androgynous—dominate, respectively, two other city-centered works of this period, "Street-Haunting: A London Adventure" (1930) and *Orlando*
(1928). In "Street-Haunting" Woolf envisions for herself the kind of
journey she recommends to Mary Carmichael. The ramble appears to

[7] Virginia Woolf, *A Room of One's Own* (New York: Harcourt, Brace, 1957), pp. 93–94;
emphasis added.
[8] Ibid., p. 101.

be an experience of the present, however, and not a projection into the future; and yet the rambler herself is wholly disembodied, a spectral figure (as the essay's title might suggest) whose pleasure derives in part from shedding the self and assuming—in imagination—the identities of those she observes. She becomes a generic walker, using the pronoun "we" in place of "I," and is then transmuted into an "eye"— "a central oyster of perceptiveness, an enormous eye."[9] Like the "solar eye" Certeau invokes, Woolf's eye seems to float above the scene, alighting to consume the treasures of Oxford Street or enter the mind of a washerwoman, but never allowing herself to "dig deeper than the eye approves."[10] She is not so much the flaneur, who enjoys anonymity but has a privileged sense of his authority and visible person, as an invisible presence whose being dissolves and disperses.

In *Orlando*, where the fluid boundary between male and female which Woolf contemplates in *A Room of One's Own* is realized in the central character, the city inspires Orlando, changed from male to female, to return to masculine dress. Thrust as a woman into eighteenth-century London, she finds her pleasure in the great metropolis marred by the attentions of men: "Was it impossible then to go for a walk without being half suffocated, presented with a toad set in emeralds, and asked in marriage by an Archduke?" The company of Mr. Pope and her realization that, although a wit might praise her and drink her tea, he would in no way "respect her opinions" or "admire her understanding," cause her to meditate longingly upon her past.[11] She goes to her bedroom cupboard, removes an old suit of her male clothes, and goes out into the night city dressed as a man. In Leicester Square she encounters a prostitute, Nell, and goes with her to her chambers, only to reveal her femaleness at the moment when Nell displays herself, ready for sex. Laughter and relief are Nell's response; she had not really wanted the company of men that night any more than Orlando had, and the two join a group of whores for the camaraderie Orlando had missed in the company of London wits. The period of her life that follows becomes all but unrepresentable. The narrator tells us: "As we peer and grope in the ill-lit, ill-paved, ill-ventilated courtyards that lay about Gerrard Street and Drury Lane at that time, we

[9] Virginia Woolf, "Street-Haunting: A London Adventure," in *Collected Essays* (London: Hogarth Press, 1967), 4:156.

[10] Ibid., 4:157.

[11] Virginia Woolf, *Orlando, A Biography* (New York: Harcourt Brace, 1956), pp. 191–92, 214.

seem now to catch sight of her and then again to lose it. What makes
the task of identification still more difficult is that she found it conven-
ient at this time to change frequently from one set of clothes to another.''[12] Orlando's urban habit of wearing men's clothing goes beyond
the mere disguise of cross-dressing. Only by calling upon her masculine
past and her masculine self can she as a woman enjoy the company of
her own sex and escape the oppressive company of men.

Clarissa Dalloway escapes objectification on the city streets by virtue
of her age and the consequent erasure of her sexuality. No longer
herself—''not even Clarissa any more; this being Mrs. Dalloway''—she
walks up Bond Street with the sense that her own body is like a garment
she wears. Her aging skin disguises her to the point of invisibility: ''She
had the oddest sense of being herself invisible; unseen; unknown; there
being no marrying, no more having of children now.''[13] Although Mrs.
Dalloway derives protection from being past the age of sexual attractiveness, her freedom nonetheless has a bittersweet quality, for sexual
possibility is what establishes a woman's identity on the street even while
it makes the streets impassable. *Mrs. Dalloway* begins with Clarissa's superannuation and ends with Elizabeth Dalloway's initiation into the
sexual politics of the street. ''It was beginning,'' the narrator intones
as Elizabeth waits for the bus at Victoria Street. ''People were beginning
to compare her to poplar trees, early dawn, hyacinths, fawns, running
water, and garden lilies; and it made her life a burden to her.'' Clarissa
understands that her daughter has crossed into that phase of her life
from which she has already exited; she can see that ''the compliments
were beginning.'' And the narrative itself performs the aestheticizing
role of the street: it compares ''the beautiful body in the fawn-coloured
coat'' to the figurehead of a ship, her cheeks to white-painted wood,
and her eyes to sculpture.[14]

But Elizabeth herself, although registering as a burden her new status
as object of erotic curiosity, proceeds to navigate the city with confidence. She enters what Charlotte Brontë's Lucy Snowe calls ''the heart
of city life,'' and, like Lucy, she prefers the Strand and Cornhill to the
West End and Westminster.[15] Indeed, the very experience of these new

---

[12] Ibid., p. 220.

[13] Virginia Woolf, *Mrs. Dalloway* (New York: Harcourt Brace, 1953), p. 14.

[14] Ibid., pp. 204, 206.

[15] Charlotte Brontë, *Villette* (London: Dent, 1983), p. 43. In the chapter titled ''London'' Lucy devotes two pages of her narrative to her brief sojourn in the metropolis
before describing her impulsive flight to the Continent. Lucy's pleasure in the city is, as

parts of the city suggests to Elizabeth the possibility of a future unlike her mother's or her father's:

> It was quite different here from Westminster, she thought, getting off at Chancery Lane. It was so serious; it was so busy. In short, she would like to have a profession. She would become a doctor, a farmer, possibly go into Parliament, if she found it necessary, *all because of the Strand.*
>
> The feet of those people busy about their activities, hands putting stone to stone, minds eternally occupied not with trivial chatterings (comparing women to poplars—which was rather exciting, of course, but very silly), but with thoughts of ships, of business, of law, of administration . . . made her quite determined, whatever her mother might say, to become either a farmer or a doctor.[16]

Westminster, the seat of government, is her father's territory, Bond Street, with its opportunities for the consumption of luxury goods, her mother's. The Strand, with its bustling mix of classes and types, professions and commerce, might be Elizabeth's, and it fills her with aspiration and with the exhilarating sense that "she was a pioneer, a stray, venturing, trusting."[17] I end with Elizabeth Dalloway's sense of possibility and with Woolf's recognition that for women yet to come the city might be a locus of expansion and emancipation, that, even as others compare them to hyacinths and early dawn, they might nonetheless become explorers and adventurers: "She penetrated a little further in the direction of St. Paul's. She liked the geniality, sisterhood, motherhood, brotherhood of this uproar. It seemed to her good."[18] Mrs. Dalloway, disguised by advancing age, gives way to Elizabeth, undisguised and poised to take on the city before, she hopes, some form of incognito is required.

---

she puts it, an "irrational" one and is inseparable from the daring and even the danger of navigating it alone.

[16] Woolf, *Mrs. Dalloway*, p. 207; emphasis added.

[17] Ibid., p. 208.

[18] Ibid., p. 209.

Bibliography

Primary Sources

Acton, William. *Prostitution.* Ed. Peter Fryer. London: MacGibbon and Kee, 1968.

Baudelaire, Charles. *The Painter of Modern Life and Other Essays.* Trans. Jonathan Mayne. New York: Garland Publishing, 1978.

Becker, George J., ed. *Documents of Modern Literary Realism.* Princeton: Princeton University Press, 1963.

Beik, Doris, and Paul Beik, eds. *Flora Tristan, Utopian Feminist: Her Travel Diaries and Personal Crusade.* Bloomington: Indiana University Press, 1993.

Bell, Lady. *At the Works: A Study of a Manufacturing Town (Middlesbrough).* London: Edward Arnold, 1907.

Booth, Charles, ed. *Life and Labour of the People in London.* London: Macmillan, 1892.

Bosanquet, Mrs. Bernard. *Rich and Poor.* London: Macmillan, 1896.

———. *Social Work in London, 1869 to 1912: A History of the Charity Organisation Society.* London: John Murray, 1914.

Certeau, Michel de. *The Practice of Everyday Life.* Trans. Steven F. Rendall. Berkeley: University of California Press, 1984.

Chadwick, Edwin. *Report on the Sanitary Condition of the Labouring Population of Great Britain.* 1842. Ed. M. W. Flinn. Edinburgh: University of Edinburgh Press, 1965.

Collet, Clara. "The Economic Position of Educated Working Women, A Discourse Delivered in South Place Chapel, Finsbury, February 2, 1890." London: E. W. Allen, 1890.

Craske, May. "Girl Life in a Slum." *Economic Review* 18 (1908): 184–89.

Cronwright-Schreiner, S. C., ed. *The Letters of Olive Schreiner, 1876–1920.* London: T. Fisher Unwin, 1924.

De Quincey, Thomas. *Confessions of an English Opium Eater.* Harmondsworth: Penguin, 1971.

———. *Literary Reminiscences.* Boston: Ticknor and Fields, 1851.

Dickens, Charles. *Bleak House.* 1853. Harmondsworth: Penguin, 1985.

———. *Dombey and Son: Wholesale, Retail and for Exportation.* 1848. Harmondsworth: Penguin, 1970.

———. *The Personal History, Adventures, Experience and Observation of David Copperfield, The Younger of Blunderstone Rookery.* 1850. New York: Signet, 1962.

———. *The Posthumous Papers of the Pickwick Club.* 1837. Harmondsworth: Penguin, 1972.

———. *Sketches by Boz; Illustrative of Every-day Life and Every-day People.* 1837. London: Chapman and Hall, 1867.

Disraeli, Benjamin. *Sybil, or the Two Nations.* Harmondsworth: Penguin, 1980.

Egan, Pierce. *Life in London.* London: John Camden Hotten, 1869.

Engels, Friedrich. *The Condition of the Working Class in England.* Trans. W. O. Henderson and W. H. Chaloner. Stanford: Stanford University Press, 1968.

Faucher, Leon. *Manchester in 1844.* Trans. with notes by "A Member of the Manchester Athenaeum." London: Frank Cass, 1969.

Fielding, K. J., ed. *The Speeches of Charles Dickens.* London: Harvester, 1988.

Gaskell, Elizabeth. *Elizabeth Gaskell: Four Short Stories.* London: Pandora Press, 1981.

———. *The Letters of Mrs. Gaskell.* Ed. J. A. V. Chapple and Arthur Pollard. Manchester: Manchester University Press, 1966.

———. *Mary Barton.* 1848. Harmondsworth: Penguin, 1970.

———. *North and South.* 1855. Harmondsworth: Penguin, 1970.

———. *Ruth.* 1853. London: Dent, 1967.

Gissing, George. *London and the Life of Literature in Late Victorian England: The Diary of George Gissing.* Ed. Pierre Coustillas. Hassocks, Sussex: Harvester Press, 1978.

Harkness, Margaret. *George Eastmont: Wanderer.* London: Burns and Oates, 1905.

———. *In Darkest London: A Story of the Salvation Army.* London: William Reeves, 1891.

———. Letters to Beatrice Potter, 1878. Passfield Papers. Section II–1–ii. London School of Economics and Political Science.

———. *Out of Work.* London: Swan Sonnenschein, 1888.

Higgs, Mary. *Glimpses into the Abyss.* London: P. S. King and Son, 1906.

Hill, Octavia. *Homes of the London Poor.* London: Macmillan, 1883.

Hunt, Leigh. *Leigh Hunt's Political and Occasional Essays.* Ed. Lawrence Huston Houtchens and Carolyn Washburn Houtchens. New York: Columbia University Press, 1962.

Jameson, Anna. *The Diary of an Ennuyée.* Boston: Ticknor and Fields, 1860.

Kay, James Phillips. *The Moral and Physical Condition of the Working Classes Employed in the Cotton Manufacture in Manchester.* Manchester: E. J. Morten, 1969.

Keating, Peter, ed. *Into Unknown England, 1866–1913.* Manchester: Manchester University Press, 1976.

Kingsley, Mary H. *Travels in West Africa.* London: Virago, 1982.

Lamb, Charles. *The Essays of Elia and Eliana.* London: George Bell and Sons, 1883.

————. *The Letters of Charles Lamb.* Ed. E. V. Lucas. London: J. M. Dent and Sons, 1935.

————. *The Works of Charles Lamb.* Ed. William MacDonald. London: J. M. Dent and Co., 1903.

Levy, Amy. "A Ballad of Religion and Marriage." Houghton Library, Harvard University. N.d.

————. *The Complete Novels and Selected Writings of Amy Levy, 1861–1889.* Ed. Melvyn New. Gainesville: University Press of Florida, 1993.

————. *A London Plane Tree and Other Verse.* New York: Frederick A. Stokes, 1890.

————. *A Minor Poet and Other Verse.* London: T. Fisher Unwin, 1884.

————. *Reuben Sachs.* London: Macmillan, 1888.

————. *The Romance of a Shop.* Boston: Cupples and Hurd, 1889.

London, Jack. *The People of the Abyss.* N.p.: Joseph Simon, 1980.

Mayhew, Henry. *London Labour and the London Poor.* London: Griffin, Bohn, and Co., 1861–62.

Montagu, Lady Mary Wortley. *The Letters and Works of Lady Mary Wortley Montagu.* London: George Bell and Sons, 1887.

Moor, Lucy M. *Girls of Yesterday and To-day: the Romance of the YWCA.* London: S. W. Partridge, 1911.

"On the Projected Improvements of St. James's Park." *London Magazine,* n.s., 2 (July 1825): 445–52.

Orwell, George. *The Road to Wigan Pier.* New York: Berkley Publishing, 1961.

Parent-Duchâtelet, Alexandre. *De la prostitution dans la ville de Paris.* 1845. Paris: Seuil, 1981.

Phillipps, Evelyn March. "The Working Lady in London." *Fortnightly Review* 52 (August 1892): 193–203.

Redding, Cyrus. "The Tea Garden." *London Magazine* 6 (August 1822): 136–40.

Reeves, Mrs. Pember. *Round About a Pound a Week.* 1914. London: Virago, 1979.

Sala, George Augustus. *Twice Round the Clock; or the Hours of the Day and Night in London.* Leicester: Leicester University Press, 1971.

Sand, George. *Histoire de ma vie.* Paris: Calmann-Lévy, 1926.

Schreiner, Olive. *Letters.* Vol. 1. *1871–1879.* Ed. Richard Rive. Oxford: Oxford University Press, 1988.

Shepherd, Thomas, and Elmes, James. *Metropolitan Improvements, or London in the Nineteenth Century.* London: Jones and Co., 1827.

Tristan, Flora. *The London Journal of Flora Tristan, 1842.* Trans. Jean Hawks. London: Virago, 1982.

————. *Peregrinations of a Pariah, 1833–1834.* Trans. Jean Hawks. London: Virago, 1986.

————. *Promenades dans Londres.* Paris: Maspero, 1983.

————. *The Workers' Union.* Trans. Beverly Livingston. Urbana: University of Illinois Press, 1983.

Trollope, Frances. *Domestic Manners of the Americans.* New York: Dodd, Mead, 1839.

Webb, Beatrice. *The Diary of Beatrice Webb.* Ed. Norman MacKenzie and Jeanne MacKenzie. Cambridge: Harvard University Press, 1982.

————. *My Apprenticeship.* London: Longmans, n.d.

————. "Pages from a Work-girl's Diary." *The Nineteenth Century* 25 (September 1888): 301–14.

Wells, H. G. *The New Machiavelli*. Harmondsworth: Penguin, 1970.

Woolf, Virginia. *Mrs. Dalloway*. New York: Harcourt Brace, 1953.

————. *Orlando, a Biography*. New York: Harcourt Brace, 1956.

————. *The Pargiters*. Ed. Mitchell A. Leaska. New York: Harcourt Brace Jovanovich, 1977.

————. *A Room of One's Own*. New York: Harcourt Brace, 1957.

————. "Street-Haunting: A London Adventure." In *Collected Essays*. London: Hogarth Press, 1967.

Wordsworth, William. *The Prelude*. 1850. Ed. J. C. Maxwell. Harmondsworth: Penguin, 1971.

————. *Selected Poems and Prefaces*. Ed. Jack Stillinger. Boston: Houghton Mifflin/Riverside Press, 1965.

Yates, Gayle Graham, ed. *Harriet Martineau on Women*. New Brunswick, N.J.: Rutgers University Press, 1985.

Secondary Sources

Alexander, Sally. *Women's Work in Nineteenth-Century London: A Study of the Years 1820–50*. London: Journeyman Press, 1983.

Altick, Richard D. *The Shows of London*. Cambridge: Harvard University Press, 1978.

Anderson, Amanda. *Tainted Souls and Painted Faces: The Rhetoric of Fallenness in Victorian Culture*. Ithaca: Cornell University Press, 1993.

Auerbach, Nina. *Communities of Women: An Idea in Fiction*. Cambridge: Harvard University Press, 1978.

————. "Dickens and Dombey: A Daughter After All." In *Dickens Studies Annual*. Vol. 5, ed. Robert B. Partlow, Jr. Carbondale: Southern Illinois Press, 1976.

————. *Ellen Terry: Player in Her Time*. New York: W. W. Norton, 1987.

Barrell, John. *The Infection of Thomas De Quincey: A Psychopathology of Imperialism*. New Haven: Yale University Press, 1991.

Beals, Polly A. "Fabian Feminism: Gender, Politics, and Culture in London, 1880–1930." Ph.D. diss., Rutgers University, 1989.

Benjamin, Walter. *Charles Baudelaire: A Lyric Poet in the Era of High Capitalism*. Trans. Harry Zohn. London: New Left Books, 1973.

Bernstein, Carol L. *The Celebration of Scandal: Toward the Sublime in Victorian Urban Fiction*. University Park: Pennsylvania State University Press, 1991.

Bloom, Harold., ed. *Charles Dickens's "Bleak House."* New York: Chelsea House, 1987.

Bodenheimer, Rosemarie. "Private Grief and Public Acts in *Mary Barton*." In *Dickens Studies Annual*. Vol. 9, ed. Michael Timko, Fred Kaplan, and Edward Guiliano. New York: AMS Press, 1981.

Boxer, Marilyn, and Jean H. Quataert, eds. *Socialist Women: European Socialist Feminism in the Nineteenth and Early Twentieth Centuries*. New York: Elsevier, 1978.

Briggs, Asa. *The Making of Modern England, 1783–1867: The Age of Improvement.* New York: Harper and Row, 1965.

———. *Victorian Cities.* New York: Harper and Row, 1963.

Buck-Morss, Susan. "The Flaneur, the Sandwichman, and the Whore: The Politics of Loitering." *New German Critique* 39 (Fall 1986): 99–140.

Burke, Thomas. *English Night-Life: From Norman Curfew to Present Black-Out.* London: B. T. Batsford, 1941.

Butt, John, and Kathleen Tillotson. *Dickens at Work.* London: Methuen, 1968.

Byrd, Max. *London Transformed: Images of the City in the Eighteenth Century.* New Haven: Yale University Press, 1978.

Cannadine, David, and David Reeder, eds. *Exploring the Urban Past: Essays in Urban History.* Cambridge: Cambridge University Press, 1982.

Clark, Robert. "Riddling the Family Firm: The Sexual Economy in *Dombey and Son.*" *ELH* 51 (Spring 1984): 69–84.

Cole, G. D. H. *A History of Socialist Thought.* London: Macmillan, 1955.

Collins, Dorothy W. "The Composition of Mrs. Gaskell's *North and South.*" *Bulletin of the John Rylands Library* 54 (1971–72): 67–93.

Collins, Philip. *Dickens and Crime.* London: Macmillan, 1964.

———. "Dickens's Reading." *The Dickensian* 60 (September 1964): 136–51.

Corfield, Penelope J. "Walking the City Streets: The Urban Odyssey in Eighteenth-Century England." *Journal of Urban History* 16 (February 1990): 132–74.

d'Albertis, Deirdre. "Elizabeth Gaskell and the Victorian Social Text: Politics, Gender, and Genre." Ph.D. diss., Harvard University, 1991.

David, Deirdre. *Fictions of Resolution in Three Victorian Novels.* New York: Columbia University Press, 1981.

Davin, Anna. "Imperialism and Motherhood." *History Workshop* 5 (Spring 1978): 9–66.

DeLuca, V. A. *Thomas De Quincey: The Prose of Vision.* Toronto: University of Toronto Press, 1980.

Desanti, Dominique. *A Woman in Revolt: A Biography of Flora Tristan.* Trans. Elizabeth Zelvin. New York: Crown, 1976.

DeVries, Duane. *Dickens's Apprentice Years: The Making of a Novelist.* New York: Barnes and Noble, 1976.

Dexter, Walter. "The Reception of Dickens's First Book." *The Dickensian* 32 (1935–36): 43–50.

Dijkstra, Sandra. *Flora Tristan: Feminism in the Age of George Sand.* London: Pluto Press, 1992.

Dyos, H. J. and Michael Wolff, eds. *The Victorian City: Images and Realities.* London: Routledge and Kegan Paul, 1973.

Feldman, Jessica R. *Gender on the Divide: The Dandy in Modernist Literature.* Ithaca: Cornell University Press, 1993.

Foucault, Michel. *Discipline and Punish: The Birth of the Prison.* Trans. Alan Sheridan. New York: Pantheon Books, 1977.

Gallagher, Catherine. *The Industrial Reformation of English Fiction, 1832–1867.* Chicago: University of Chicago Press, 1985.

Gallagher, Catherine, and Thomas Laqueur, eds. *The Making of the Modern Body:*

Sexuality and Society in the Nineteenth Century. Berkeley: University of California Press, 1987.

George, M. Dorothy. *Hogarth to Cruikshank: Social Change in Graphic Satire*. London: Penguin, 1967.

Gilman, Sander. *Disease and Representation: Images of Illness from Madness to AIDS*. Ithaca: Cornell University Press, 1988.

Grillo, Virgil. *Charles Dickens' "Sketches by Boz": End in the Beginning*. Boulder: Colorado Associated Press, 1974.

Gross, John J., ed. *Dickens and the Twentieth Century*. Toronto: University of Toronto Press, 1962.

Gurney, Michael S. "Disease as Device: The Role of Smallpox in *Bleak House*." In *Literature and Medicine*. Vol. 9, ed. Peter W. Graham and Elizabeth Sewell. *Fictive Ills: Literary Perspectives on Wounds and Diseases*. Baltimore: Johns Hopkins University Press, 1990.

Handlin, Oscar, and John Burchard, eds. *The Historian and the City*. Cambridge: MIT Press, 1963.

Harman, Barbara Leah. "In Promiscuous Company: Female Public Appearance in Elizabeth Gaskell's *North and South*." *Victorian Studies* 31 (Spring 1988): 351–74.

Harsin, Jill. *Policing Prostitution in Nineteenth-Century Paris*. Princeton: Princeton University Press, 1985.

Hartman, Geoffrey H. *Wordsworth's Poetry, 1787–1814*. New Haven: Yale University Press, 1964.

Hayter, Alethea. *Opium and the Romantic Imagination*. Berkeley: University of California Press, 1968.

Hopkins, A. B. *Elizabeth Gaskell, Her Life and Work*. London: John Lehmann, 1952.

Hudson, Derek. *Munby, Man of Two Worlds: The Life and Diaries of Arthur J. Munby, 1828–1910*. London: John Murray, 1972.

Jeffreys, Sheila. *The Spinster and Her Enemies: Feminism and Sexuality, 1880–1930*. London: Pandora Press, 1985.

Johnson, Edgar. *Charles Dickens, His Tragedy and Triumph*. Harmondsworth: Penguin, 1977.

Kapp, Yvonne. *Eleanor Marx*. New York: Pantheon, 1976.

Keating, Peter. *The Working Classes in Victorian Fiction*. New York: Barnes and Noble, 1971.

Kidd, Alan J., and K. W. Roberts, eds. *City, Class, and Culture: Studies of Social Policy and Cultural Production in Victorian Manchester*. Manchester: Manchester University Press, 1985.

Klaus, H. Gustav, ed. *The Socialist Novel in Great Britain: Towards the Recovery of a Tradition*. New York: St. Martin's Press, 1982.

Kramer, Lawrence. "Gender and Sexuality in *The Prelude*: The Question of Book Seven." *ELH* 54 (Fall 1987): 619–37.

Langbauer, Laurie. *Woman and Romance: The Consolations of Gender in the English Novel*. Ithaca: Cornell University Press, 1990.

Lewis, Jane. *Women and Social Action in Victorian and Edwardian England*. Stanford: Stanford University Press, 1991.

Marcus, Jane. "*The Years* as Greek Drama, Domestic Novel, and Götterdämmerung." *Bulletin of the New York Public Library* 80 (Winter 1977): 276–301.

Marcus, Steven. *Dickens from Pickwick to Dombey.* New York: Simon and Schuster, 1965.

———. *Engels, Manchester, and the Working Class.* New York: Random House, 1974.

Marsh, Joss Lutz. "Good Mrs. Brown's Connections: Sexuality and Story-Telling in *Dealings with the Firm of Dombey and Son.*" *ELH* 58 (Summer 1991): 405–26.

Michie, Helena. " 'Who Is This in Pain?': Scarring, Disfigurement, and Female Identity in *Bleak House* and *Our Mutual Friend.*" *Novel* 22 (Winter 1989): 199–212.

Miller, J. Hillis. *The Disappearance of God: Five Nineteenth-Century Writers.* Cambridge: Harvard University Press, 1963.

Miller, J. Hillis, and David Borowitz. *Charles Dickens and George Cruikshank.* Los Angeles: William Andrews Clark Memorial Library, University of California, 1971.

Moers, Ellen. "*Bleak House*: The Agitating Women." *The Dickensian* 69 (January 1973): 13–24.

———. *Literary Women: The Great Writers.* New York: Doubleday, 1976.

Nadel, Ira Bruce, and F. S. Schwarzbach, eds. *Victorian Artists and the City.* New York: Pergamon Press, 1980.

Nead, Lynda. *Myths of Sexuality: Representations of Women in Victorian Britain.* London: Basil Blackwell, 1988.

Neff, Wanda Fraiken. *Victorian Working Women: An Historical and Literary Study of Women in British Industries and Professions, 1820–1850.* New York: Columbia University Press, 1929.

Nicolson, Nigel. *Portrait of a Marriage.* London: Weidenfeld and Nicolson, 1973.

Nord, Deborah Epstein. *The Apprenticeship of Beatrice Webb.* Ithaca: Cornell University Press, 1989.

Olsen, Donald J. *The City as a Work of Art: London, Paris, Vienna.* New Haven: Yale University Press, 1986.

———. *The Growth of Victorian London.* London: B. T. Batsford, 1976.

Paulson, Ronald. *Hogarth: His Life, Art, and Times.* New Haven: Yale Univesity Press, 1971.

Pfautz, Harold W., ed. *Charles Booth on the City.* Chicago: University of Chicago Press, 1967.

Pinchbeck, Ivy. *Women Workers and the Industrial Revolution, 1750–1850.* London: Virago, 1969.

Pollak, Ellen. " 'Things Which Must Not Be Exprest': Teaching Swift's Scatological Poems about Women." In *Teaching Eighteenth-Century Poetry,* ed. Christopher Fox. New York: AMS Press, 1990.

Pollock, Griselda. *Vision and Difference.* London: Routledge, 1988.

Pope, Norris. *Dickens and Charity.* London: Macmillan, 1978.

Reid, J. C. *Bucks and Bruisers: Pierce Egan and Regency London.* London: Routledge and Kegan Paul, 1971.

Riga, Frank P., and Claude A. Prance. *Index to the London Magazine.* New York: Garland, 1978.

Ross, Ellen. *Love and Toil: Motherhood in Outcast London, 1870–1918.* New York: Oxford University Press, 1993.

Rubenius, Aina. *The Woman Question in Mrs. Gaskell's Life and Work.* Uppsala: Lundequistka Bokhanden, 1950.

Ryan, Mary P. *Women in Public Places: Between Banners and Ballots, 1825–1880.* Baltimore: Johns Hopkins University Press, 1990.

Savage, Gail. " 'The Willful Communication of a Loathsome Disease': Marital Conflict and Venereal Disease in Victorian England." *Victorian Studies* 34 (Autumn 1990): 35–54.

Schor, Hilary M. *Scheherezade in the Marketplace: Elizabeth Gaskell and the Victorian Novel.* Oxford: Oxford University Press, 1992.

Schwarzbach, F. S. *"Bleak House:* The Social Pathology of Urban Life." In *Literature and Medicine.* Vol. 9, ed. Peter W. Graham and Elizabeth Sewell. *Fictive Ills: Literary Perspectives on Wounds and Diseases.* Baltimore: Johns Hopkins University Press, 1990.

———. *Dickens and the City.* London: Athlone, 1979.

Sharps, John Geoffrey. *Mrs. Gaskell's Observation and Invention: A Study of Her Non-Biographic Works.* Fontwell, Sussex: Linden Press, 1970.

Shattock, Joanne, and Michael Wolff, eds. *The Victorian Press: Samplings and Soundings.* Leicester: Leicester University Press, 1982.

Shesgreen, Sean. *Hogarth and the Times-of-the-Day Tradition.* Ithaca: Cornell University Press, 1983.

Smith-Rosenberg, Carroll. "The Female World of Love and Ritual: Relations between Women in Nineteenth-Century America." *Signs: Journal of Women in Culture and Society* 1 (Autumn 1975): 1–29.

Squier, Susan Merrill. *Virginia Woolf and London: The Sexual Politics of the City.* Chapel Hill: University of North Carolina Press, 1985.

———, ed. *Women Writers and the City: Essays in Feminist Literary Criticism.* Knoxville: University of Tennessee Press, 1984.

Stallybrass, Peter, and Allon White. *The Politics and Poetics of Transgression.* Ithaca: Cornell University Press, 1986.

Strumingher, Laura S. *The Odyssey of Flora Tristan.* New York: Peter Lang, 1988.

Summerson, John. *Georgian London.* Harmondsworth: Penguin, 1978.

Sypher, Eileen. "The Novels of Margaret Harkness." *Turn-of-the-Century Woman* 1 (Winter 1984): 12–26.

Vicinus, Martha. *Independent Women: Work and Community for Single Women, 1850–1920.* Chicago: University of Chicago Press, 1985.

Walkowitz, Judith R. *City of Dreadful Delight.* Chicago: University of Chicago Press, 1992.

———. *Prostitution and Victorian Society: Women, Class, and the State.* Cambridge: Cambridge University Press, 1980.

———. "Science, Feminism, and Romance: The Men and Women's Club, 1885–1889." *History Workshop* 21 (Spring 1986): 37–59.

Webb, Catherine. *The Woman with the Basket: A History of the Women's Co-operative*

Guild, 1883–1927. Manchester: Cooperative Wholesale Society's Printing Works, 1927.

Welsh, Alexander. *The City of Dickens*. Cambridge: Harvard University Press, 1986.

Williams, Raymond. *The Country and the City*. London: Chatto and Windus, 1973.

———. *Culture and Society, 1780–1950*. Harmondsworth: Penguin, 1961.

Wolff, Janet. "The Invisible *Flâneuse*: Women and the Literature of Modernity." In *The Problems of Modernity: Adorno and Benjamin*, ed. Andrew Benjamin. London: Routledge, 1989.

Yeazell, Ruth Bernard, ed. *Sex, Politics, and Science in the Nineteenth-Century Novel*. Baltimore: Johns Hopkins University Press, 1990.

Yelin, Louise. "Strategies for Survival: Florence and Edith in *Dombey and Son*." *Victorian Studies* 22 (Spring 1979): 297–319.

Index

abyss, 231–33
Acton, William, 10, 79n, 83–84, 94n, 110n, 111
actresses, 7, 8
adultery, 85, 119n
Alexander, Sally, 214n, 222
alienation. *See* crowd (male spectators' experience of)
Alison, Archibald, 52
Anderson, Amanda, 79n, 88n, 93n, 151n, 152n
androgyny, 245–47
anonymity. *See* crowd (male spectators' experience of)
Arbuthnot, John, 56
aristocracy: in *Bleak House*, 98, 109; Boz's rejection of, 49; culture of, 169–71; and London improvements, 25, 52; natural, 133. *See also* swells
Astley's circus (London), 63
At the Works (Bell), 208, 212, 227–30
audience (Dickens's male), 50, 52–54, 65, 68–71
Auerbach, Nina, 7, 92n, 184
Aurora Leigh (E. B. Browning), 197, 202, 214–15
Austen, Jane, 202
authority: Charles Booth's, 212–13; of female social investigators, 207–8, 235; Gaskell's, 137, 138n, 144, 145, 177; Harkness's, 196; as issue in *North and South*, 166–69, 173, 176; and Tristan, 127

Bacup (Lancashire), 191, 192
Baker Street (London), 201
"A Ballad of Religion and Marriage" (Levy), 188
Barrell, John, 45n
Barrett, Elizabeth, 139, 197, 214–15
bars, 117, 126
Barton, Bernard, 38, 39n
Baudelaire, Charles, 2, 4–6, 43
"A Beautiful Young Nymph Going to Bed" (Swift), 74
Beckett, Gilbert à, 53
beggars, 12, 29, 35, 72–73; "Elia" on, 39–40; Redding on, 21, 23; Wordsworth on, 6–7, 22, 40, 61
Bell, Florence, 208, 212, 219, 227–31, 233, 236
Bell's Life in London, 51
Benjamin, Walter, 2, 5, 23–24, 27n, 30–31, 39, 143n
Bernstein, Carol, 49n
Bitter Cry of Outcast London, 200
Blackheath (London), 24
Blackwood's, 41
Blain, Virginia, 99, 104n, 106n
Blake, William, 11, 21, 39, 74; on venereal disease, 8–9, 75, 94
Bleak House (Dickens), 86n, 143, 162, 164, 211; disguises in, 238, 241–44; female sexuality in, 81, 82, 84–85, 96–109, 111, 152, 238
Bodenheimer, Rosemarie, 149n, 150n, 153n, 154n

bohemian culture, 2, 4–6, 20, 30–46, 50, 60n, 77–78, 118, 200n

Bond Street (London), 4, 244, 247, 248

Booth, Charles, 14, 212–13, 217–19, 239; Beatrice Webb's work with, 189, 191, 193, 212

Booth, William, 194, 231

Bosanquet, Helen, 208, 212, 219–22, 226, 227, 230, 231, 236

Boswell, James, 19, 36

"Boz." *See* Dickens, Charles: as "Boz"

"Bridge of Sighs" (Hood), 78–79

Briggs, Asa, 52n, 137

British Museum (London), 61, 200

Brontë, Charlotte, 100n, 151, 165, 178n, 200, 247

brothels, 117, 126, 128

Browning, Elizabeth Barrett, 139, 197, 214–15

Browning, Robert, 49n

Buckingham Palace (London), 25

Buck–Morss, Susan, 1n, 11

Burdett–Coutts, Angela, 164

Burke, Thomas, 27n

Burlington Arcade (London), 4, 245

Burns, John, 204

Burns, Mary, 145

Burton, Decimus, 27

Butler, Josephine, 123n

Byrd, Max, 19n

cafés, 27, 117

Cairo, 123

Cambridge University, 231. *See also* Girton; Newnham

Canaletto, 22

Captain Lobe (Harkness), 194–95

Carlton House (London), 27

Carlyle, Thomas, 82, 132

Cassatt, Mary, 117

celibacy, 100–101, 105–6, 111, 183, 203, 205. *See also* spinsters

Cenci, Beatrice, 131, 155–56, 176

Certeau, Michel de, 238, 246

Cervantes, Miguel de, 70

Chadwick, Edwin, 102n

Chalk Farm (London), 21

Chamberlain, Joseph, 187

Chancery Lane (London), 248

Chapman, Edward, 157, 159

Charity Organization Society (COS), 189, 211, 212, 219, 222, 223

charity schools, 21, 23, 47

charity work, 14, 47, 208, 209–11, 219, 222, 240; "sentimental," 29; women's navigation of streets to do, 4n, 182, 240. *See also* slumming; "visiting"

Chartism, 145, 149

chastity, 85, 88–92, 95, 111, 133, 140–41, 149–53, 173

Chazal, André (Tristan's husband), 115, 126n, 129

Chelsea (London), 56

Cheyne Walk (London), 56, 187

childbirth, 228–30, 233

A Child of the Jago (Morrison), 194

children: of beggars, 72–73; death of, 45n, 80, 143, 146–48, 151; of fallen women, 7, 8, 33; on mothers working outside home, 220–21; nourishment of, 212, 223–26; and Opium Eater, 41, 42; in poverty, 102n, 103; as prostitutes, 127–28; rearing of, 166, 214; as sweeps, 39, 40, 61, 63; and Thackeray's persona, 76–77; Tristan's, 115n, 129, 133n. *See also* illegitimacy

"The Chimney Sweeper" (Blake), 39n

chimney sweeps, 39, 40, 61, 63

cholera, 50, 51, 79, 83, 93n, 94, 103, 110, 162n, 165, 176

Christian imagery, 45, 134, 170n

city. *See* London; Manchester; Paris; public space

A City Girl (Harkness), 193–95

Clark, Robert, 87n

class difference: and childbirth, 228–30, 233; Dickens's collapse of, 50, 63–65, 68, 81–111; Gaskell's attempts to bridge, 13, 147–48, 151, 168–70; and geographical separation, 28–29, 147; Harkness's portrayal of, 193–97, 203, 206; Higgs on, 232–34; middle-class women's obscuring of, 216–19, 221–24, 234–35; Orwell on, 239–40; Tristan's concerns about, 121–22; urban observers' interest in, 2. *See also* aristocracy; disguise(s); industrial conflict; middle–class; working–class

clubs, 182, 183n, 184, 217

coffeehouses, 27, 47

Cole, G. D. H., 133n

Collet, Clara, 212, 214–15, 217–18

Collins, Philip, 60n, 64n, 77n

Colosseum (London), 27–28

"A Complaint of the Decay of Beggars in
the Metropolis" (Lamb), 39, 40
concubinage. *See* harems
*The Condition of the Working Class in
England* (Engels), 141, 147
Confessions of an English Opium Eater (De
Quincey), 5, 20, 30, 40–46
Cons, Emma, 189–90
consumerism, 1, 4, 37, 235
contagion. *See* disease
Contagious Diseases Acts, 9–10, 79n, 83,
85, 123n, 162
contamination. *See* disease
contrast (as literary device), 31–32, 48,
147–48, 168–69, 171, 229
Conversations on Political Economy (Marcet),
139
Corbin, Alain, 82, 83
Corfield, Penelope J., 13n, 27n
Cornhill (London), 247
Cornhill Magazine, 60n
COS. *See* Charity Organization Society
The Country and the City (Williams), 11, 12,
138
Courtney, Leonard, 187
Covent Garden (London), 26, 55, 58, 69
Cranford (Gaskell), 178n
Craske, May, 217
crocodile imagery, 4, 45, 46, 244–45
cross–dressing (women's), 4, 120–21,
237, 241, 246–47. *See also* disguise(s)
crowd (male spectators' experience of):
alienation from, 1–3, 6–8, 43, 50;
anonymity in, 2, 4, 24, 30, 39, 43, 237;
encounters in, 21–24, 48, 62–63;
invisibility in, 1, 2, 24, 30, 33, 39, 143,
238, 239; invulnerability in, 33, 143. *See
also* public space
crowd (women's experience of), 3–4,
143; absence from, 4, 15, 227–28;
eroticization by, 3n, 4–6, 27n, 43, 155–
56, 173–78; sense of exposure in, 12,
142, 143–44, 155–57, 172–74, 177,
178, 206, 235; sense of trespass in, 12,
118, 174–78, 184, 206, 207, 244;
sexual vulnerability in, 3, 4, 12, 137,
144, 155, 156, 182, 201, 206, 216, 230,
232–34, 240, 243, 244, 247–48; women
as spectacle in, 2–7, 13, 15, 27n, 66–
68, 125–28, 174, 235–36. *See also*
disguise(s); public space
Cruikshank, George, 31, 58, 66–68, 237

Cruikshank, Isaac Robert, 31
Culture and Society (Williams), 145–46
"The Curate's Walk" ("Spec"), 76–77

Daguerre, Louis, 27
d'Albertis, Deirdre, 162n, 163n
Damascus, 123
dandy, 5n, 55. *See also* swells
Daniel Deronda (Eliot), 203
David, Deirdre, 173n
David Copperfield (Dickens), 9, 83
Davin, Anna, 214n
death, 178; of children, 45n, 80, 143,
146–48, 151
De la prostitution dans la ville de Paris
(Parent–Duchâtelet), 79n
DeLuca, V. A., 46
Demos (Gissing), 195
De Quincey, Elizabeth, 45n
De Quincey, Thomas, 5, 20, 30, 40–48,
58, 74
Desanti, Dominique, 133nn
DeVries, Duane, 54
Diary of an Ennuyée (Jameson), 130–32
Dickens, Charles, 11–12, 143; as "Boz,"
1, 49–80, 237; fallen women as threat
to middle–class in works by, 81–111;
and Gaskell, 164–65, 172; as urban
observer, 2, 19. *See also titles of works by*
Dickens, Charley, 74n
diet (working–class), 224–25
Dijkstra, Sandra, 117, 126n
dioramas, 22, 27, 30–31
disease [contagion, contamination,
pollution], 238; fallen women's
association with, 2–3, 6, 8–11, 44, 50–
51, 75–76, 81–85, 93–94, 110–11, 162–
64; as link between classes, 8–11, 75–
76, 81–85, 93–94, 96, 102–4, 162–63;
as metaphor for city, 50, 95–96, 104;
and sin, 44–45, 83–86, 93–94, 96–97,
102–4; urban observers' interest in, 2.
See also Contagious Diseases Acts; urban
blight; *specific diseases*
disguise(s): Beatrice Webb's, 184, 191–92,
206, 230, 240; of beggars, 35; foreign
dress as, 119–21, 135, 240–41; as
journalist, 239; as Opium Eater's, 43; and
respectability, 126–29, 152–53, 241; as
self-transformation, 119, 120, 241;
Tristan's, 4n, 118–22, 184, 241, 242;
among urban observers, 237; as

disguise(s) (*cont.*)
  vagrants, 230, 232, 235–36, 238–40;
  women's cross–dressing as, 4, 120–21,
  237, 241; 246–47. *See also* personae;
  veils
Disraeli, Benjamin, 140, 151, 239
distancing techniques, 35–36, 38–40, 50,
  63, 66, 75, 127, 156
divorce, 94n, 116n, 216
Dobson, Austin, 197
dock labor, 189, 190, 208
Dock Strike (London, 1889), 193–96
Dombey and Son (Dickens), 11–12, 81, 82,
  84, 86–99, 101, 110–11, 152, 164
domestic life: and impressionist painters,
  117; national concern about, 14, 140–
  42, 150, 209, 213–14, 222–23, 228,
  231–34; as proper sphere for middle-
  class women, 107, 183, 190, 207, 208–
  12, 214, 240; and venereal disease, 8–
  11, 75–76, 94, 110; women social
  investigators' ambivalence about, 14,
  181, 184, 190, 207–36; working–class,
  132–34, 207–36. *See also* children;
  fathers; marriage; mother(s)
Domestic Manners of the Americans
  (Trollope), 130
domestic service, 139, 150
domestic violence, 71–73, 124, 195, 223,
  226
Down and Out in Paris and London
  (Orwell), 230
dressmakers, 150, 151, 161, 164–65, 178
"The Drunkard's Death" (Boz), 62–63,
  80
Drury Lane (London), 26, 37, 68, 246
Dyos, H. J., 28–29

East End (London), 4n, 32, 107n, 182,
  186, 189–94, 208, 217–22
East London (Booth), 191
"The Economic Position of Educated
  Working Women" (Collet), 214–15
Economic Review, 217
Edinburgh Review, 158
education (for women), 14, 124, 132,
  134, 140n, 215, 221–22. *See also* charity
  schools
Egan, Pierce, 20, 49; contrasted with Boz,
  54, 68, 70, 73; distancing techniques
  of, 42, 48, 66; on Newgate Prison, 35–
  36, 64; and prostitutes, 33–34, 47–48,

74, 79; as urban observer, 30–37, 41,
  58, 76, 237–38
Egg, Augustus, 104n
"Elia." *See* Lamb, Charles
Eliot, George, 203, 205
Ellis, Havelock, 185n
Elmes, James, 28, 29–30
encounters (urban solitary), 21–24, 48,
  62–63
Engels, Friedrich, 140, 141, 144–45, 147,
  150, 193
eroticization (of women). *See* crowd
  (women's experience of)
eugenics, 213, 228–30
"Eurydice" (H.D.), 199
Evening Chronicle (London), 51
exile, 94, 135, 157, 164–65, 178, 204
exposure. *See* crowd (women's experience
  of); writers (female): fears of exposure
eye imagery: and all–seeing narrator, 1,
  238, 246; bird's–eye (panoramic) views,
  21–25, 27–28, 35; *camera obscura* views,
  33, 237; and male ramblers, 208. *See
  also* invisibility

Fabian Society, 183n, 185, 204, 222. *See
  also* Fabian Women's Group
Fabian Women's Group (FWG), 209, 212,
  222–27, 232
factory workers, 191, 212; analogues
  between women and, 149–50, 153–54,
  156; female, 12, 139–41, 143–45, 150–
  51, 156, 160, 217–19; male, 132, 143–
  44, 168–70. *See also* working–class
fairy tales, 90n, 168
fallen women, 27n, 78–79, 165–66, 176,
  246; association of, with contagion, 2–
  3, 6, 8–11, 44, 50–51, 75–76, 81–85,
  93–94, 110–11, 162–64; as bohemian
  man's double, 4–6, 15, 16, 43–46, 74;
  children as, 127–28; children of, 7–8,
  33; drowned, 78–79, 106n; effects of,
  on other working women, 115–236; as
  emblematic of fleeting urban relations,
  5–6, 20, 43–44, 48; as emblems of
  alienated selves, 2–3, 7–8, 15, 43; as
  emblems of urban suffering, 2, 3, 13,
  34, 46, 51, 67–68, 71–81; as
  instruments of pleasure, 3, 20, 74;
  marriages of, 10–11, 13, 81, 84; as
  sights to be consumed, 33–48; as threat
  to middle-class, 81–111; and Tristan,

116, 122–28, 132, 134–35; urban
observers' distance from, 24, 30–80;
variety of portrayals of, 2–3. *See also*
chastity; Contagious Diseases Acts;
crowd (women's experience of);
disease; prostitution; urban observers
family. *See* domestic life
Fanny Hill (Cleland), 89n
fathers, 8, 84, 151, 221, 225–28
Faucher, Léon, 140–42, 150
Fawcett, Millicent, 205
Feldman, Jessica R., 5n
femininity: definition of, 118; female
social investigators' personae of, 208;
Nightingale's unconventional, 165–66;
recovery of, 118; as sign of
respectability, 126–29
feminism: and female social investigators,
208, 215–16, 221, 223–27, 234;
women's avoidance of, 181–206. *See also*
"woman question"
Figaro in London, 53
filles publiques. *See* fallen women
"finish," 125–29
"The First of May" (Boz), 63n
flânerie, 11, 116
flaneurs, 1, 2n, 4, 11, 30, 43, 118, 235,
237, 238, 240. *See also* urban observers
flâneuse, 11–12, 184, 201–2
"flash girls," 217
Fleet Prison (London), 71
Fortnightly Review, 215
Foucault, Michel, 24–25
"Found Drowned" (Watts), 106n
Fourier, Charles, 134
"The Four Times of the Day" (Hogarth),
58–60
Fox, Celina, 53n
Fox, Eliza, 159, 170n
French culture, 104n, 121, 244
From the Abyss (Masterman), 231
FWG. *See* Fabian Women's Group

Gallagher, Catherine, 149n
Garnett, Richard, 185n
Gaskell, Elizabeth, 211, 227, 241;
ambivalence of, as public person, 12,
137, 138n, 143–44, 148–49, 157–60,
173, 174, 235; as urban observer, 11–
14, 137–78, 230
Gaskell, Marianne, 158
Gaskell, William, 138, 146, 158

Gauguin, Clovis, 115n
Gauguin, Paul, 115n, 133n
George, Dorothy, 24
George Eastmont, Wanderer (Harkness), 193,
195
George IV (King of England), 19, 21, 25–
30, 38
Gilman, Sander, 85
"Girl Life in a Slum" (Craske), 217
Girton College (Cambridge University),
218
Gissing, George, 189, 193–95, 200–202,
216
Glimpses into the Abyss (Higgs), 208, 230–
34
gout, 101
governesses, 130–31, 200
Gray, Donald, 22, 53
Greenwood, James, 230, 239
Greg, W. R., 79n, 109–10
Grillo, Virgil, 49n, 54n
Gurney, Michael S., 103n

H. D. (Hilda Doolittle), 199
"Hackney–Coach Stands" (Boz), 57
Hagar, 131
harems, 123–24, 141
Harkness, Margaret, 183–87, 192–97,
200n, 203–6, 215
harlots. *See* fallen women
Harman, Barbara, 174n
Harrison, Frederic, 205
Hartman, Geoffrey, 22
Hayter, Alethea, 41n
Hazlitt, William, 20–21, 38
"Helen" (H.D.), 199
Helen of Troy, 155, 156, 199
Hemyng, Bracebridge, 10–11
Higgs, Mary, 14–15, 208, 219, 230–35,
240
Hill, Octavia, 189–90, 211, 212, 222
Hogarth, William, 39, 58–60
"Holy Thursday" (Blake), 21
home. *See* domestic life; homelessness
homelessness, 19, 43, 70, 230–34
Hood, Thomas, 49n, 78–79
Hook, Theodore, 49n
"Horatio Sparkins" (Boz), 55
Hornor, Thomas, 27
"The Hospital Patient" (Boz), 61–62, 73–
75
Household Words, 140n, 172

Howitt's Journal of Literature and Popular Progress, 143
Hugo, Victor, 2
Hunt, Leigh, 49n, 55–58
husbands. *See* fathers
Hyde Park (London), 25, 27, 193, 194

illegitimacy, 88, 101–2, 115, 163, 164, 244
impressionists, 117–18, 126
incognito. *See* disguise(s)
In Darkest England and the Way Out (Booth), 194, 231
In Darkest London (Harkness), 194–95
industrial conflict, 137, 139, 145–59. *See also* class difference; socialism
industrialization, 127n
inheritance: Gaskell on, 152–53, 164, 176; as theme in *Bleak House*, 96–109, 152, 242–43; as theme in *Dombey and Son*, 86–87, 93–95, 152; Tristan's, 115
"In the Abyss" (Wells), 231
invisibility. *See* crowd (male spectators' experience of); narrators; voyeurs; women: aging
invulnerability. *See* crowd (male spectators' experience of)
Iron, Ralph, 196. *See also* Schreiner, Olive
iron manufacture, 208, 212, 227–30
irony, 39–40, 63n, 128, 196

Jack the Ripper, 183
Jameson, Anna, 130–32, 155
Jane Eyre (Brontë), 100n, 151, 200
Jeffreys, Sheila, 183n
Jerrold, Douglas, 53
Jews, 186, 188–92, 197–204
Johnson, Edgar, 74n
journalism and journalists, 9, 40–41, 52–54, 60n. See also *specific journals*

Kapp, Yvonne, 203n
Katherine Buildings (London), 187, 189, 193
Kay, James, 83, 84
Keating, Peter, 194, 231
Kidd, Alan J., 138n
Kipling, Rudyard, 193–95, 217

lady's maids, 121–22, 170–71
Lamb, Charles ("Elia"), 20, 70; as urban observer, 2, 30, 36–42, 47, 49, 55–58, 61, 63
Lamb, Mary, 36n
Lambeth (London), 209, 212, 222–27
Langbauer, Laurie, 111n
Laqueur, Thomas, 101n
Law, John, 196. *See also* Harkness, Margaret
Levy, Amy, 183–86, 188–89, 197–206, 215
Lewis, Jane, 220n
Life and Labour of the People in London (Booth), 212
Life in London (Egan), 30, 31–36, 41, 47–48, 64, 73, 79, 237–38
The Life of Charlotte Brontë (Gaskell), 178n
literary forms. *See* novels; sketches
Liverpool, 154–57
London: alienation from, 1–3, 6–8, 43, 50; Dickens's depiction of, 2, 19, 49–61, 81, 86, 93; encounters with solitary figures in, 21–24, 48, 62–63; as encyclopedic, 31–32, 39; as female, 37; female communities in, 14, 181–206; fleeting nature of relations in, 5–6, 20, 43–44, 48; Gaskell on, 167–77; illustrations of, 22–24, 31–32, 58–60; improvements to, under George IV, 19–21, 25–30, 48, 52; Lamb on, 2, 36–40; Shaw on, 2; as stage, 12, 15, 29–49, 51–52, 63, 237; as symbol of social crisis, 13; Tristan's view of, 13, 115–16; variety of readings of, 2. *See also* crowd; fallen women; poverty; public space; urban observers; *names of streets, buildings, and areas of*
London, Jack, 231, 235, 239
"London" (Blake), 8–9, 74, 75, 94
London Bridge, 3n, 57
"The Londoner" (Lamb), 37, 38, 40
"London in July" (Levy), 198
London Journal (Tristan), 13, 132
London Labour and the London Poor (Mayhew), 10, 76
London Magazine, 20, 23, 29, 36, 40, 41
A London Plane Tree (Levy), 197–99, 201
Low Life, 60n

"Maid of Buttermere," 7, 8
Manchester ("Milton"), 13, 137–39, 142–45, 147, 155, 157, 167–77, 227
Mann, Tom, 204

Manning, Thomas, 36, 38

Marcet, Mrs. Jane, 139

Marcus, Jane, 186

Marcus, Steven, 70, 71, 92n, 127n, 140n, 144–45, 147n

marginality: of communities of single women, 183–84, 186, 188, 192, 195–97; of Dickens's characters, 50; of English Jews, 197, 200; of fallen women, 5–6, 43, 44; of male writers, 2, 4–6, 20, 30–36, 43, 44; Tristan's, 13, 115–16, 120–22, 133–35; of women, 14

marriage: alternatives to, 215–16; of fallen women, 10–11, 13, 81, 84; and female social investigators, 208, 221–22, 225–27, 234; and Gaskell, 138, 151, 172, 176–78; and Levy, 202, 203–4; and polygamy, 123–24; as prostitution, 87–88, 111, 133; Tristan's, 115, 116, 126n, 129, 130, 133n; Trollope's, 130; and venereal disease, 10, 94, 110; women's rejection of, 186–89. *See also* domestic life; domestic violence

Marsh, Joss Lutz, 89n

Martin Chuzzlewit (Dickens), 176n

Martineau, Harriet, 123–24, 139, 140n

Marvell, Andrew, 38

Marx, Eleanor, 185, 186, 200n, 203

Marx, Karl, 132

Mary Barton (Gaskell), 13, 131n, 139, 142–60, 176, 178, 227, 241

Marylebone (London), 56

masquerade. *See* disguise(s)

Masterman, C. F. G., 231, 239

maternalism. *See* mother(s): ideology about

Maternity: Letters from Working Women (Women's Cooperative Guild), 235

Mayhew, Henry, 10, 76, 77, 219, 231n

"Medea" (Levy), 199–200, 202

"Meditations in Monmouth Street" (Boz), 57

men: fears of, about contamination by women, 6–11; gaze of, 176–77; rage of, 71–75; Tristan on, 124–25; women's work as threat to, 140, 142. *See also* crowd (male spectators' experience of); ramblers; urban observers (male); writers (male)

Méphis (Tristan), 133n

Metropolitan Improvements (Shepherd and Elmes), 28, 29–30

Metropolitan Magazine, 50

Metropolitan Sanitary Association, 94n, 107n

Michie, Helena, 105n

middle–class: communities of single women from, 14, 181–206; domestic life as proper sphere for women of, 107, 183, 190, 207, 208–12, 214, 240; fear of lower classes by, 2, 9, 50, 65–68; fear of violence among, 145–46; Gaskell as, 13, 178; ideology about working–class life by, 139–42, 177, 213–14, 234; increased opportunities for women from, 215–18; links between prostitutes and, 8–11, 51, 75–76, 79, 81–85, 94, 110, 162–63, 216; literary depiction of city as, 49–55, 76–77, 79, 81, 85–86; in Manchester, 138–39, 158–60, 174; navigation of city streets by women from, 4n, 168–69, 182–83, 215, 240; social investigators' lack of interest in, 230. *See also* charity work; class difference; disease; marginality; social investigation; urban observers; "visiting"

Middlesbrough, 208, 212, 227–30

Mill, John Stuart, 147n

Miller, J. Hillis, 54n, 62, 63n

A Minor Poet and Other Verse (Levy), 199

mirrors, 105–6, 243

Mrs. Dalloway (Woolf), 247–48

Mrs. Warren's Profession (Shaw), 2

modernity, 5, 11–12, 117

Moers, Ellen, 85, 99n, 131, 139

Montague, Lady Mary Wortley, 75n, 119, 240–41

Moor, Lucy, 215

Moore, George, 26, 193, 195

More, Thomas, 56

Morisot, Berthe, 117

Morning Chronicle (London), 51, 76

Morning Post (London), 54

Morrison, Arthur, 193–95, 217n

Morten, Honnor, 193n

mother(s): absence of, 156, 157; authority of, 127–28; and dying children, 80; Esther Summerson as, 100–101, 107, 109; fallen women as, 7–8, 33, 151; ideology about, 213–14, 220–27, 234; London as, 37; Mrs. Jellyby as, 96, 107; redemptive powers of, 129, 132, 135, 222–27, 234; state

mother(s) (*cont.*)
  support for, 222, 224–26, 232, 234–35;
    as threat to daughters' chastity, 85, 88–
    92, 95, 133; as victims, 72–73; work of,
    outside of home, 141–42, 220–22, 224.
    See also children
Munby, Arthur, 3n
My Apprenticeship (Webb), 205

narrators: all-seeing, 1, 238, 246; female,
  98–100, 195–97, 203–4, 230
Nash, John, 25, 27, 29, 52
naturalism. *See* social realism
Nead, Lynda, 9n, 73n, 82n, 83, 85, 104n
Neff, Wanda Fraiken, 139
The Nether World (Gissing), 195
New, Melvyn, 185n, 200n
New Bailey Prison (London), 165
Newgate Prison (London), 35–36, 63–65,
  75, 128–30, 132, 135
Newnham College (Cambridge
  University), 197, 200, 218
"new woman," 181, 216, 217
Night in a Workhouse (Greenwood), 230
Nightingale, Florence, 165–66, 175–76
Nightingale, Parthenope, 166, 167
Nineteenth Century, 205
North and South (Gaskell), 13, 142, 144,
  145, 155, 166–75, 177, 211, 241
Norton, Caroline, 139
nostalgia, 37–39, 49, 55–57, 63
novels: industrial, 137–78. *See also*
  narrators; *specific novels*
nursing (healing), 162–66, 175–76

occupations (for women), 10, 14, 121–22,
  129–31, 139–40, 150, 160–61, 170–71,
  187, 196, 200–201, 215, 217–18, 221,
  248. *See also* "women's work"
The Odd Women (Gissing), 189, 195, 200–
  202
"The Old Benchers of the Inner
  Temple" (Lamb), 37–38
Oldham Workhouse, 231
Oliver Twist (Dickens), 64, 73–74, 81,
  111n
Olsen, Donald J., 25n, 52
Opium Eater. *See* De Quincey, Thomas
"Orientals," 44–46, 120
Orlando (Woolf), 245, 246–47
Orwell, George, 230, 239–40
Our Mutual Friend (Dickens), 106n

"Our Next–Door Neighbor" (Boz), 79n
Out of Work (Harkness), 193, 194

paintings: impressionist, 117–18, 126;
  Jameson on, of women, 131–32. *See also*
  Cruikshank, George; Hogarth, William
Pamela (Richardson), 151
Panopticon, 24–25, 35
panorama (urban), 1, 12, 20–25, 27, 35–
  36, 48, 238
Parent–Duchâtelet, Alexandre, 10, 79n,
  127n
The Pargiters (Woolf), 3–4, 182, 183, 201,
  244
pariah. *See* fallen women; Tristan, Flora;
  writers (female): fears of exposure
Paris, 27n, 116, 117, 119n
Parliament (British), 120–21
Past and Present (Carlyle), 82
Past and Present (Egg), 104n
patriarchy. *See* feminism; "woman
  question"
"The Pawnbroker's Shop" (Boz), 68, 81
People of the Abyss (London), 231, 235, 239
personae, 38–39; Boz's, 54–55; of Egan,
  Lamb, and De Quincey, 30; of female
  social investigators, 208; Thackeray's,
  76–77; women writers' use of, 190–93,
  196, 198–200, 205
Peru, 115, 116, 119, 241
Phillips, Evelyn March, 193n, 215, 216
"Philosophy" (Levy), 199
Piccadilly (London), 4, 241
The Pickwick Papers (Dickens), 70–72, 76,
  79
pimps, 34, 125
plague, 9, 110
Pollak, Ellen, 74n
Pollock, Griselda, 117, 118
pollution. *See* disease; urban blight
polygamy, 123–24
Pope, Norris, 93n
Potter family, 186, 187. *See also* Webb,
  Beatrice Potter
poverty: children in, 102n, 103, 212; in
  cities, 19, 28–30, 50; middle-class
  women's link to, 12, 209–11; as natural
  order, 47–48; and prostitution, 109–10,
  232–34; Tristan's, 115; unnaturalness
  of, 93; urban observer's interest in, 2.
  See also beggars; charity work; Fabian
  Society; homelessness; slums; social

investigation; social realism; social reform; "visiting"

"The Praise of Chimney Sweepers" (Lamb), 39, 63n

The Prelude (Wordsworth), 7–8, 22, 40

Pride and Prejudice (Austen), 202

Primrose Hill (London), 21–23, 25, 29, 35

"The Prisoner's Van" (Boz), 75, 80, 81, 85

prisons: Boz on, 63–65, 71, 75; and Gaskell, 147n, 165; and Panopticon, 24, 35; Tristan on, 127n, 128–30, 132, 135; unnaturalness of, 93. *See also* exile

Promenades dans Londres (Tristan), 115–35, 241

prostitution: economic analyses of, 109–10, 124–25, 151–52, 161–62; Egan on, 34, 74, 79; Faucher's views on, 140–41; as transitional occupation, 10–11, 84. *See also* fallen women

"Prostitution in London" (Hemyng), 10–11

pseudonyms, 38–39, 196, 205

public space, 1, 109–10; borders of, 117; male, 27, 37, 69–73, 117, 125–28, 134–35, 196; women in, 3–4, 7, 13–14, 72–75, 117–18, 142, 154–65, 173–78, 208–14, 240, 277; women's absence from, 227–28. *See also* crowd; domestic life; factory workers; fallen women; London; social investigation; writers (female)

Pugin, Augustus, 27

Punch, 76

Punch in London, 53

Pycroft, Ella, 189

racialism, 44–45

ramblers: men as, 1–4, 11, 20–23, 29, 30, 37, 55–62, 208; view of the poor by, 43; women as, 172, 177. *See also* urban observers

"The Reasons that Induced Dr S[wift] to write a Poem call'd The Lady's Dressing room" (Montague), 75n

"Recollections of the South Sea House" (Lamb), 36, 38, 56

"The Record of Badalia Herodsfoot" (Kipling), 194, 217n

Redding, Cyrus, 20–23, 29, 30, 47

Reeves, Maud Pember, 208–9, 212, 219, 222–27, 230, 231, 236

Reform Bill, 25, 29, 52

Regency period, 19–30, 48, 52, 73

Regent's Park (London), 25, 27, 28

Regent Street (London), 25, 26, 52, 55

rent collecting, 14, 186, 187, 189, 211, 223, 240

Reuben Sachs (Levy), 185, 188, 197, 200, 201n, 202–4

Revue des deux mondes, 140

Reynolds, J. H., 36

Reynolds, Stephen, 239

Rich and Poor (Bosanquet), 208, 219–22

Richardson, Samuel, 151

The Road to Wigan Pier (Orwell), 230, 239–40

Robson, Anne, 159

The Romance of a Shop (Levy), 189, 200–202

A Room of One's Own (Woolf), 245, 246

Ross, Ellen, 208, 214n, 223n, 225n, 229n, 234

Round About a Pound a Week (Reeve), 208–9, 222–27

Rubenius, Aina, 150n

Ruth (Gaskell), 145, 159–66, 178

Ryan, Mary, 10n

Ryan, Dr. Michael, 127n

Sackville–West, Vita, 4, 241

St. James's Park (London), 25, 29

St. Paul's (London), 25, 27–28, 35, 55, 248

Saint–Simon, comte de, 134

Sala, George Augustus, 60, 76, 77–79

Salvation Army, 4n, 194–95, 231

Sand, George, 4, 118–19, 241

sanitary reform, 9, 83, 93, 94n, 110

Savage, Gail, 94n

Schor, Hilary M., 137n, 152n, 157n

Schorske, Carl, 58

Schreiner, Olive, 135, 185, 196, 204

Schwarzbach, F. S., 58, 94n, 96n, 103n

"Scotland–Yard" (Boz), 57

Scott, John, 36

seamstresses ("trouser hands"), 160–61, 178, 191, 195, 240

Sesame and Lilies (Ruskin), 200

settlement houses, 14, 182, 190, 193n, 220n

"Seven Dials" (Boz), 65–68, 75

Seven Dials (London), 65–68, 195

"Shabby–Genteel People" (Boz), 61

Shakespeare, William, 40

Sharps, John Geoffrey, 147nn, 162n

Shaw, George Bernard, 2, 216

Shepherd, Thomas, 29

"Shops and Their Tenants" (Boz), 55

Showalter, Elaine, 110n

Sims, George, 239

sketches [literary form], 1, 2, 12, 19–25, 30–40, 49–80. See also *specific sketches*

Sketches by Boz, 49–80

slumming, 27, 189. *See also* "visiting"

slums, 19, 29–35, 50, 65–68, 98, 109, 147, 193–94, 217, 219; unnaturalness of, 93

smallpox, 83, 103–4, 110, 162n, 243–44

Smirke, Robert, 25, 26

Smith–Rosenberg, Carroll, 183n

Soane, John, 25

Social Democratic Federation, 196, 200

social investigation: Boz's, 62–65; of prostitution, 9–11, 123; role of disguise in, 238–40; satires of, 76; view of the poor in, 43; women's involvement in, 14–15, 184, 186, 189–93, 196, 205–36. *See also* poverty; urban blight; "visiting"; *specific social investigators*

socialism: in communities of single women, 184, 186, 192–97, 206; on motherhood, 223; in *North and South*, 170; and Tristan, 115, 133–34. *See also* Fabian Society

social realism (naturalism), 184, 193–95, 206

social reform, 88n, 94n, 207

social service. *See* social investigation

Socrates, 199

Songs of Experience (Blake), 21, 39

Songs of Innocence (Blake), 39

"Spec." *See* Thackeray, William Makepeace

spectacle. *See* crowd (women's experience of); London: as stage

spectators. *See* urban observers

spinsters ("glorified"), 4n, 181–84, 186–88, 205, 209, 215, 221–22. *See also* celibacy

Sporting Anecdotes (Egan), 36

Squier, Susan Merrill, 182nn, 192

stage. *See* theater

Stallybrass, Peter, 75n

Stanley, Henry M., 195

Steele, Richard, 56

sterility (sexual), 94n, 101–2, 110

stigmatization: of authors, 159; of bodies, 105; of femininity, 241; of illegitimate children, 163; by veiling, 241–44

the Strand (London), 25, 37, 247–48

"Street Haunting" (Woolf), 192, 245–46

"The Streets—Morning" (Boz), 58, 60–61, 72, 237

"The Streets—Night" (Boz), 72–75, 79

strollers, 1–4, 43. *See also* urban observers

Stumingher, Laura S., 133n

suffrage (women's), 183, 205, 216, 221, 226–27

Summerson, John, 25

sweatshop. *See* tailoring trade

swells, 30–36, 49, 54, 70

Swift, Jonathan, 56, 74

Sybil (Disraeli), 151, 239

Sypher, Eileen, 195, 196

syphilis. *See* venereal disease

"Table Talk" (Hazlitt), 20–21

tailoring trade (sweatshop), 189–91, 208, 240

taint. *See* disease; inheritance

Talbot, James Beard, 127n

"The Tea Garden" (Redding), 20–23, 29, 30, 47

textile manufacturing, 139–40

Thackeray, William Makepeace ("Spec"), 1, 60n, 76–77

theater (stage): backstage as male public space, 117; Boz's demystification of, 63; Boz's use of elements from, 65–68; London as, 12, 15, 19–49, 51–52, 237

Theatre Royal (Haymarket), 26

"The Three Eras of Libbie Marsh" (Gaskell), 143–44

The Time Machine (Wells), 231n

"To E." (Levy), 199

Tom and Jerry. *See* Egan, Pierce

Tonna, Charlotte, 139

The Town, 53, 54

The Trades of East London (Booth), 218

Trafalgar Square (London), 25

tramp (on the), 14–15, 208, 230

"Travels in London" ("Spec"), 76–77

trespass. *See* crowd (women's experience of)

Tristan, Flora, 4n, 13, 115–22, 184, 230, 235, 241, 242

Trollope, Frances, 130, 139

"trouserhands." *See* seamstresses
"The Tuggs's at Ramsgate" (Boz), 55
Turkey, 119n, 241
Twice Round the Clock (Sala), 60, 76, 77–79
"Two o'Clock A.M." (Sala), 78
typhus, 82, 83, 110, 162n, 163–64

unemployment, 194–95
Union ouvrière (Tristan), 132
university women, 218–19
urban blight [pollution], 9n, 19, 25n, 80, 83. *See also* disease; fallen women; sanitary reform; social reform
urbanization, 13
urban observers (female): Gaskell's experience as, 137, 147n; women's difficulties with being, 3–4, 11–15, 116–35, 137–78, 184–86, 192, 205–8, 232–36, 240–48. *See also* crowd; social investigation; urban observers (male); "visiting"
urban observers (male), 1–8, 11–12, 20–23, 30–36, 137, 237–40; ambivalence of, about fallen women, 49–51, 66–81; in Boz's sketches, 50, 54–55, 61–65, 67–68, 75–77, 79–80; fallen women as threat to middle–class, 81–111; fallen women's distance from, 24, 30–48. *See also* crowd; eye imagery; flaneurs; ramblers; strollers; urban observers (female)
urban space. *See* London; public space

Vauxhall Gardens (London), 24, 63
veils, 104, 237, 241–44
venereal disease, 8–11, 75–76, 83, 85, 94, 102, 104, 110. *See also* Contagious Diseases Acts
Vicinus, Martha, 3, 4n, 181n, 182, 183n, 190, 196n
Victorian period: attitudes of, 52, 73, 76–77, 79n, 82n, 83, 85; journalism in, 53–54; social service during, 209–19
Villette (Brontë), 100n, 247
"visiting," 14, 166, 169, 186, 208–14, 223, 227, 240, 241
"A Visit to Newgate" (Boz), 63–65, 80
voyeurs, 33, 202, 237–38
vulnerability. *See* crowd (women's experience of)

"Waiting at the Station" ("Spec"), 76, 77
Walkowitz, Judith R., 4n, 79n, 123n, 162, 181n, 182n, 200n
Ward, Mary (Mrs. Humphrey), 205
Waterloo Bridge (London), 62, 71, 78
Waterloo Road (London), 125
Watts, G. W., 106n
Webb, Beatrice Potter, 183, 184, 186–93, 196, 197, 200n, 204–5, 208, 215; and Booth, 189, 191, 193, 212; disguises of, 184, 191–92, 206, 230, 240
Webb, Catherine, 235
Webb, R. K., 147n
Webb, Sidney, 185, 200n, 204
Weekly True Sun, 56
Wells, H. G., 216, 231
Welsh, Alexander, 50, 81n, 82n
West, Benjamin, 56
West End (London), 4, 25, 27, 29, 32, 247
Westminster (London), 247–48
Westminster Bridge (London), 21, 78
Westminster Review, 109–10
White, Allon, 75n
whores. *See* fallen women
Wilde, Oscar, 200
Williams, Raymond: on Blake, 8, 9n; on Dickens, 82; on *Mary Barton,* 138, 145–46, 148, 149; on urban observers, 1, 11, 12
"Wise in Her Generation" (Levy), 200
Wolff, Janet, 11
Wolff, Michael, 53n
Wollstonecraft, Mary, 134, 221
"woman question": Bosanquet on, 222; Dickens on, 95–96, 99n, 107, 111; Gaskell on, 170–72. *See also* feminism
Woman's World, 200
women: acceptable roles for, in urban space, 4n, 14, 168–69, 182, 189, 208–14, 227, 240; aging, 245, 247, 248; assumptions about, on streets, 3–4, 11, 12, 14–15, 118, 123, 125, 135, 244; as commodities, 87–93, 101n, 118, 125; depiction of, as masculine, 91, 92n, 142; men's fear of contamination by, 6–11; and society's salvation, 84–85, 98–99, 110, 111, 129, 132, 135, 222–27, 234; as travelers, 115–16, 119, 123–24, 129–30, 154–55, 182, 240–41; Tristan on, 124; as urban spectacle, 2–

women (*cont.*)

7, 13, 15, 27n, 43, 66–68, 125–28, 174, 235–36; violence against, 71–73, 124, 195, 223, 226. *See also* crowd (women's experience of); disease; education; factory workers; fallen women; femininity; marriage; occupations; suffrage; "woman question"; writers (female)

Women's Cooperative Guild, 235

women's shelters, 232, 233, 236

"women's work," 183, 190, 214, 218, 234

Woolf, Virginia, 3–4, 182, 183, 186, 192, 201, 244–48

Wordsworth, Kate, 45n

Wordsworth, William, 6–8, 11, 21–22, 40, 61

working–class: changes in representation of, 24; childbirth among, 228–30, 233; domestic life of, 132–34, 207–36; Harkness's depiction of, 193–97; horizontal depictions of, 194; in Manchester, 138; Tristan's interest in, 115–16, 132–34; Webb's voice concerning, 190–93. *See also* class

difference; factory workers; homelessness; industrial conflict; socialism

writers (female): authority of, 137, 138n, 144, 145, 177; difficulties of, as urban observers, 11–14, 115–35; eroticization of, 13–14, 159–60, 173; fears of exposure, 13, 137, 138n, 143–44, 157–59; illustrations of, 197–98, 202; personae used by, 190–93, 196, 198–200, 205

writers (male) [artists], 2, 4–6, 15, 20, 30–36, 43, 44, 117–18

Wyatt, Benjamin, 26

"Xantippe" (Levy), 199

The Years (Woolf), 182, 183, 186. See also *Pargiters*

Yellin, Louise, 90n

YWCA, 215

Zenobia, 167

Zola, Emile, 194n

Zwerdling, Alex, 99n